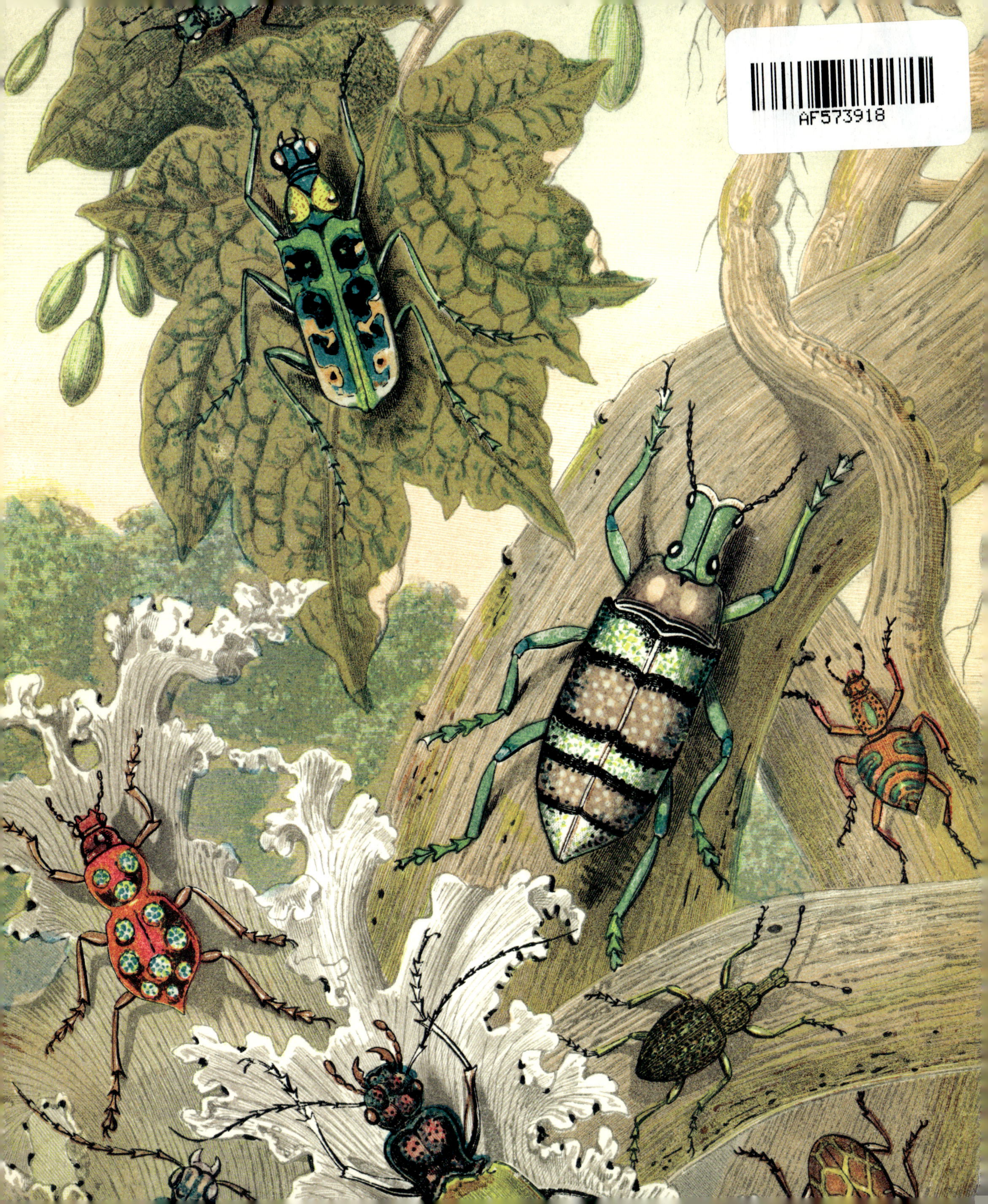

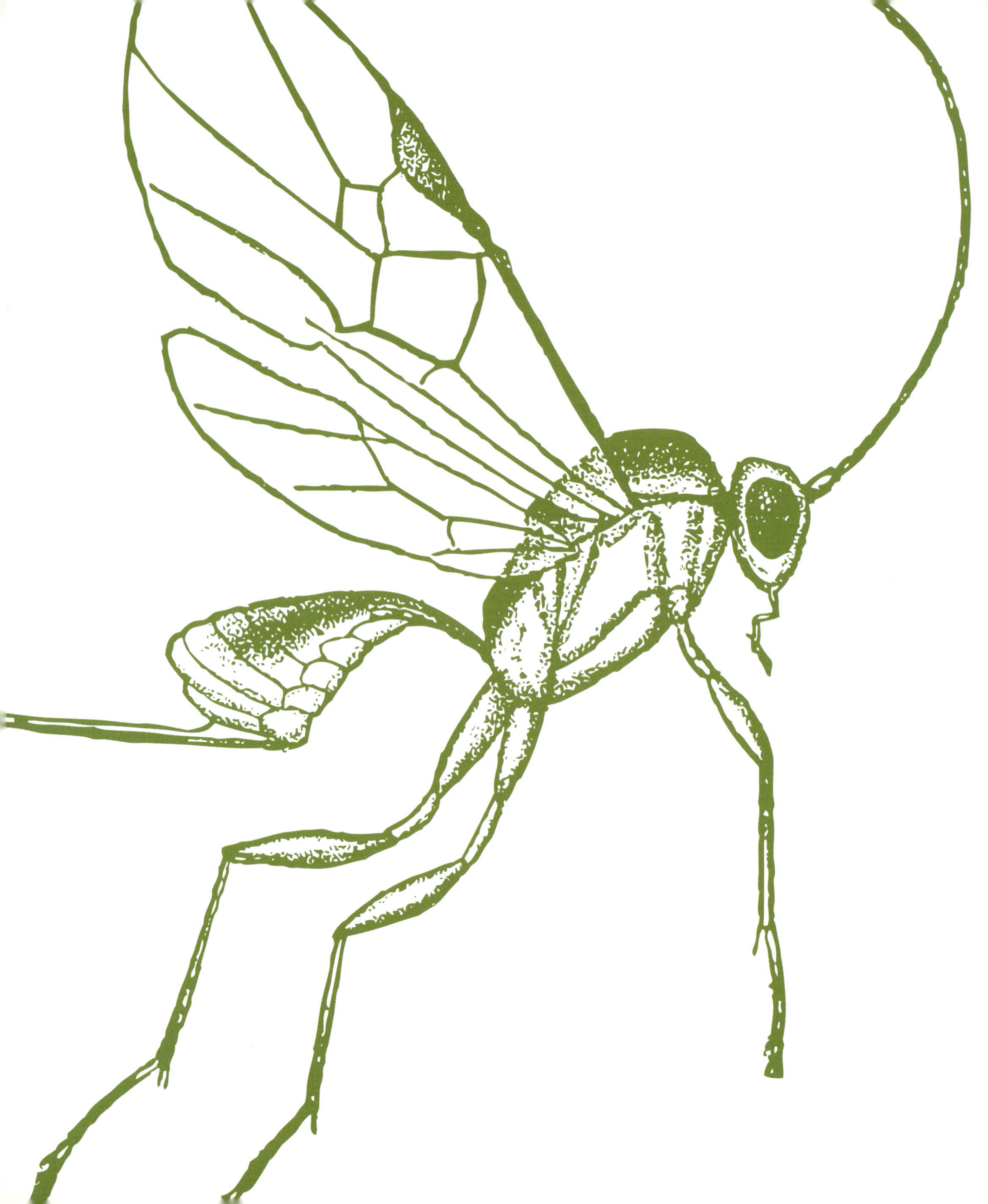

INSECTS

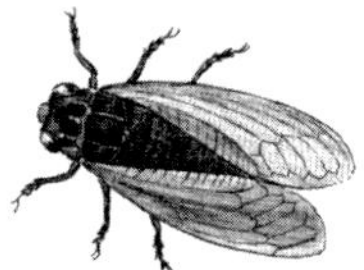

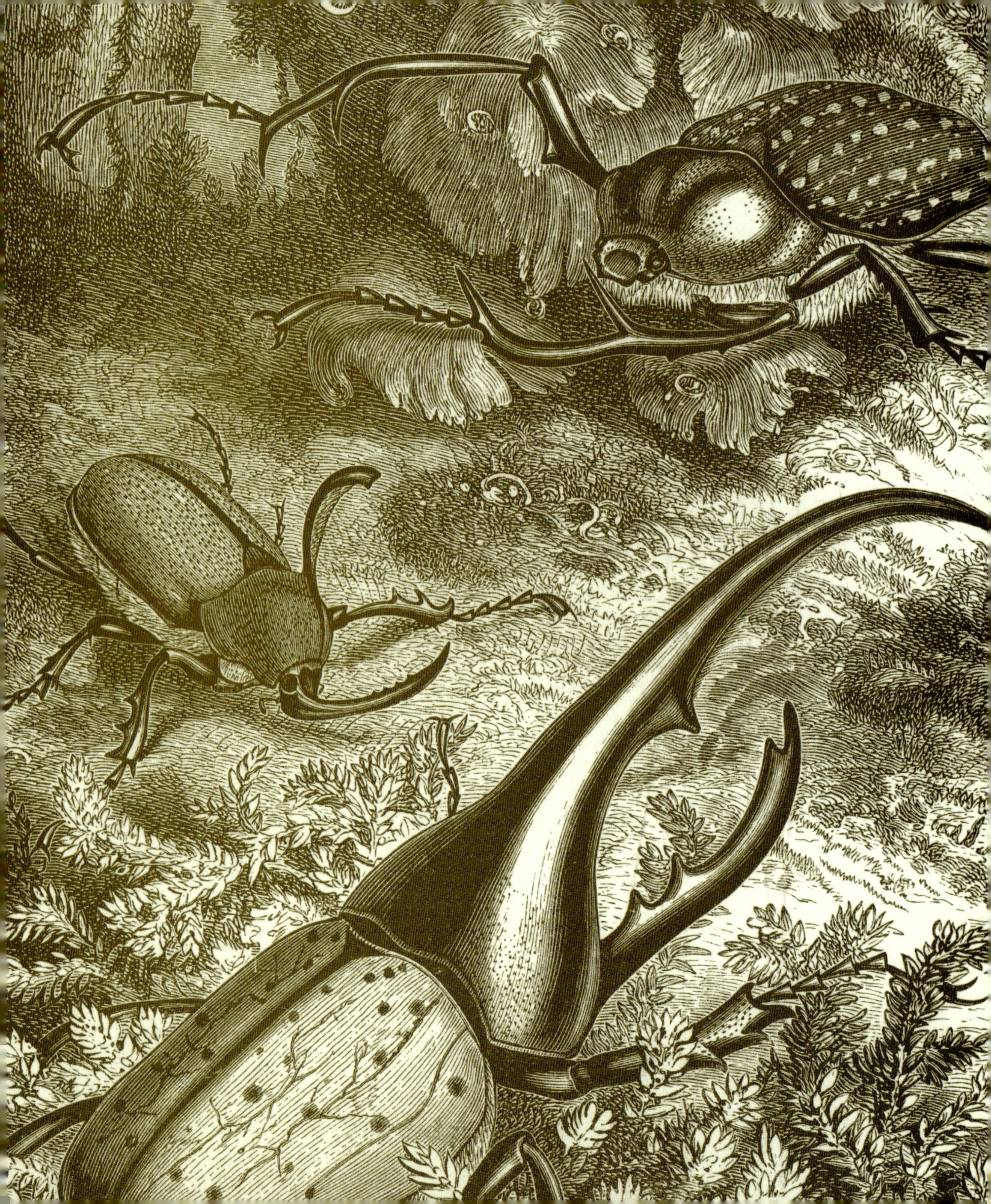

INSECTS

PICTURA

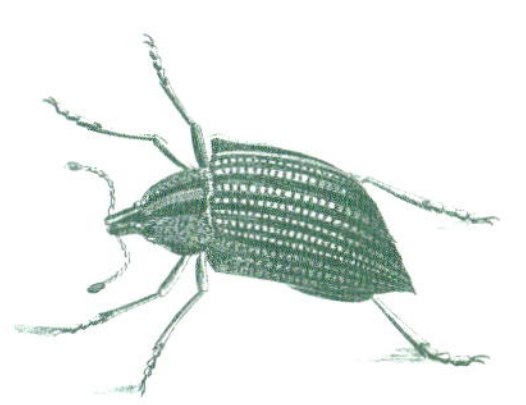

DOVER PUBLICATIONS, INC. | Mineola, New York

By Alan Weller.
Designed by Joel Waldrep.

Insects is a new work, first published by Dover Publications, Inc., in 2008.

The CD-ROM file names correspond to the images in the book. All of the artwork stored on the CD-ROM can be imported directly into a wide range of design and word-processing programs on either Windows or Macintosh platforms. No further installation is necessary.

ISBN 10: 0-486-99752-9
ISBN 13: 978-0-486-99752-0
Manufactured in the United States of America
Dover Publications, Inc., 31 East 2nd Street, Mineola, NY 11501
www.doverpublications.com

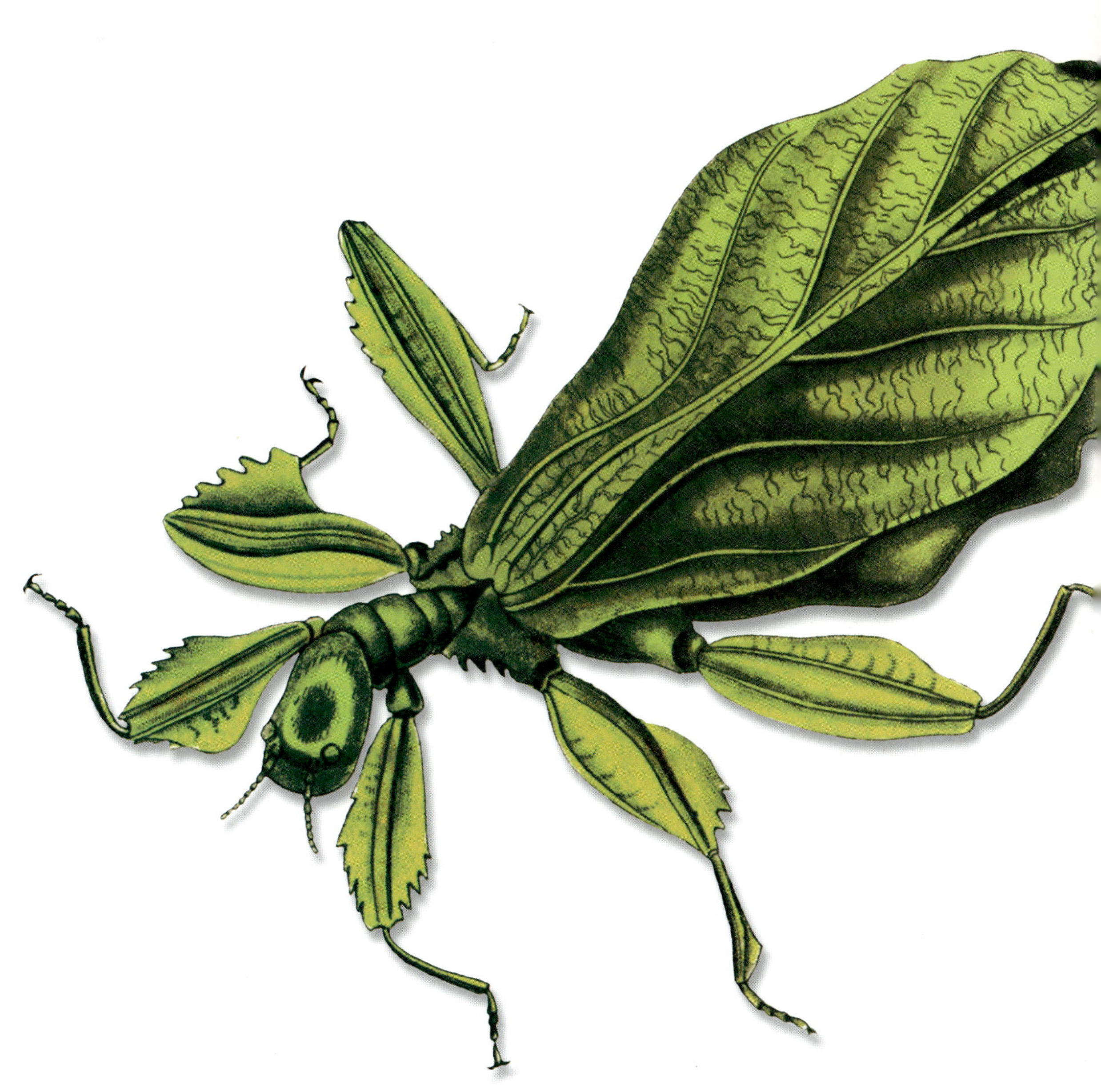

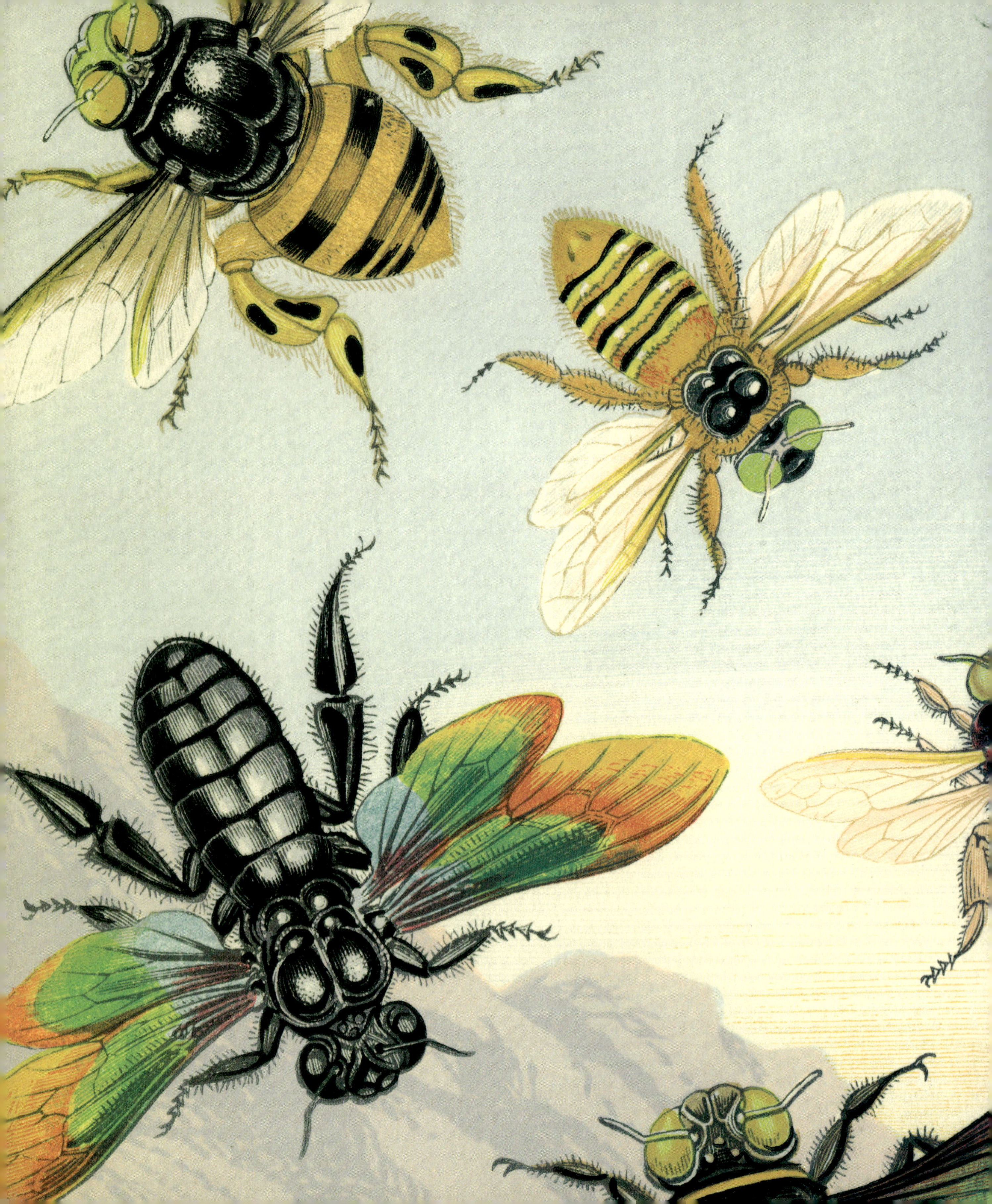

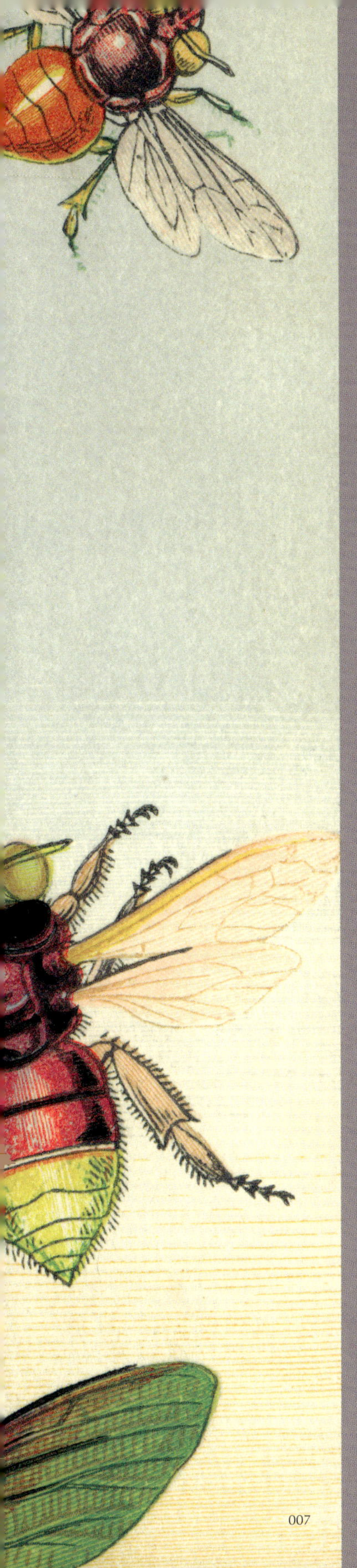

007

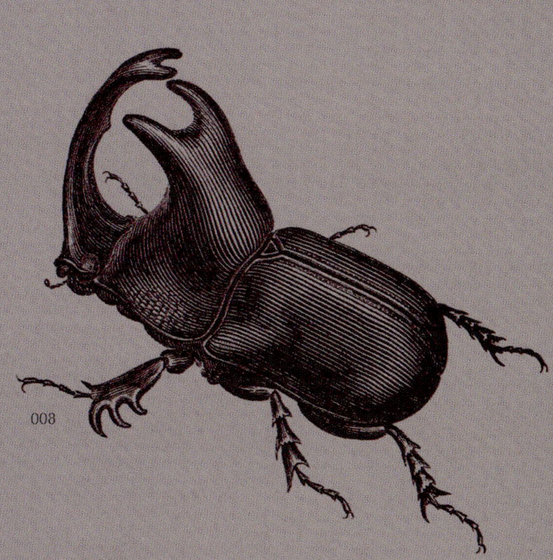

008

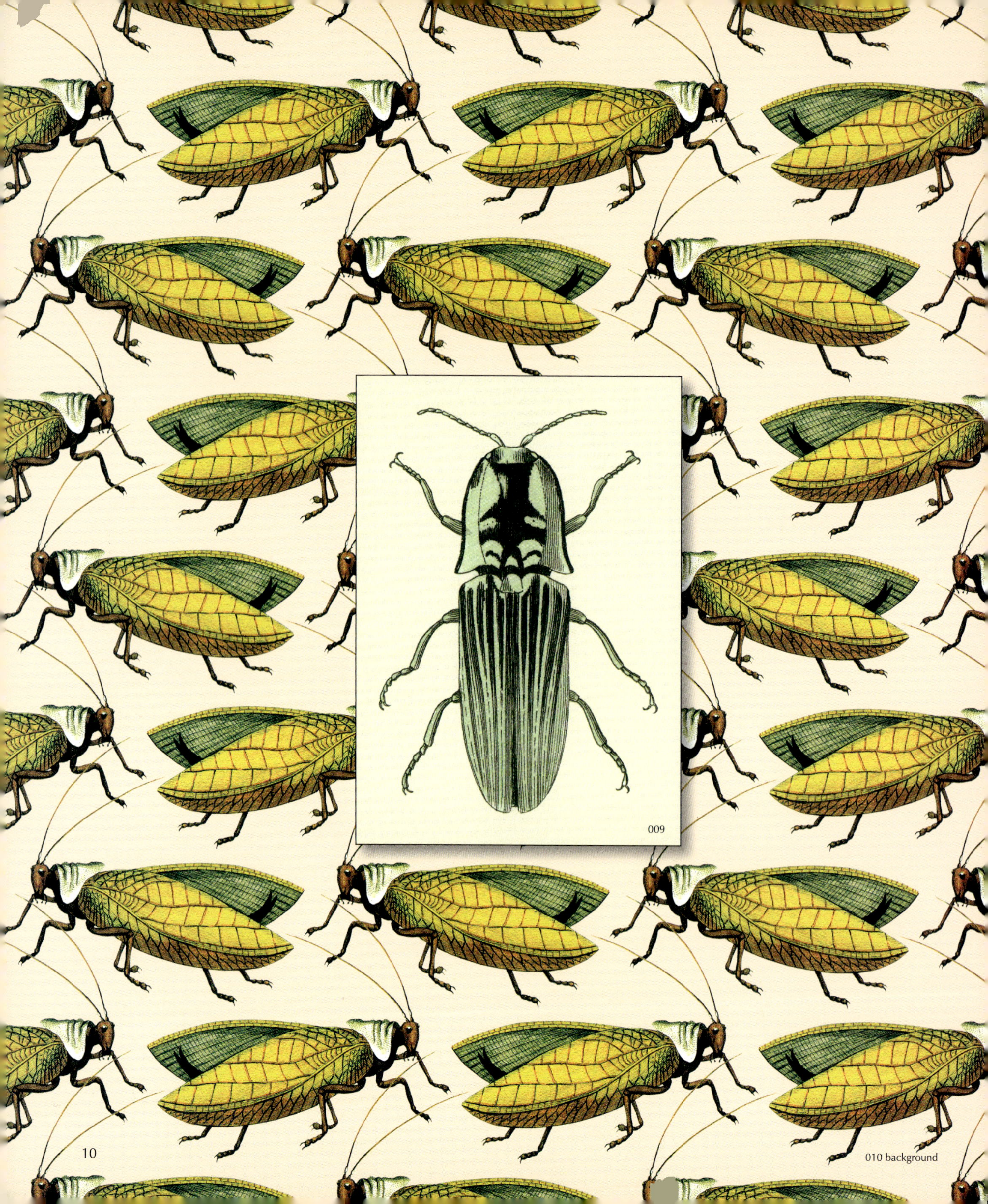

010 background

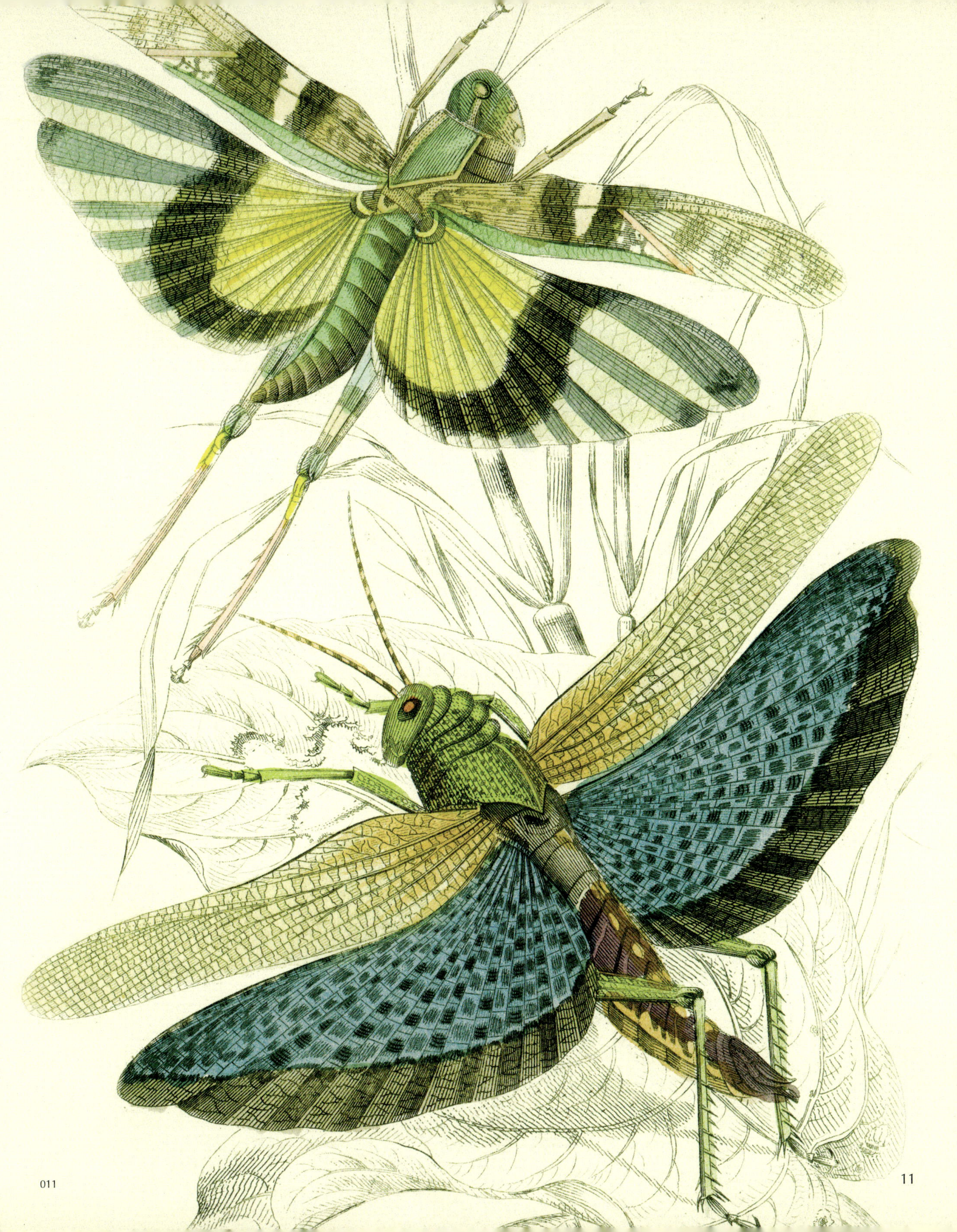

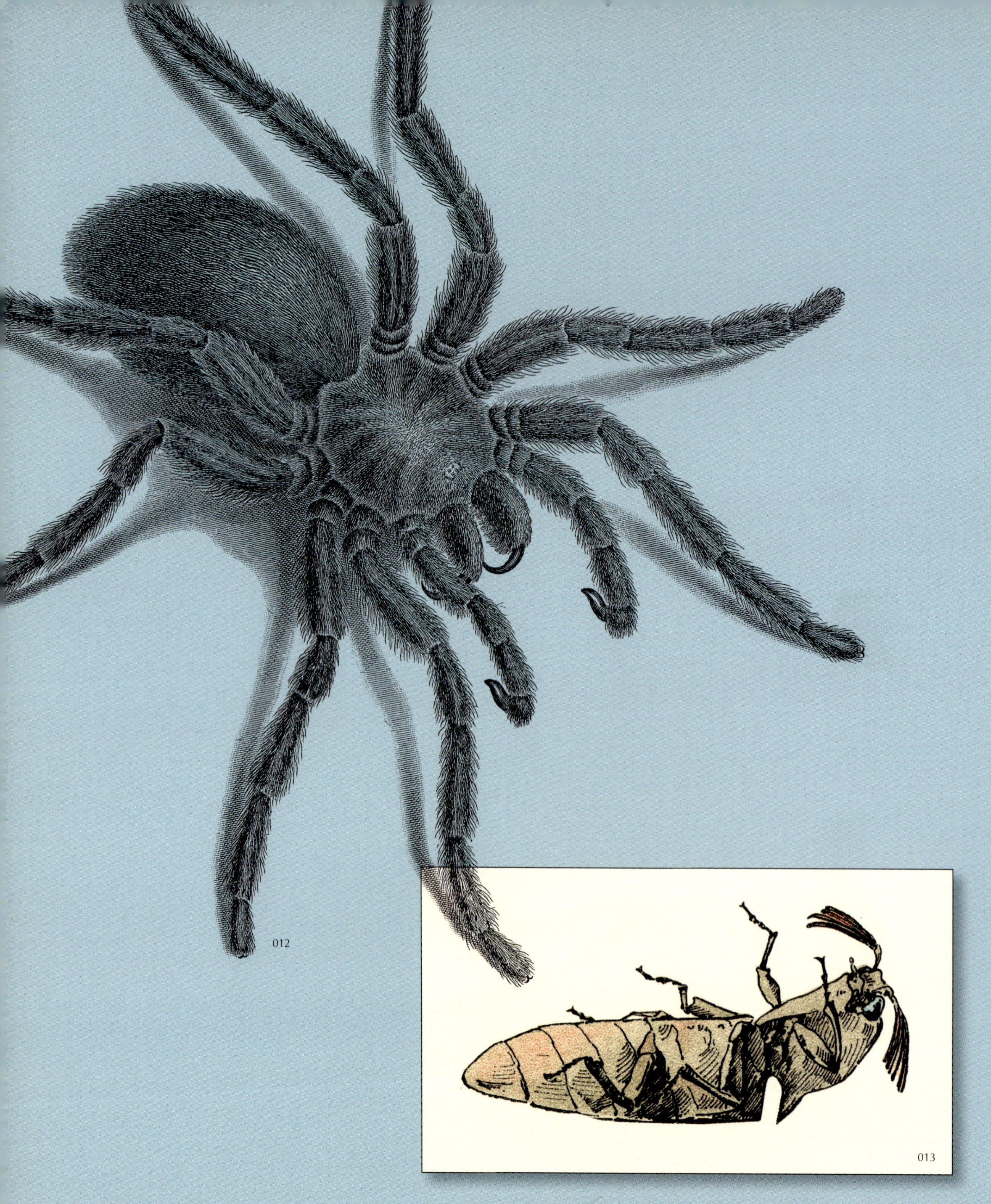

012

013

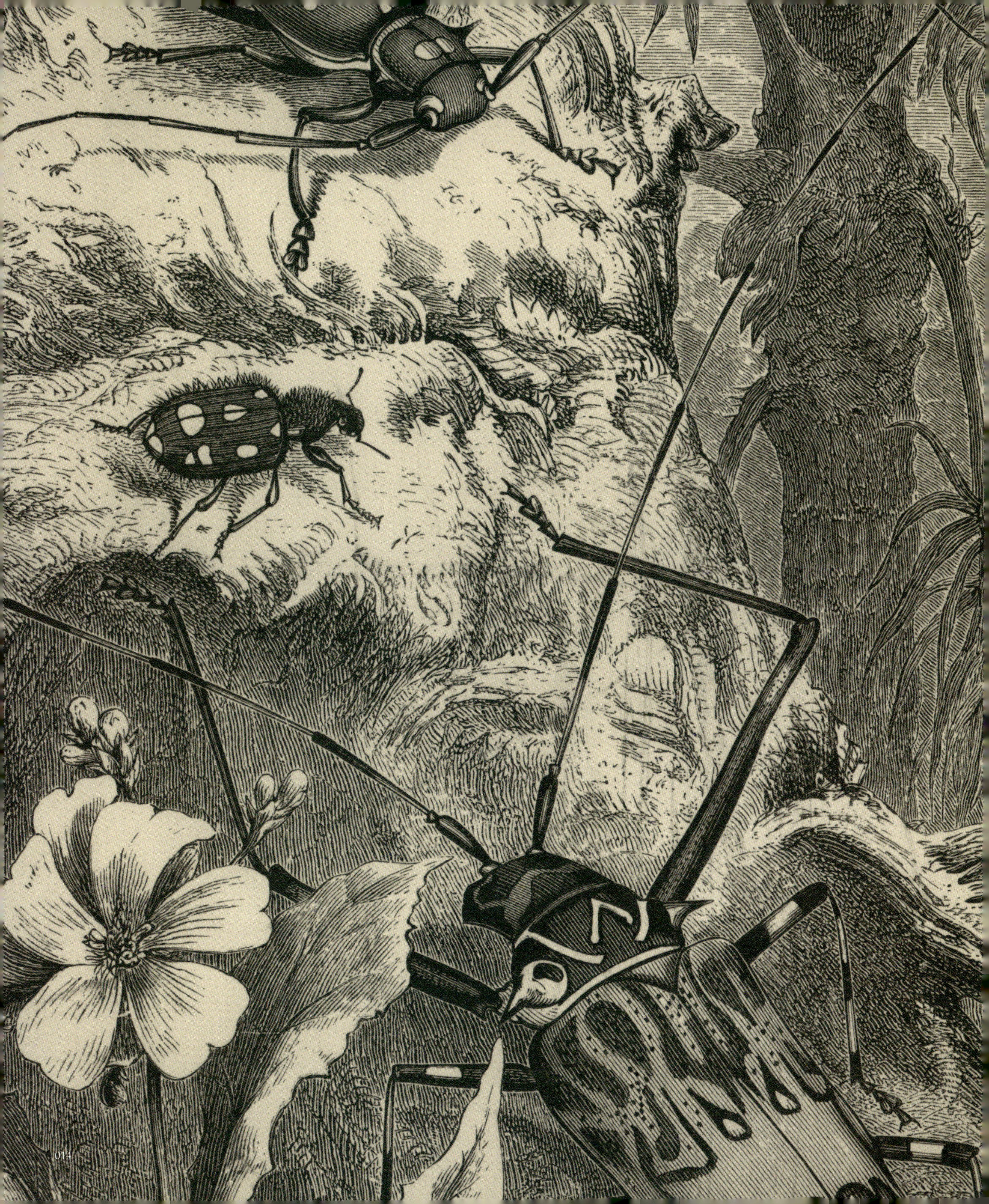

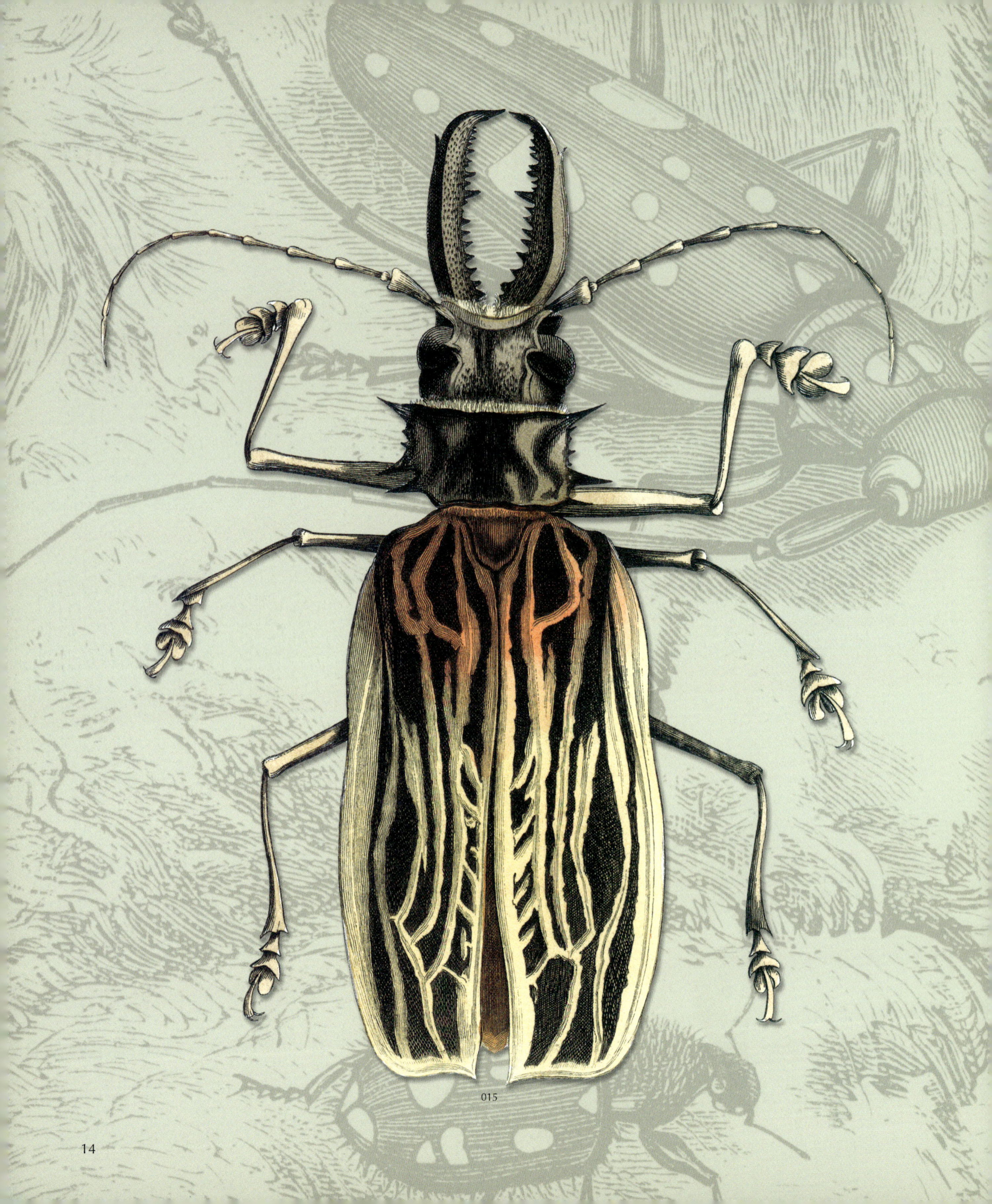

015

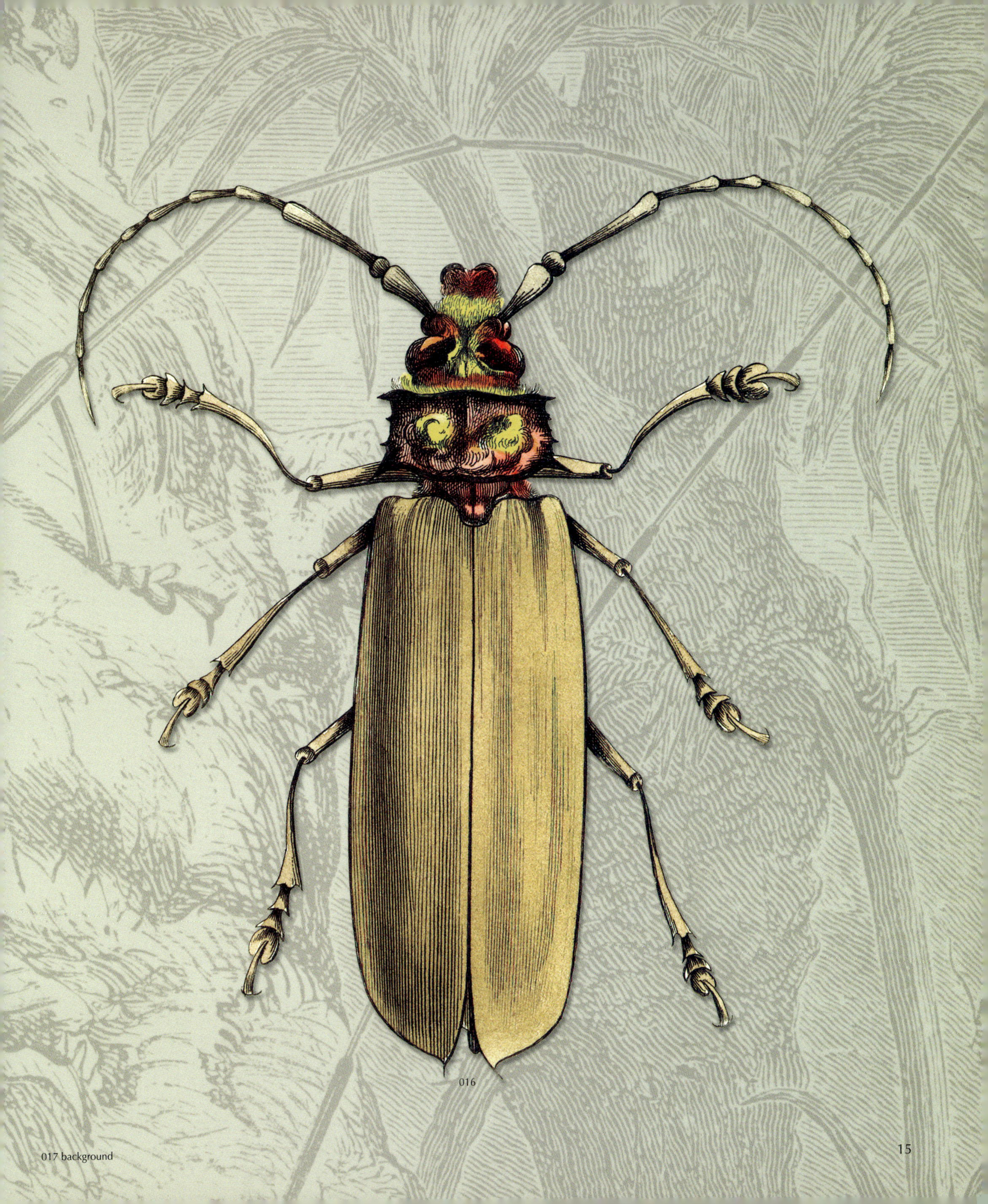

016

017 background

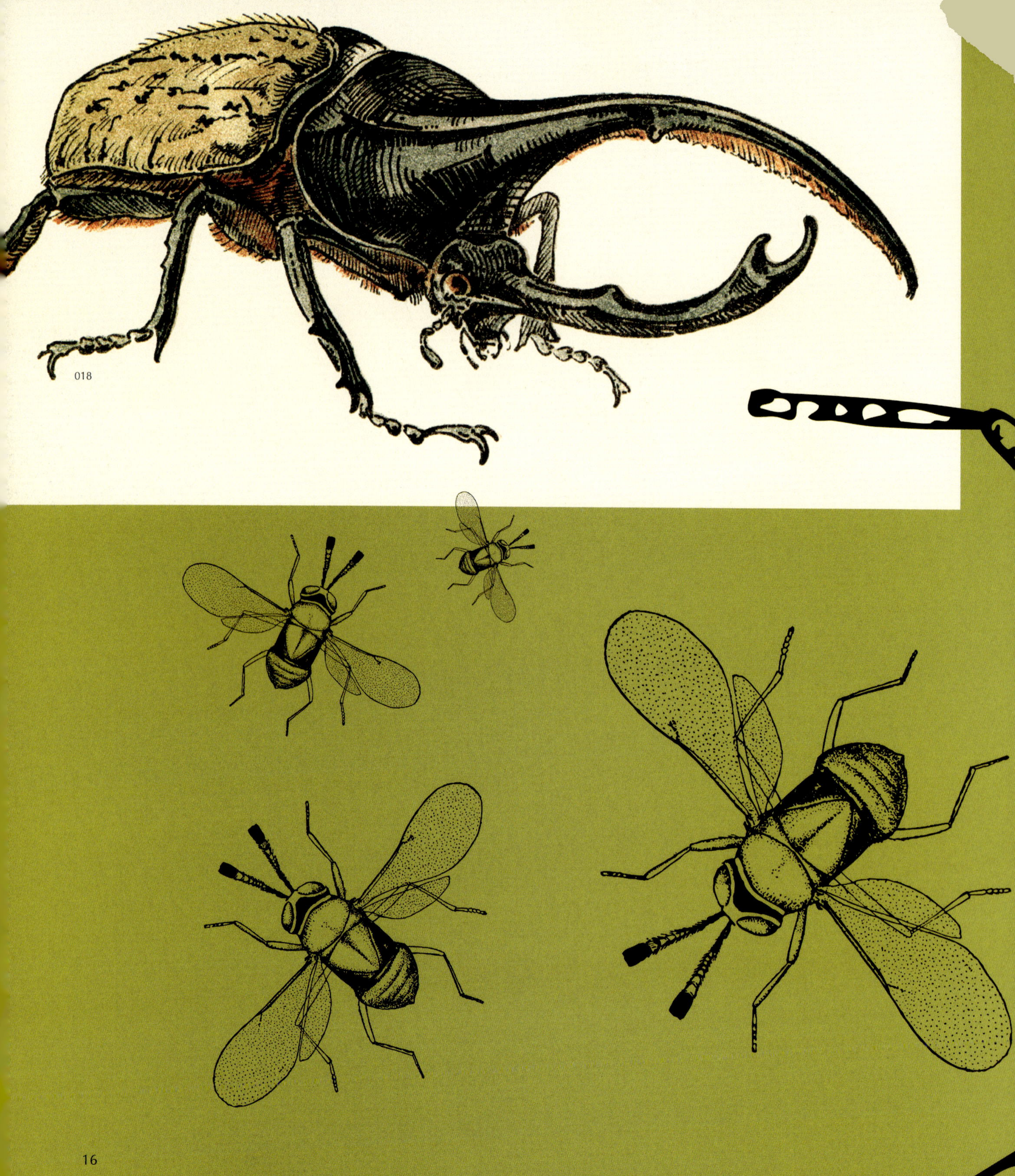
018

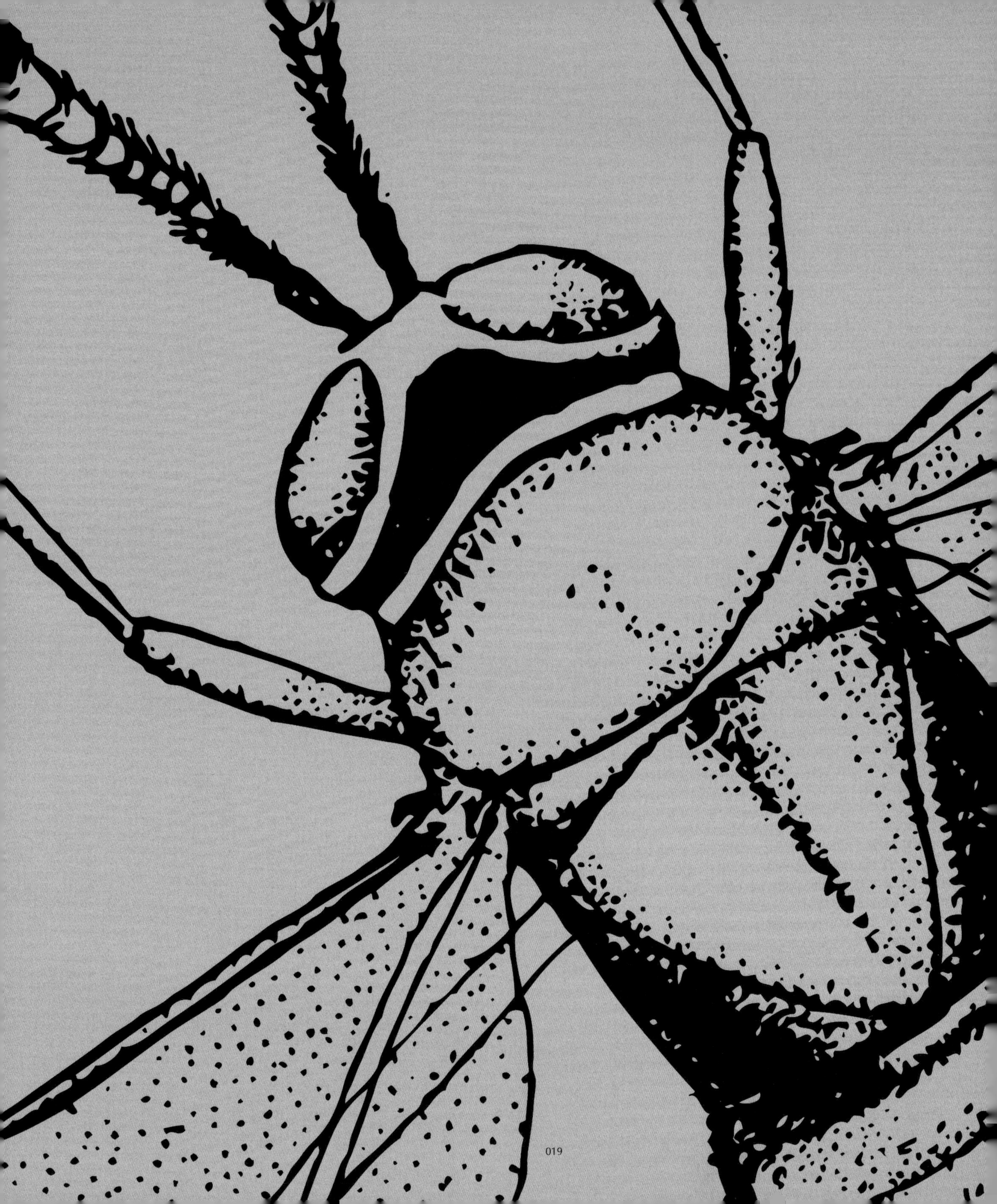

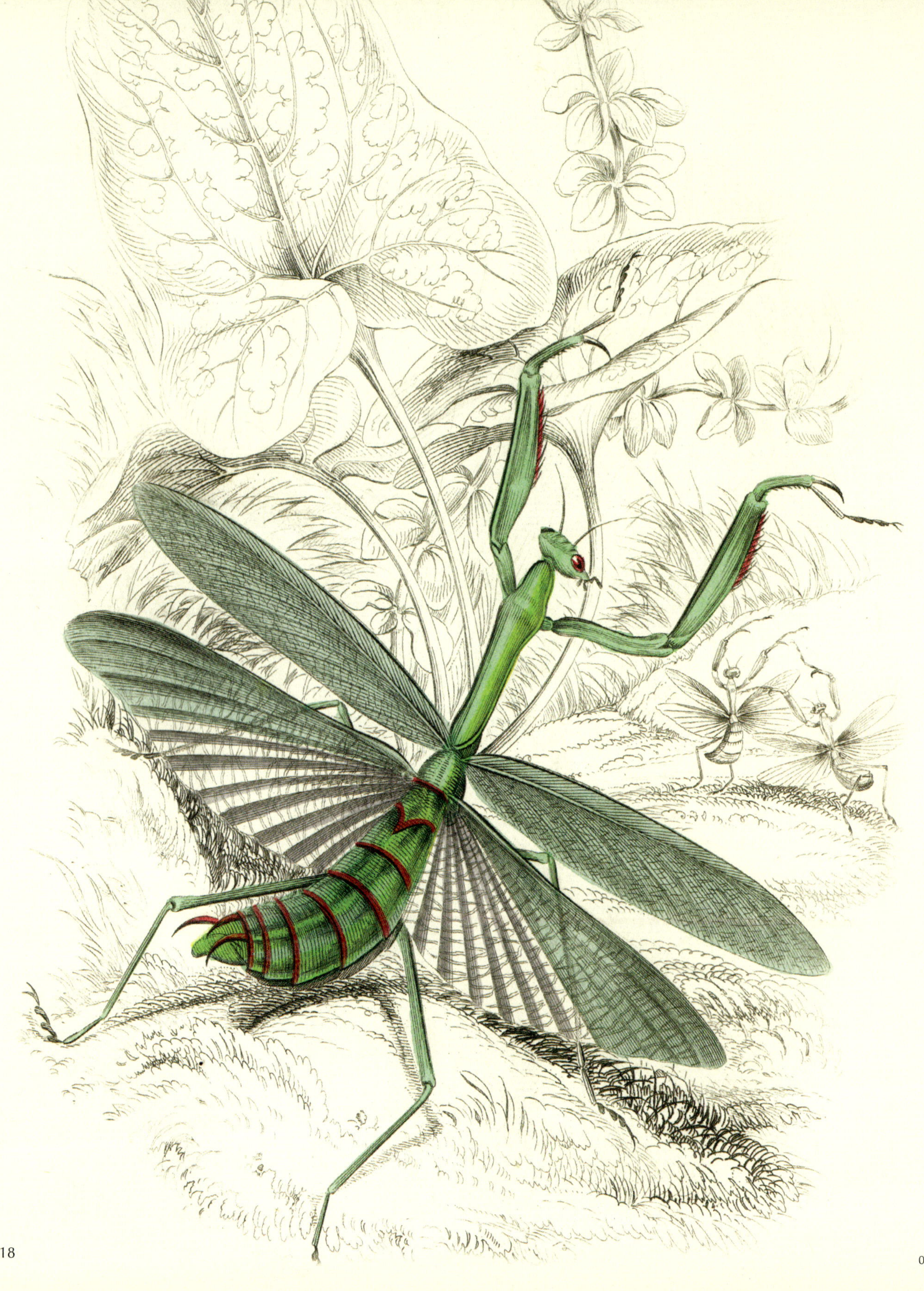

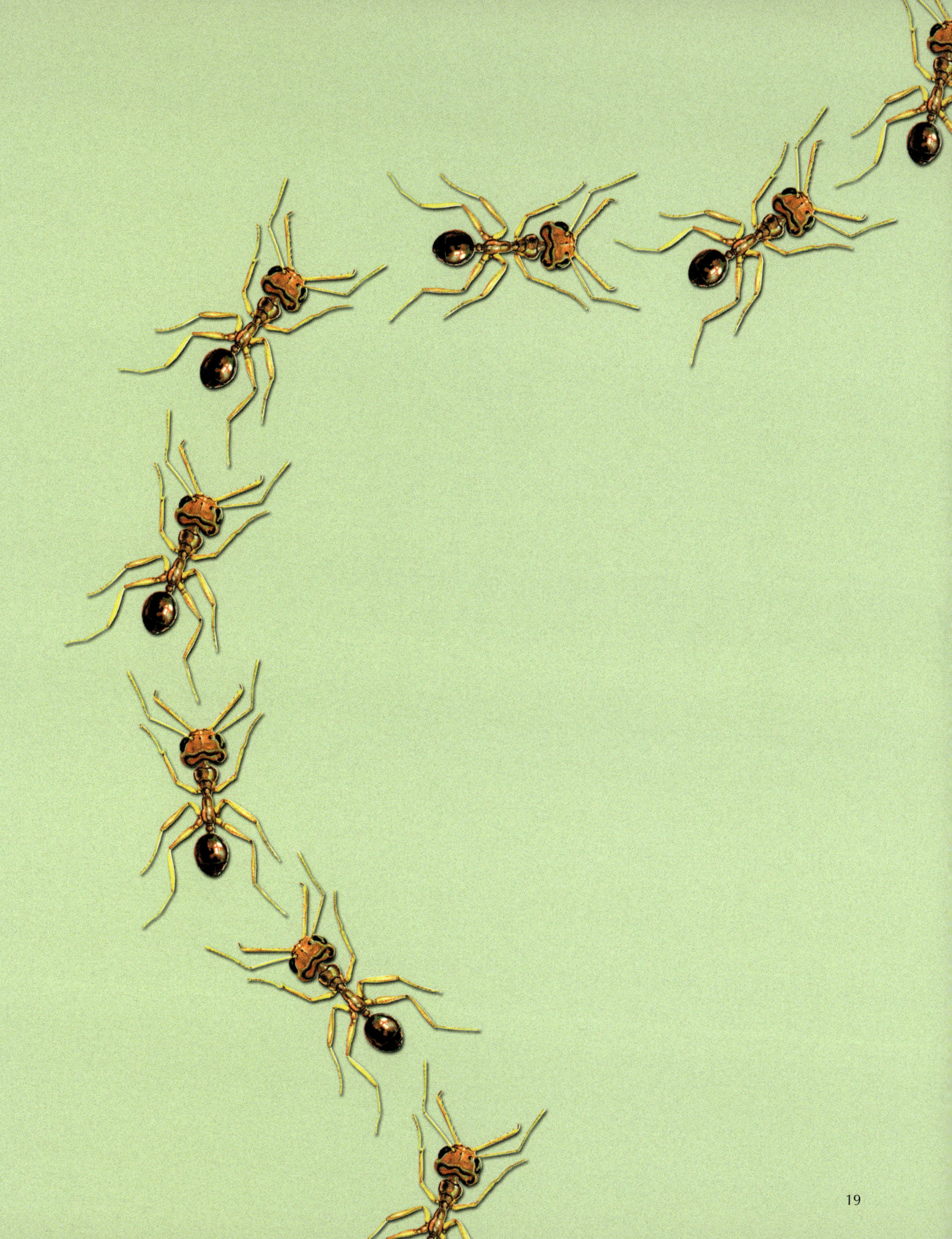

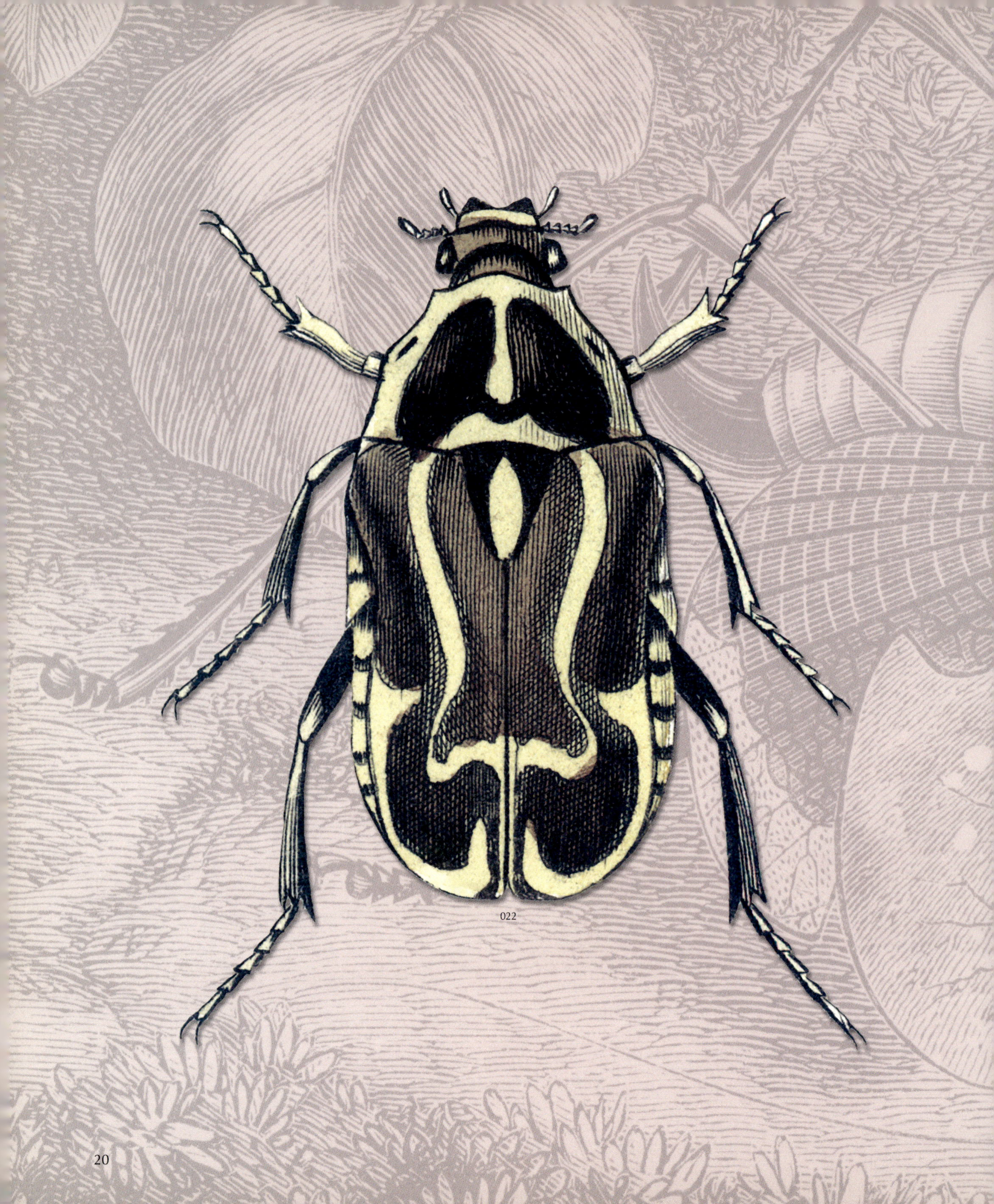

022

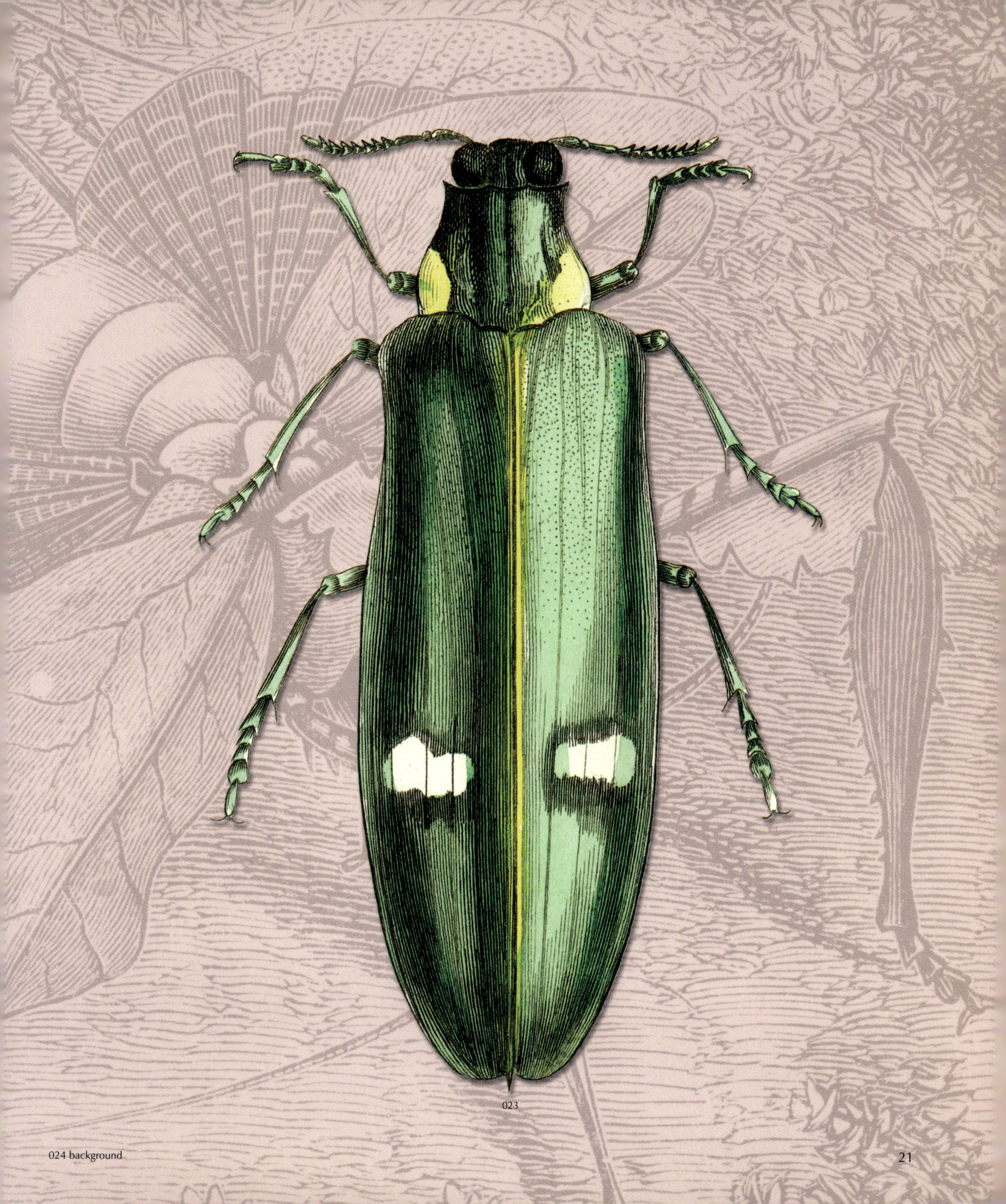

023

024 background

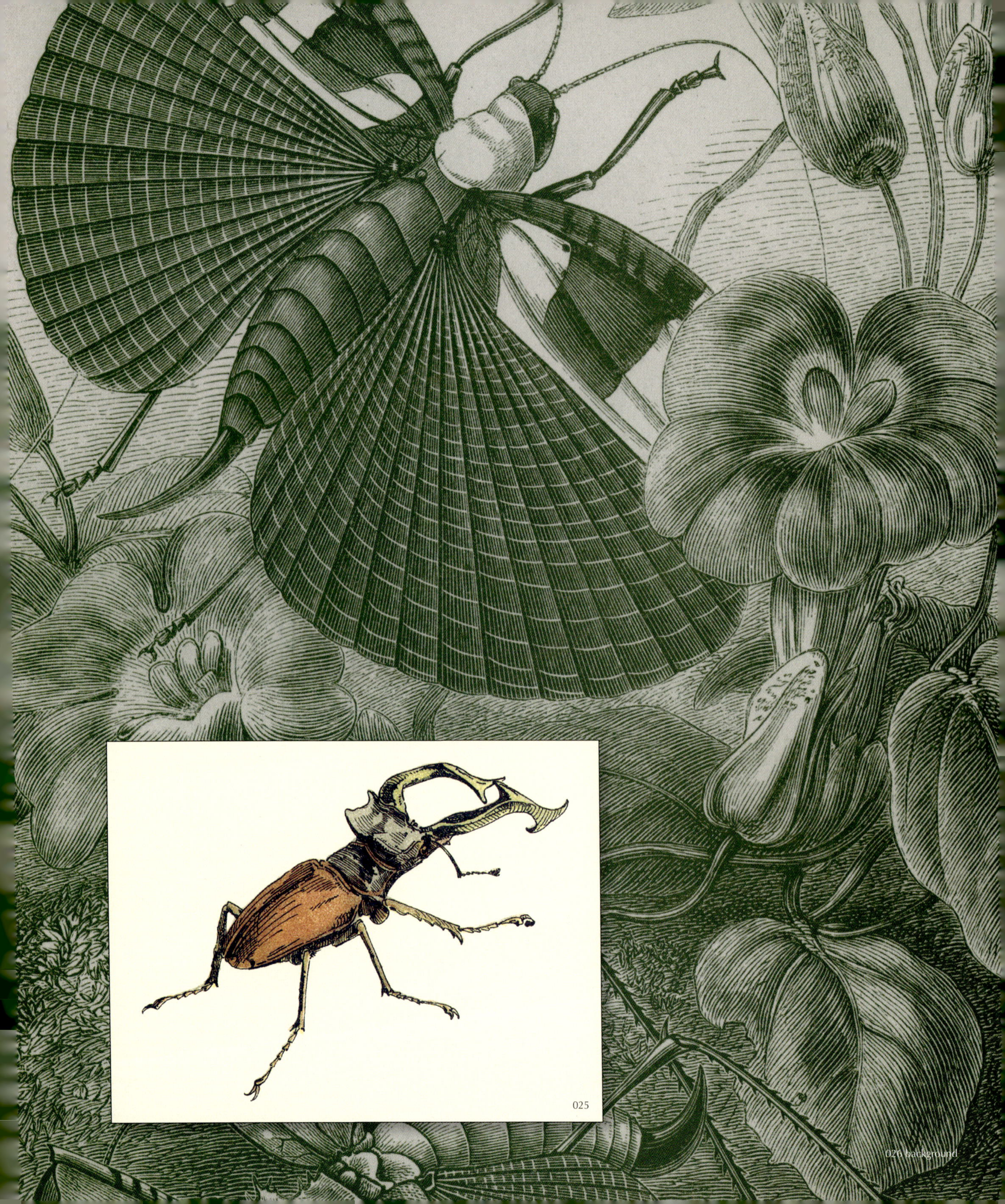

025
026 background

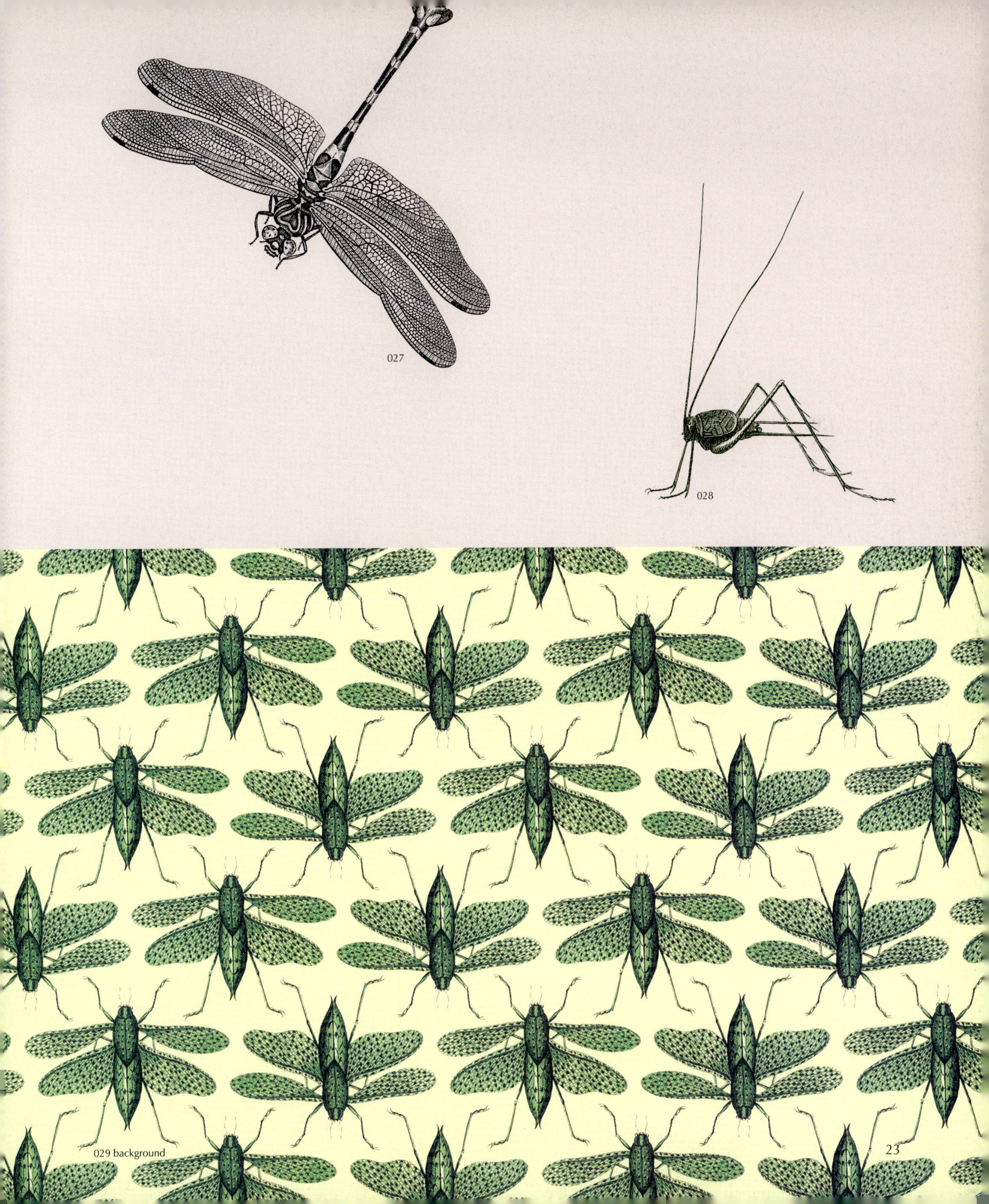

027

028

029 background

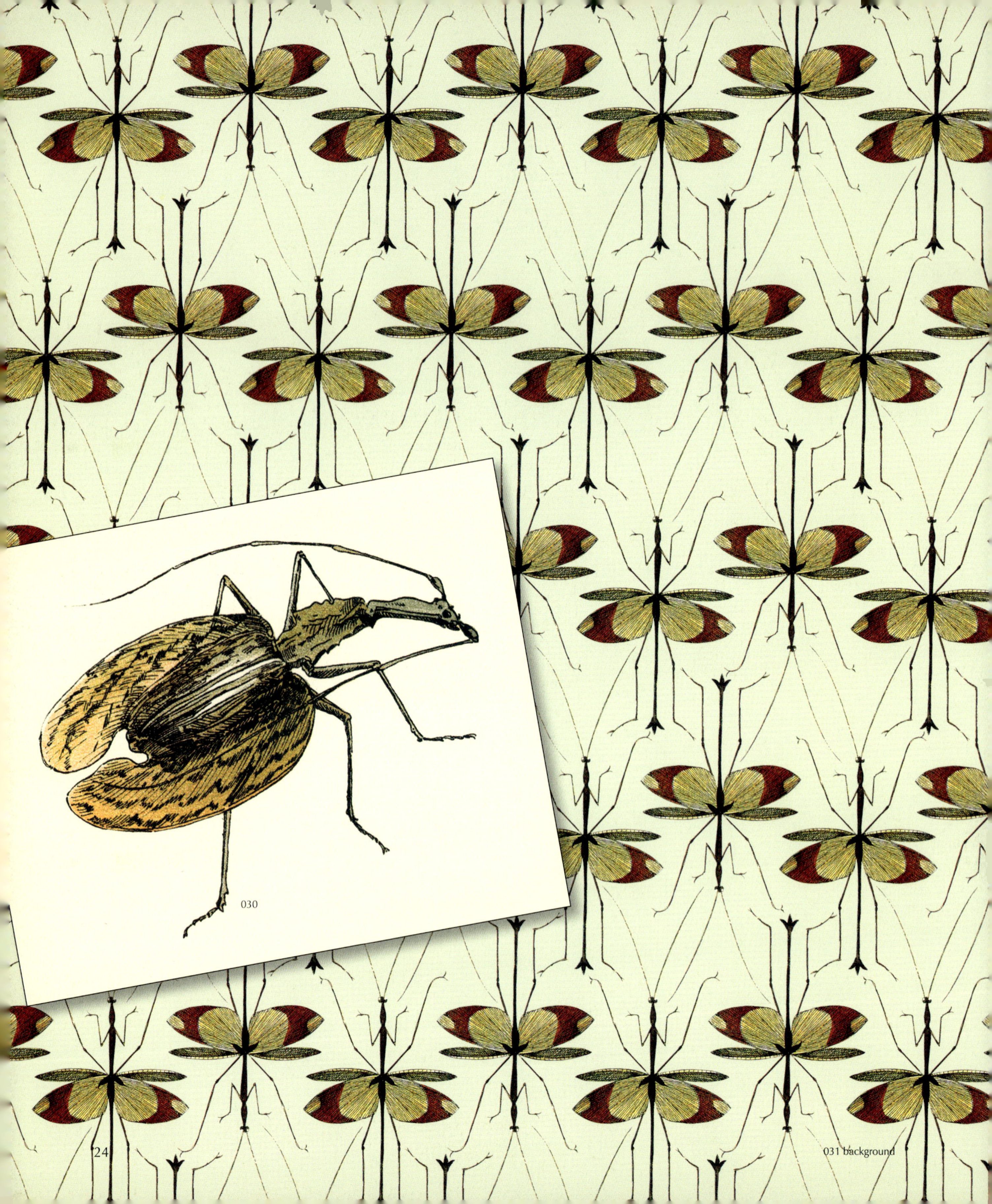

030

031 background

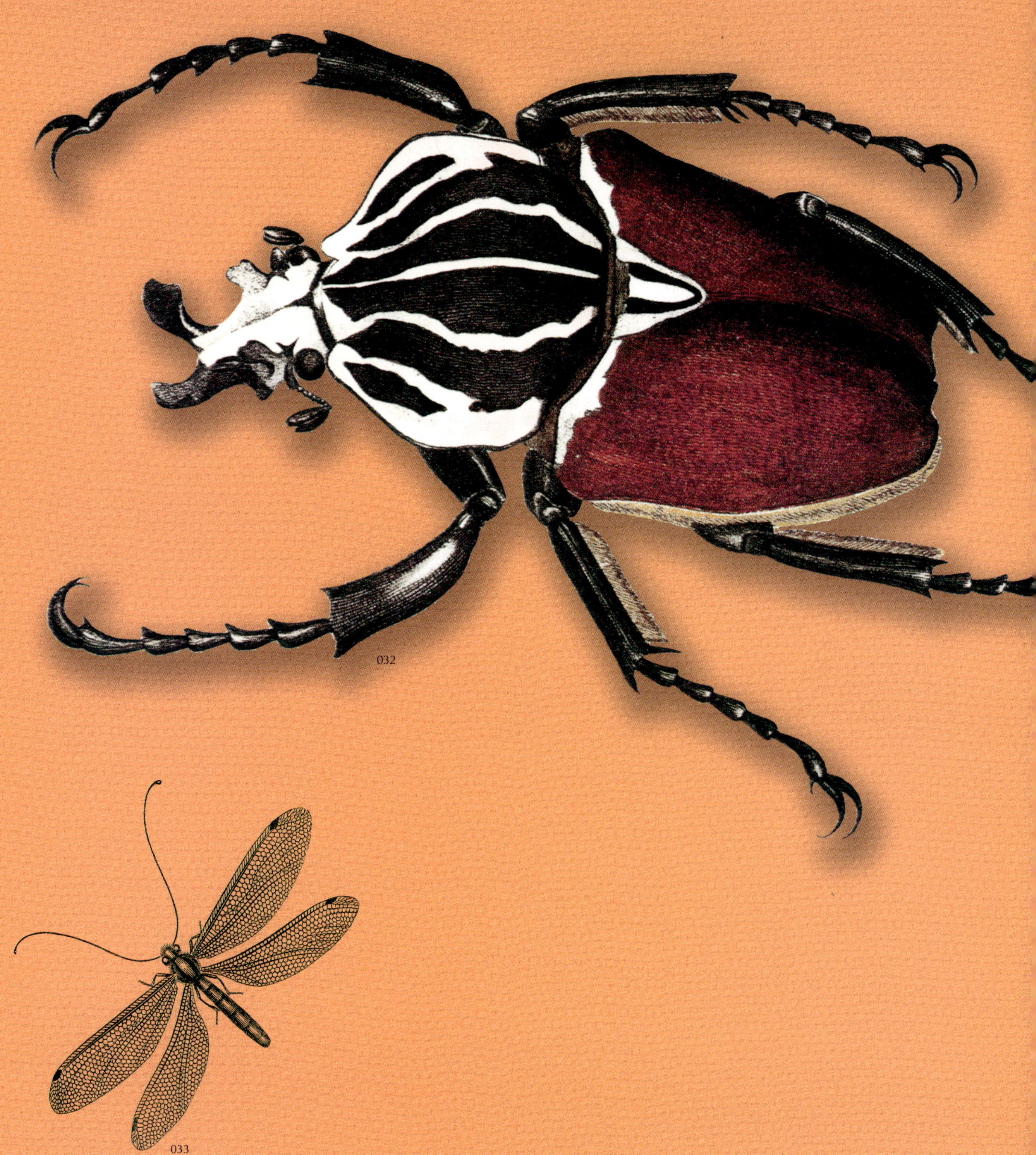

032

033

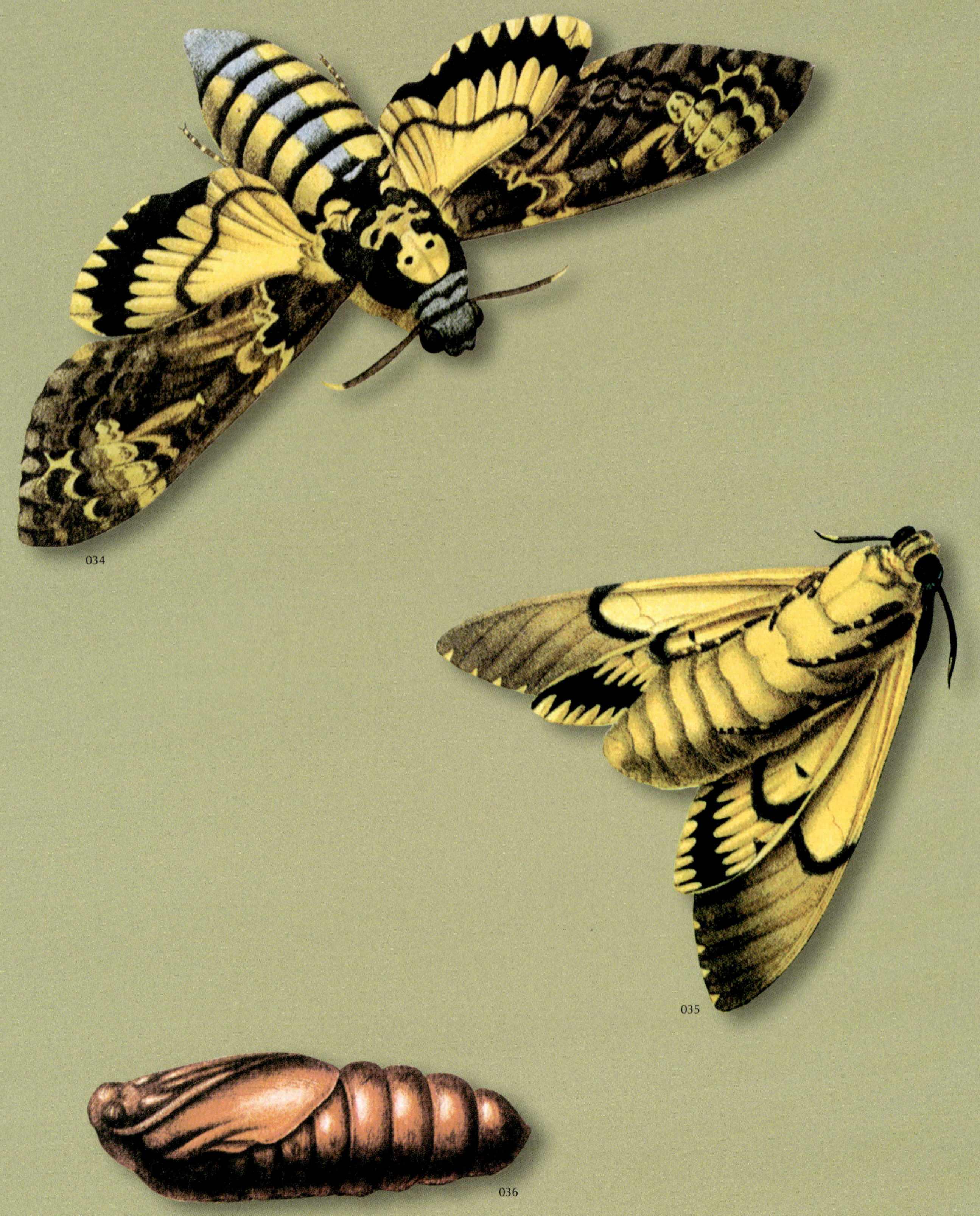
034
035
036

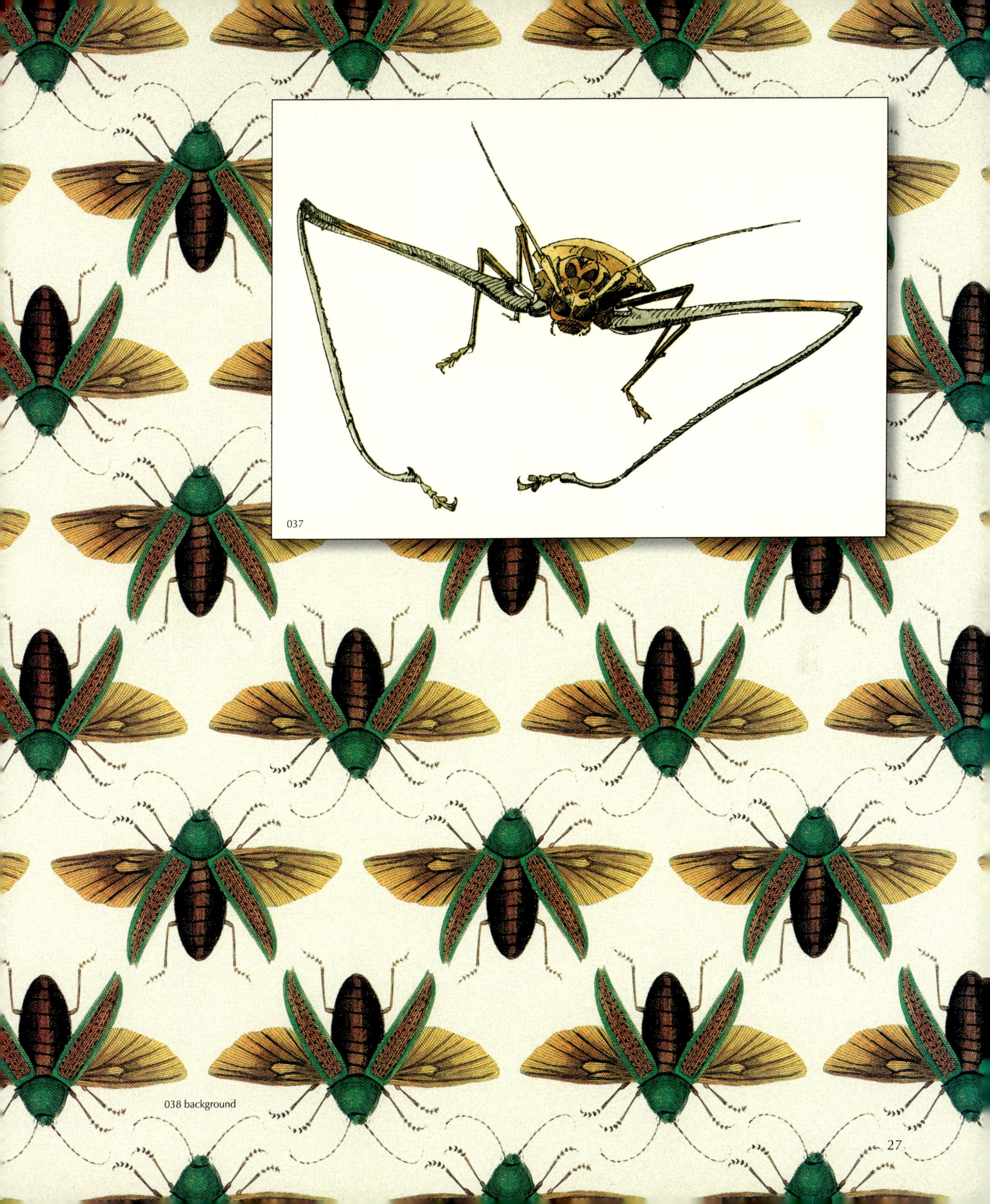
037
038 background

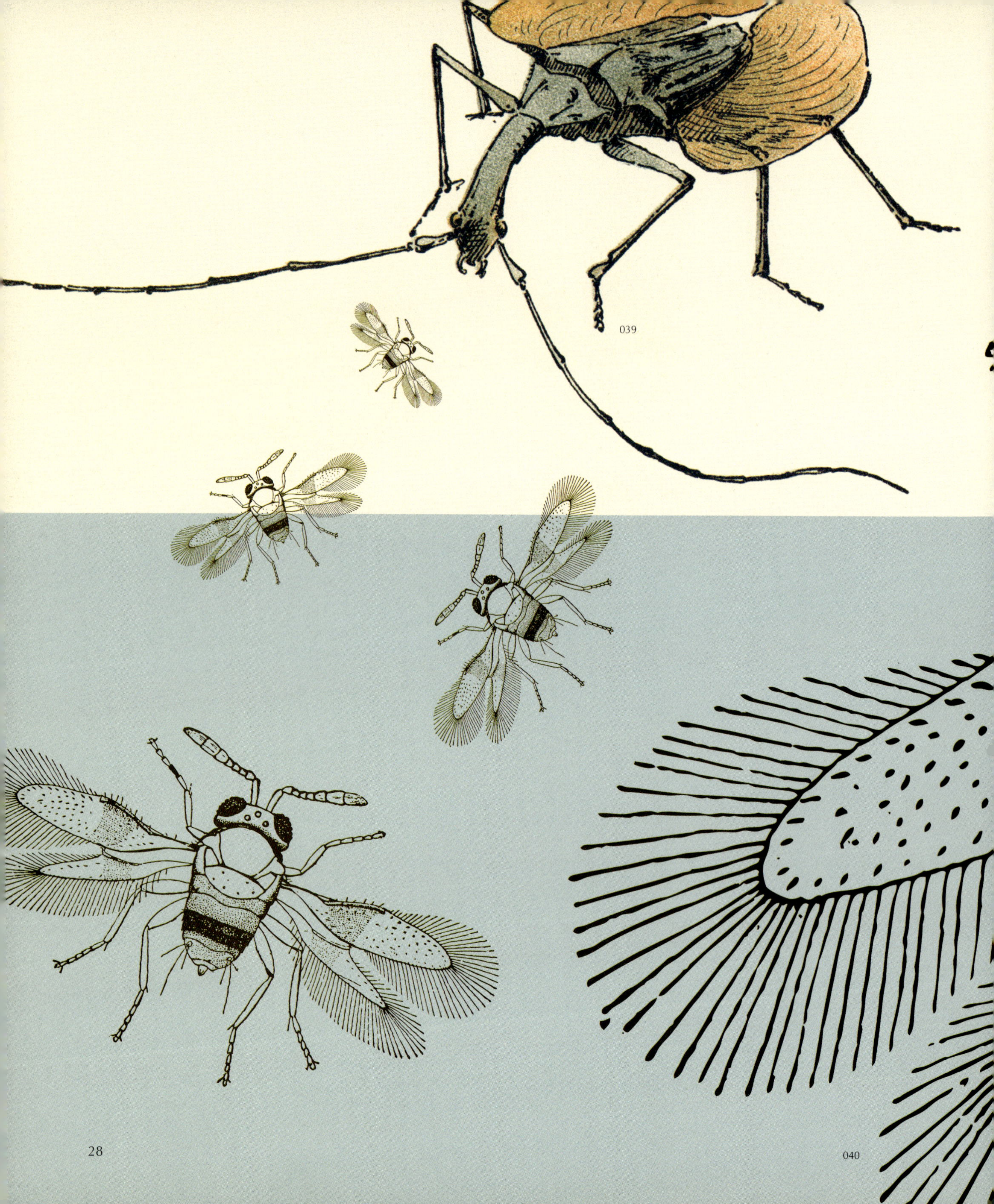
039
040

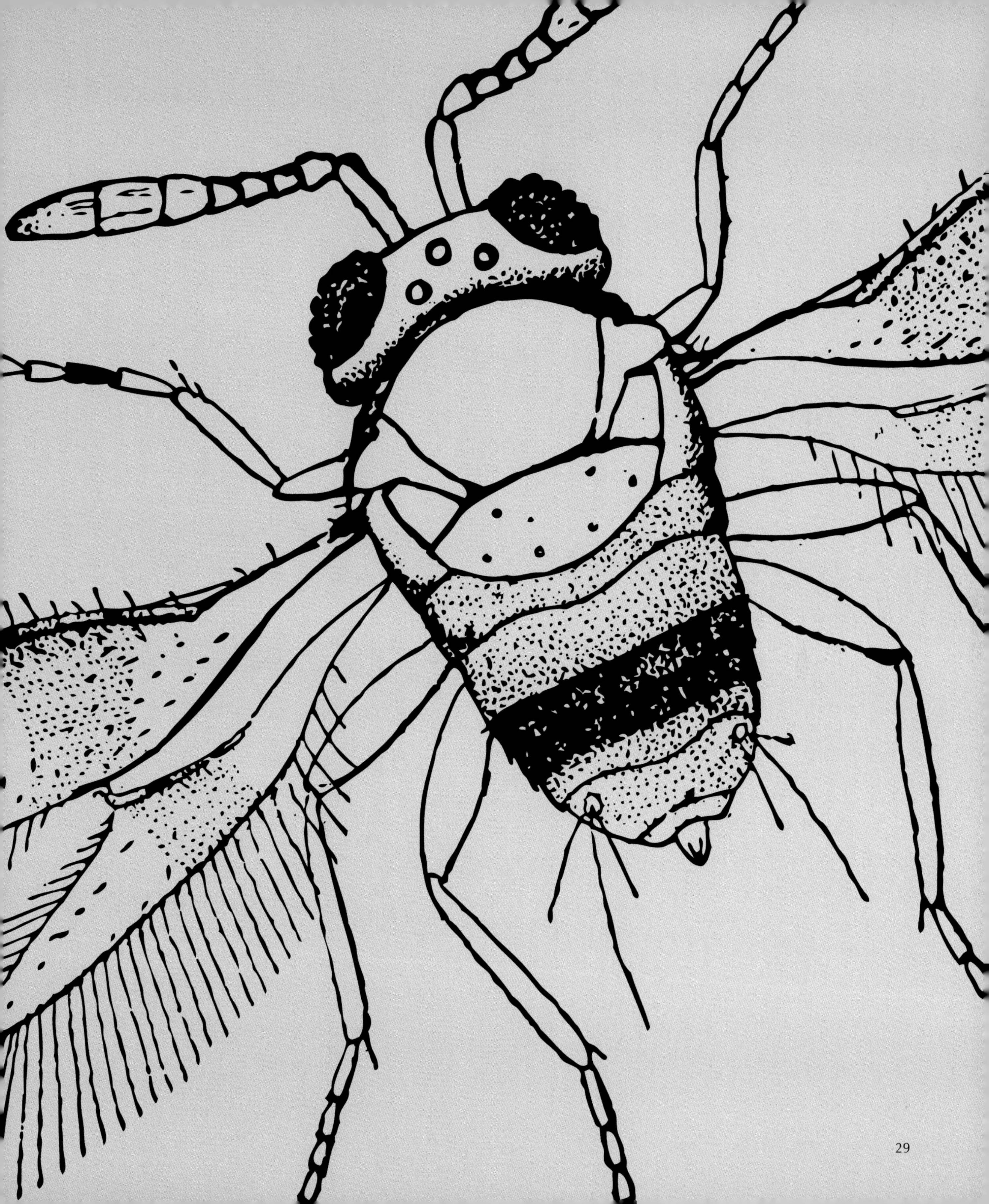

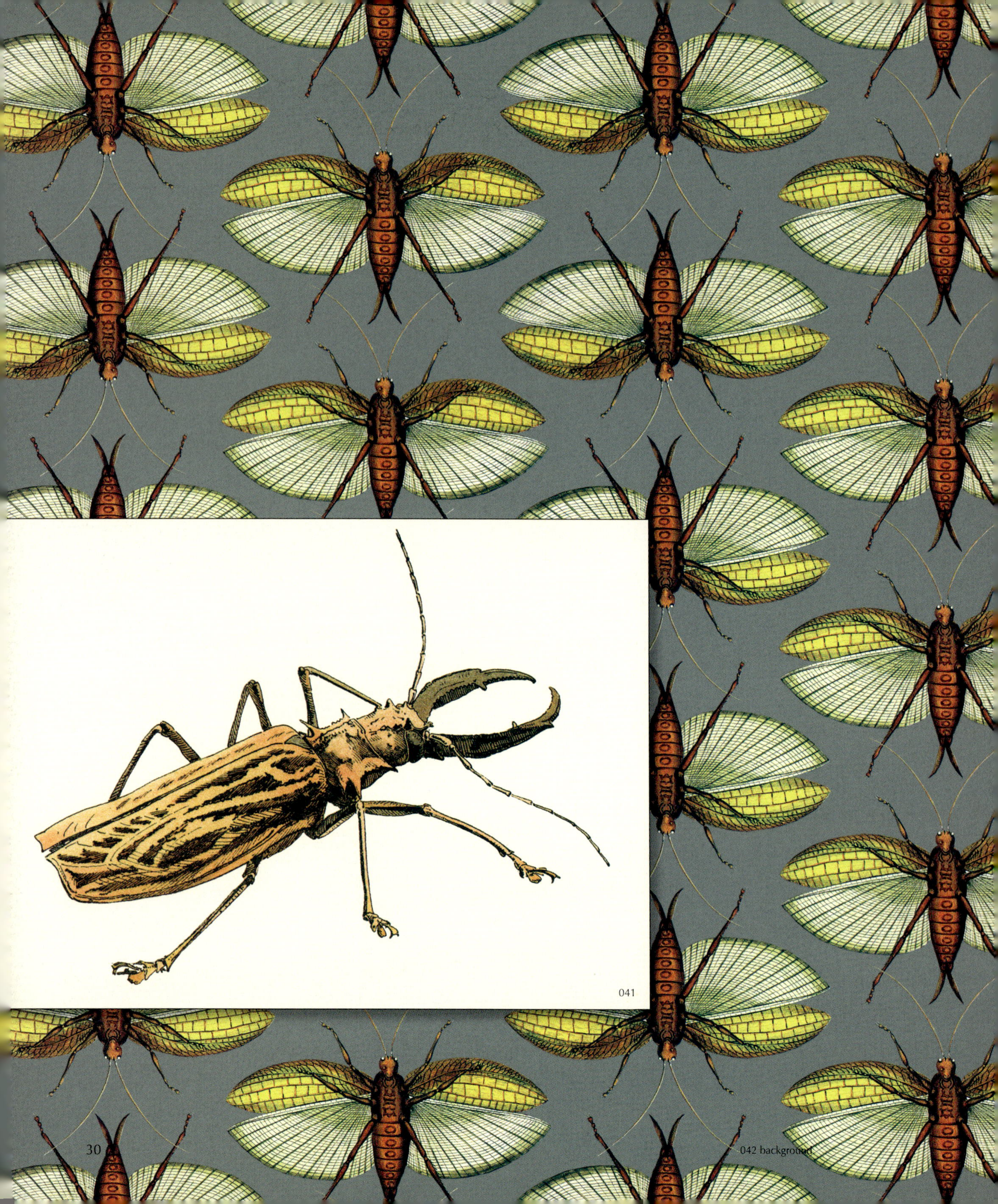
041

042 background

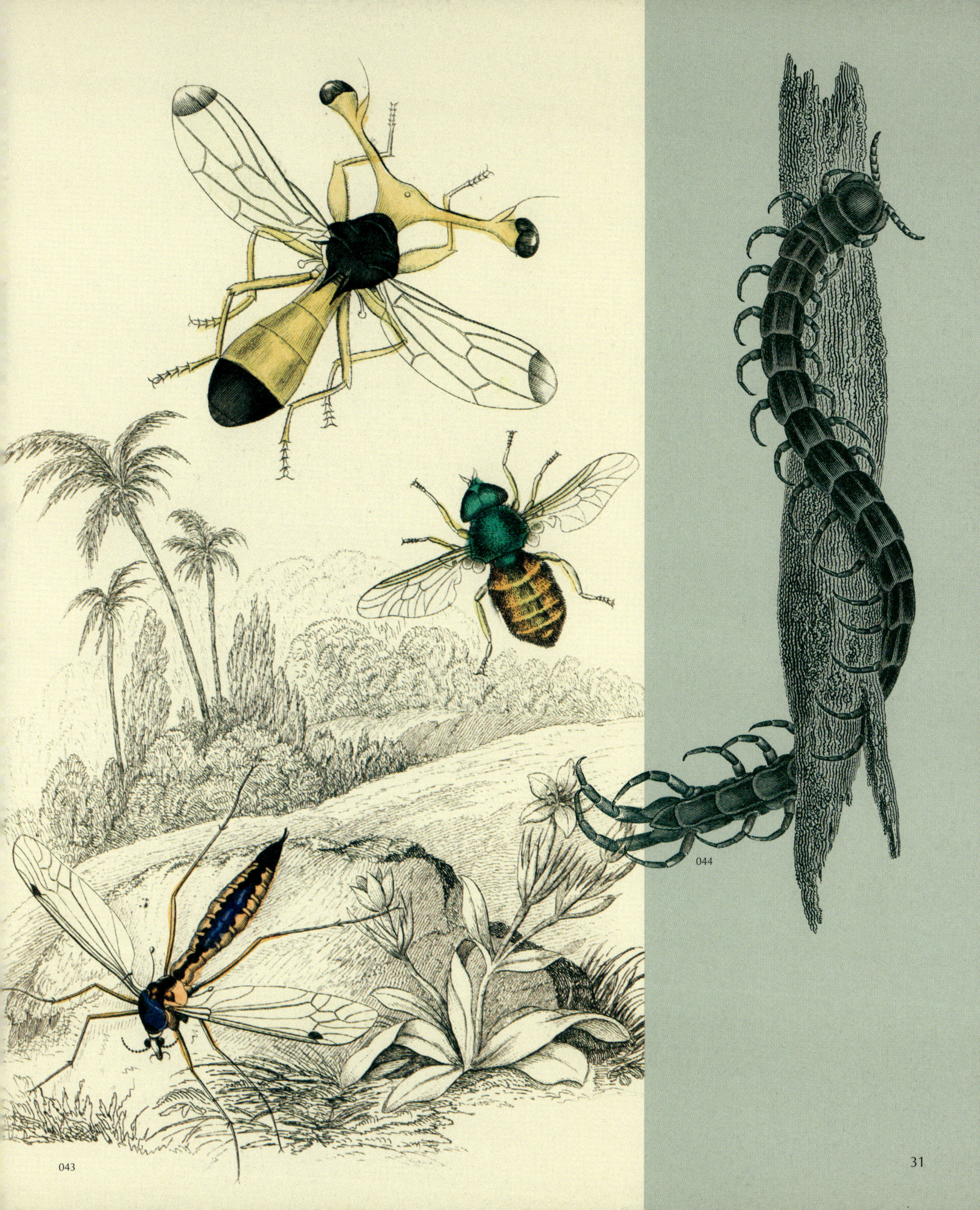
044
043

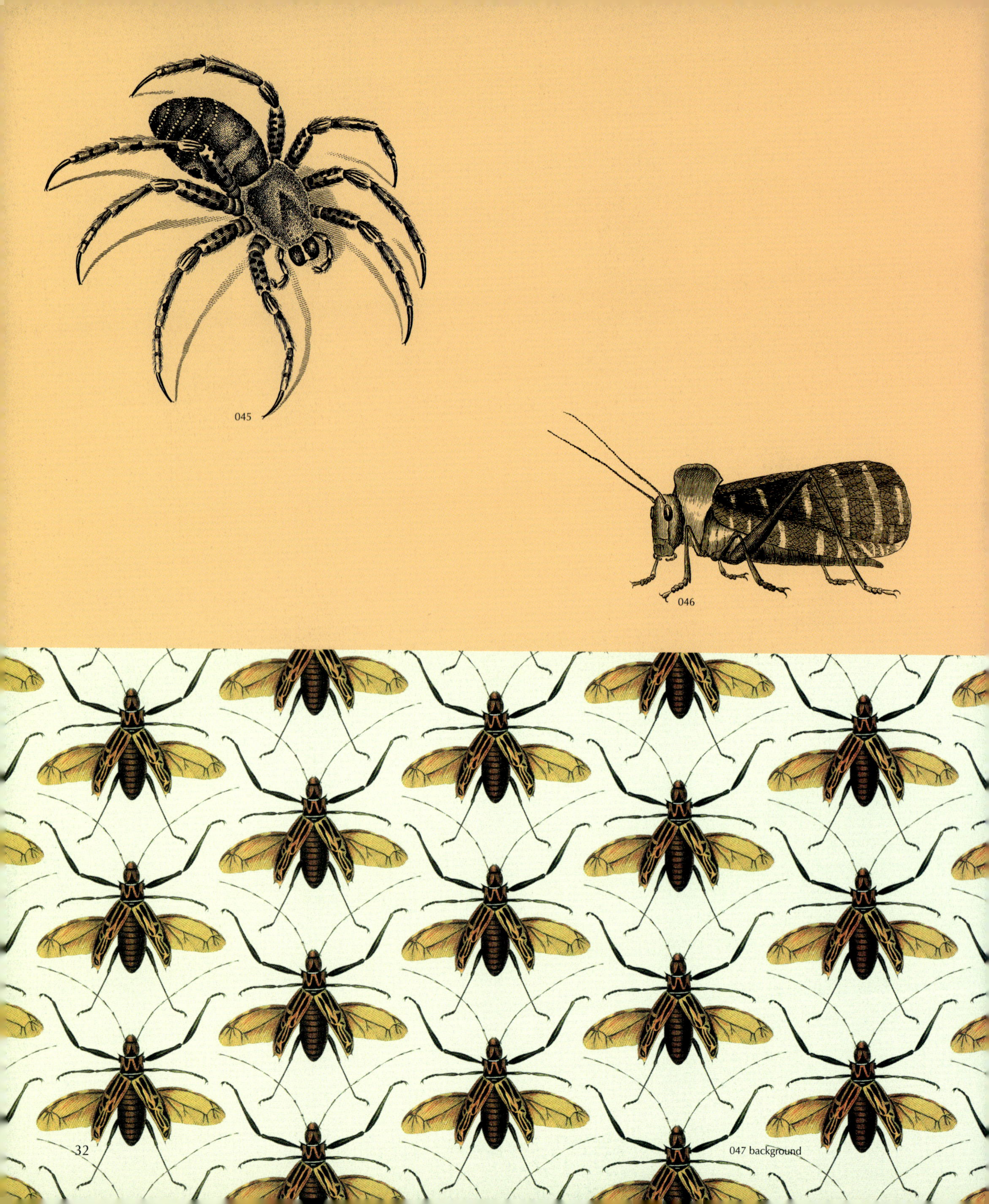

045

046

047 background

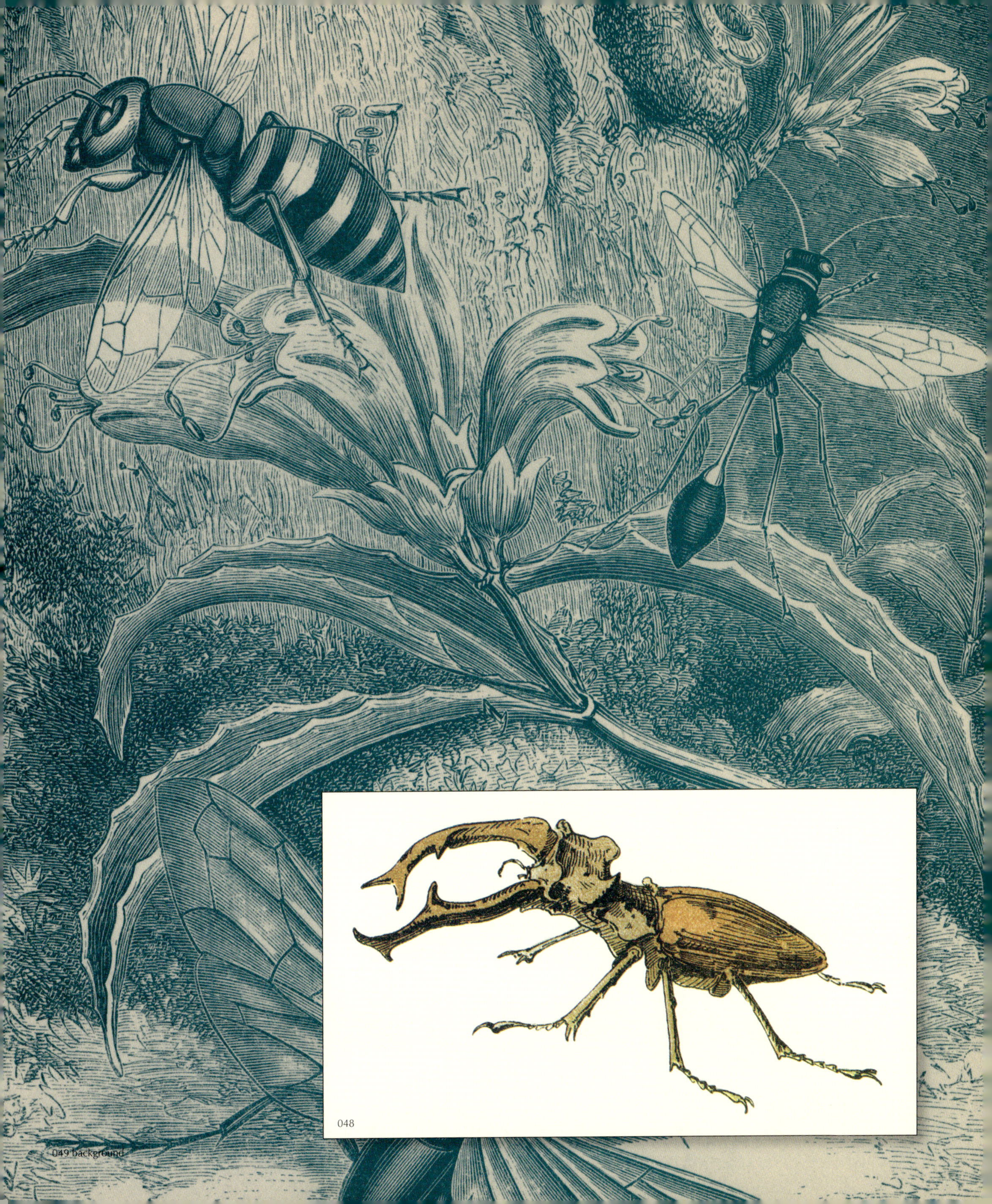
048
049 background

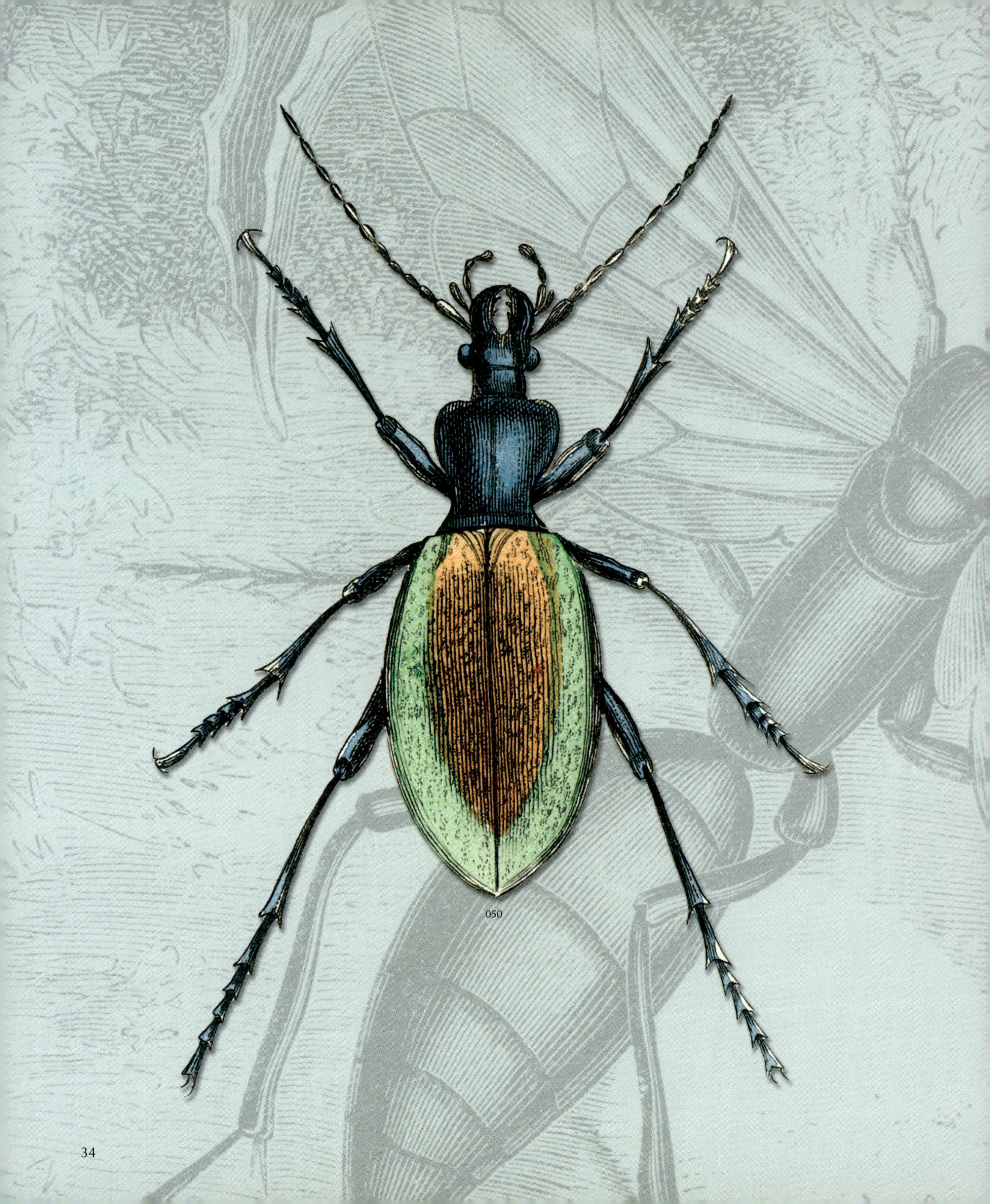
050

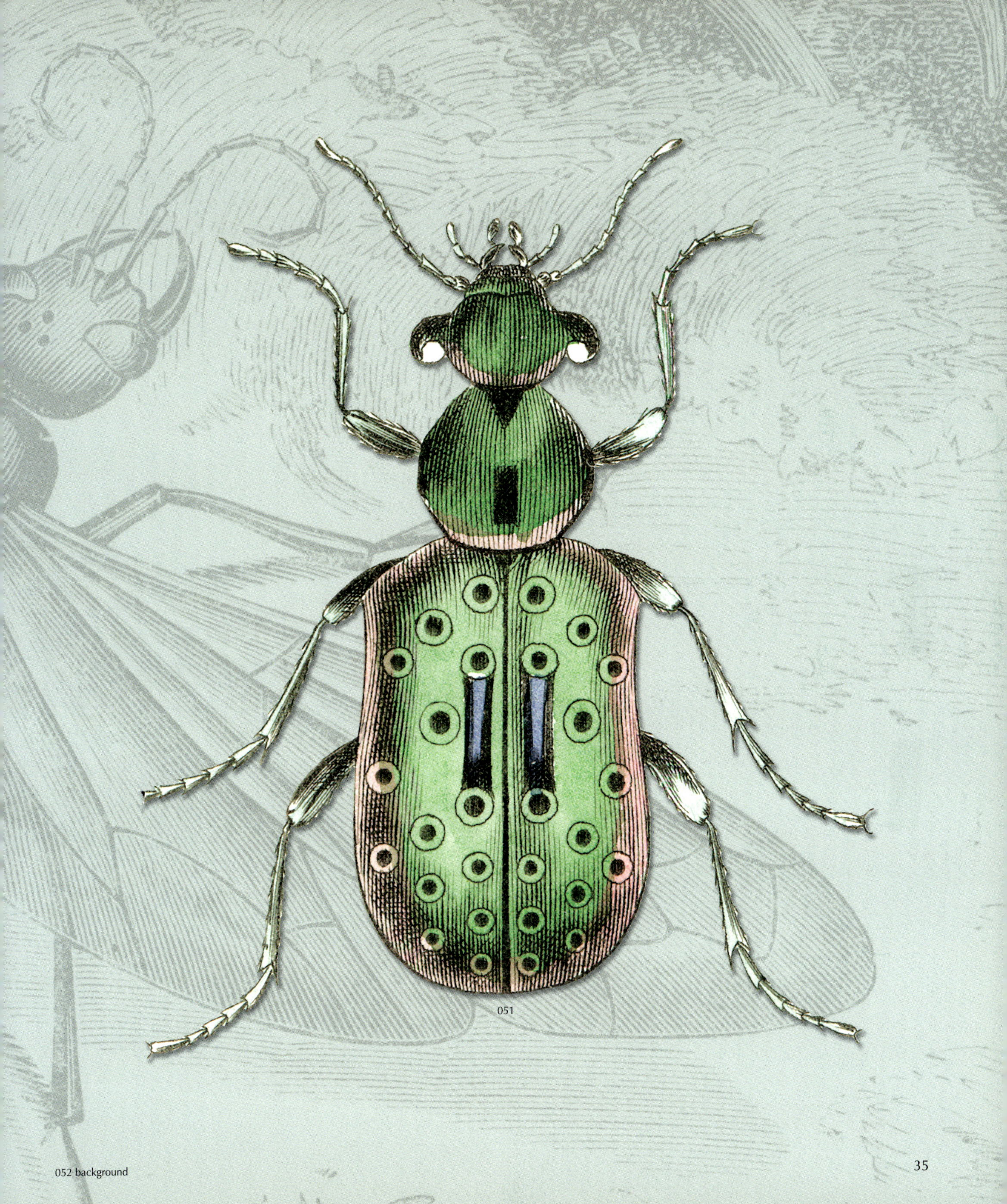

051

052 background

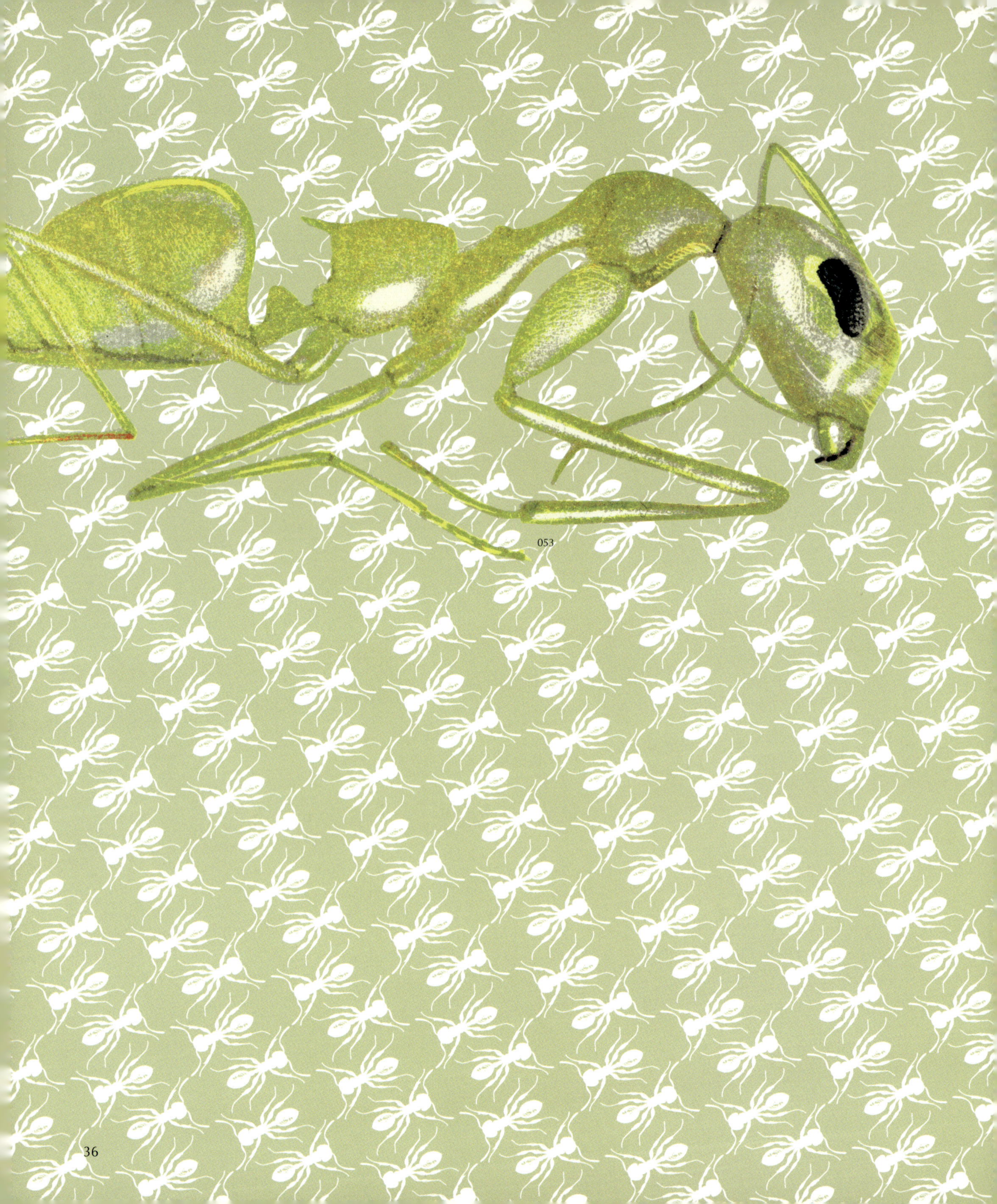
053

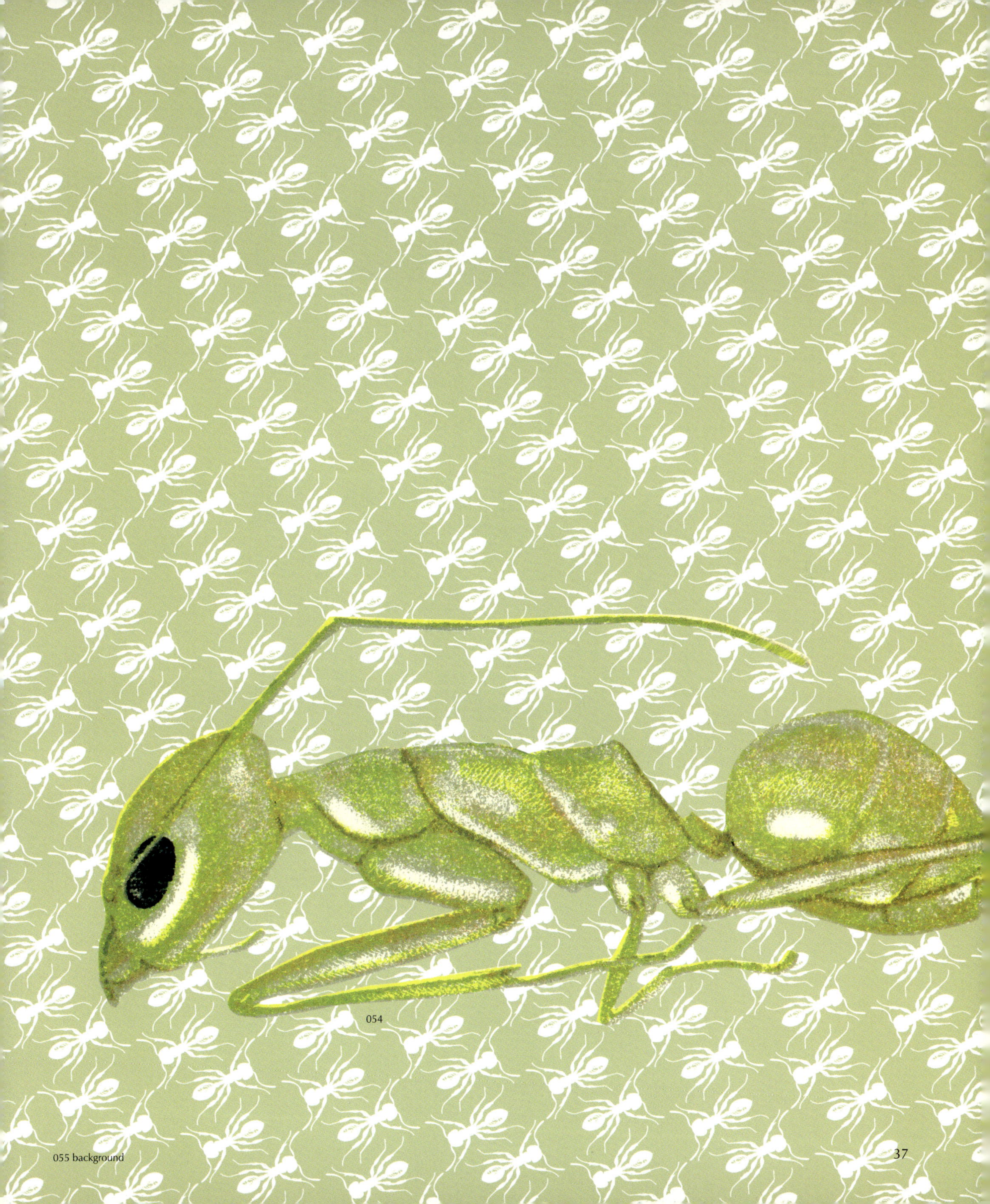

054

055 background

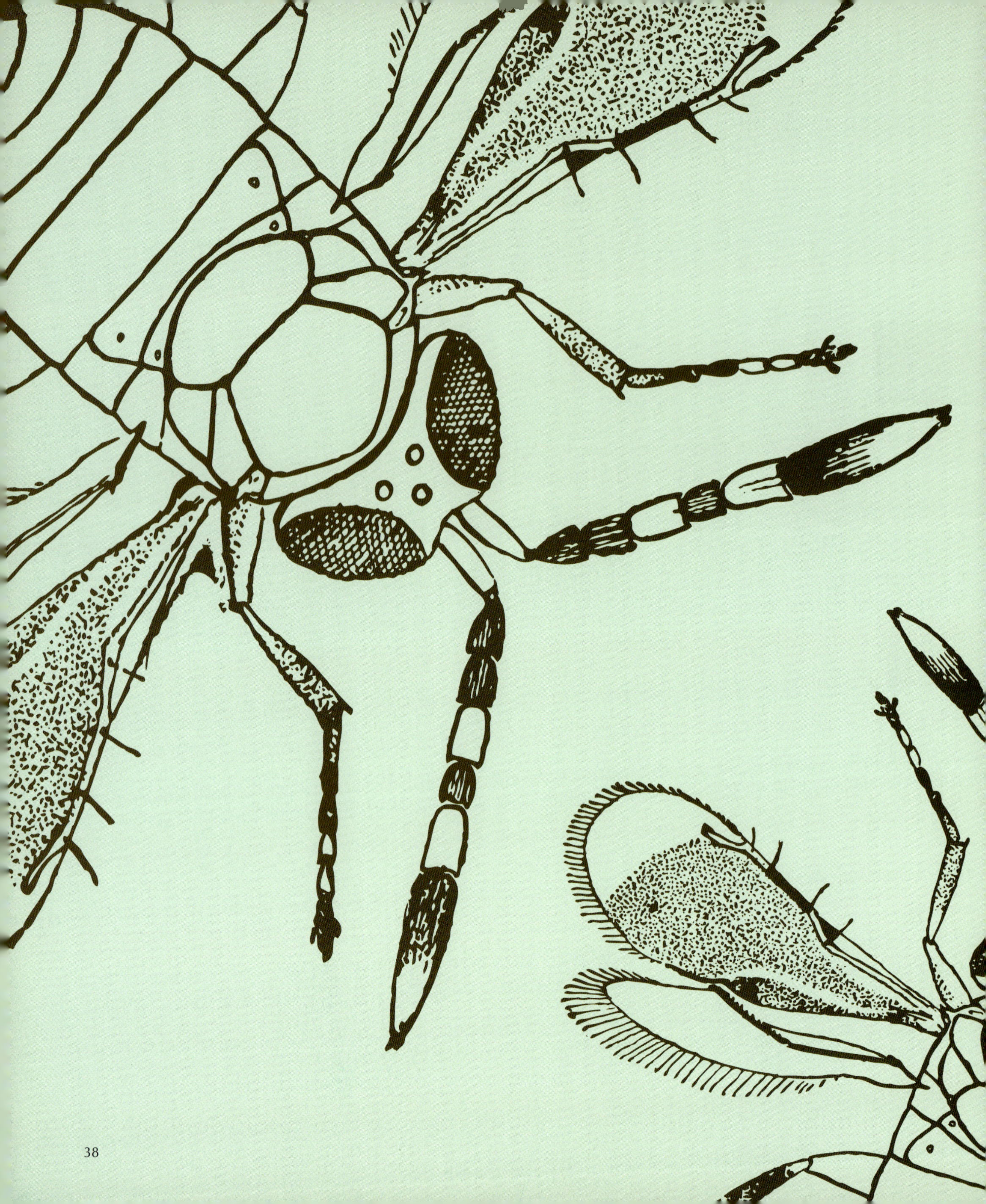

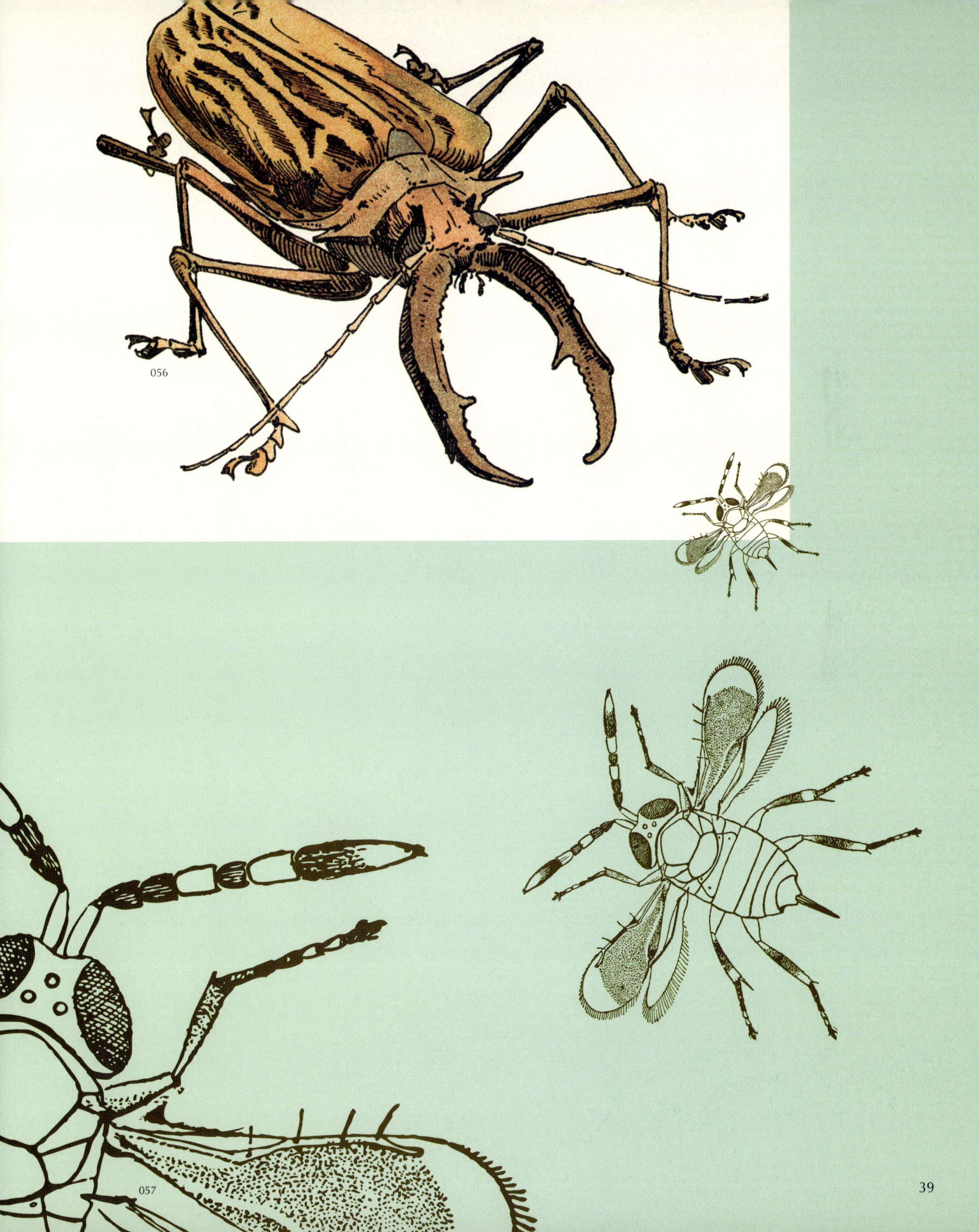
056
057

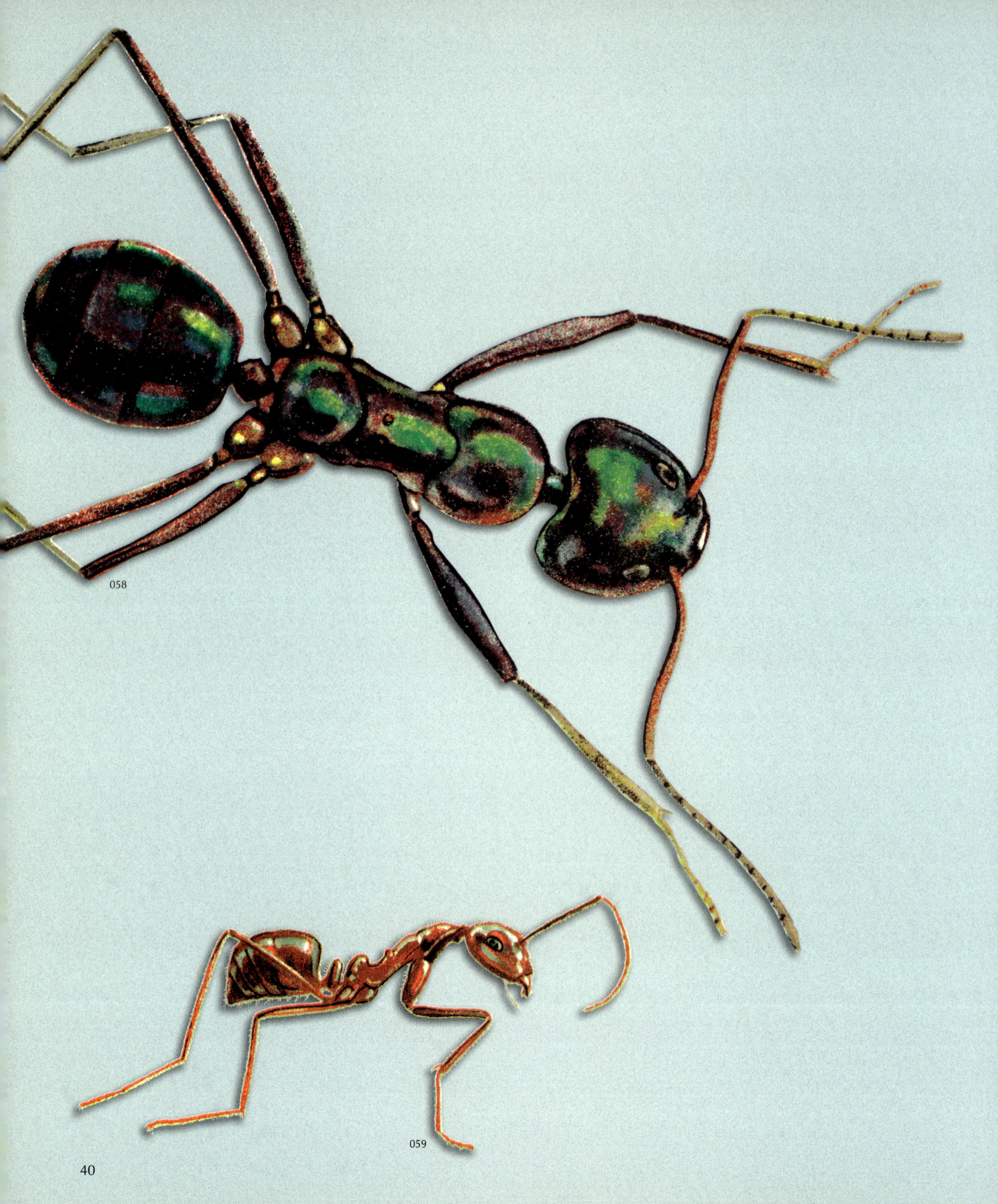
058
059

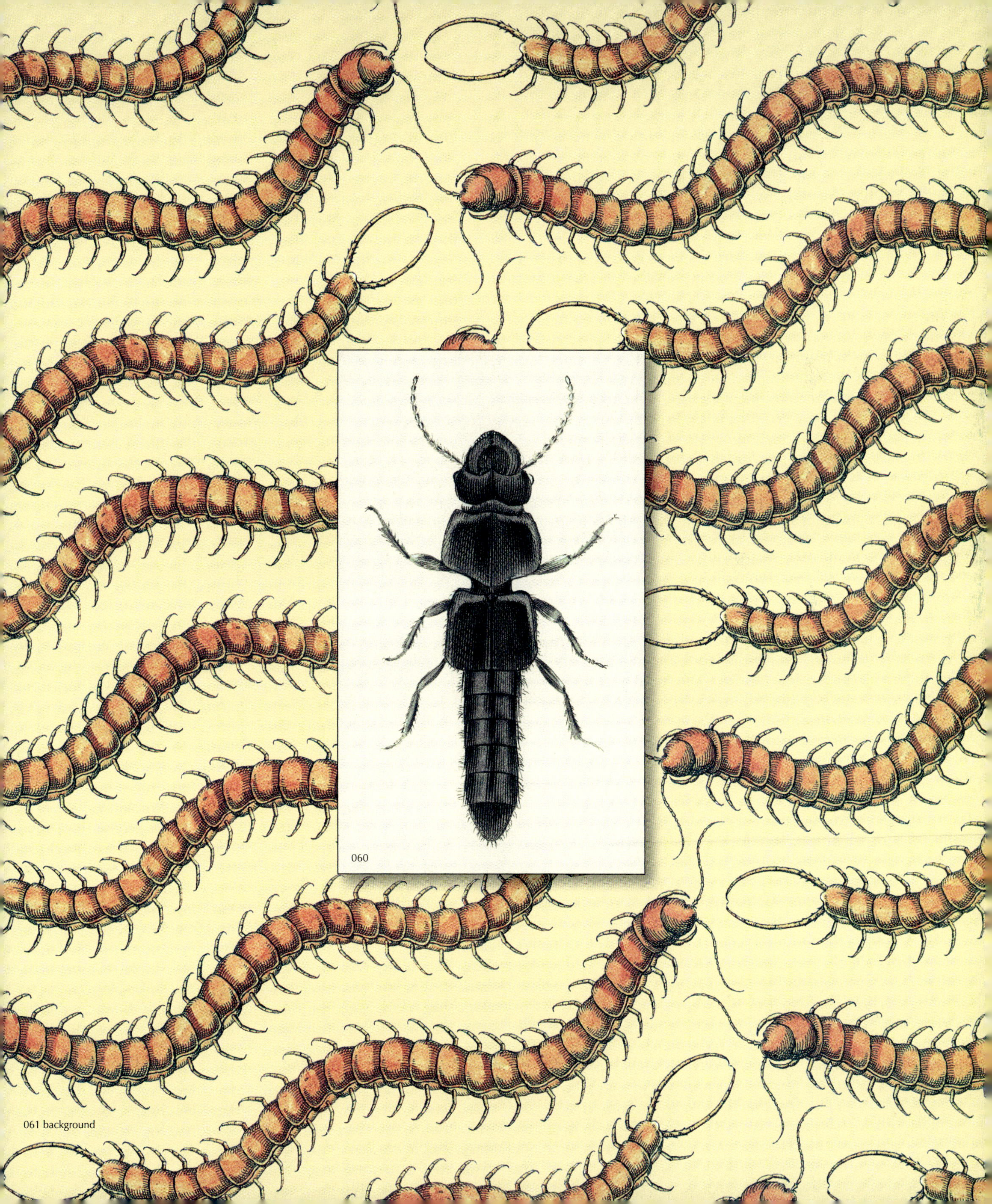

061 background

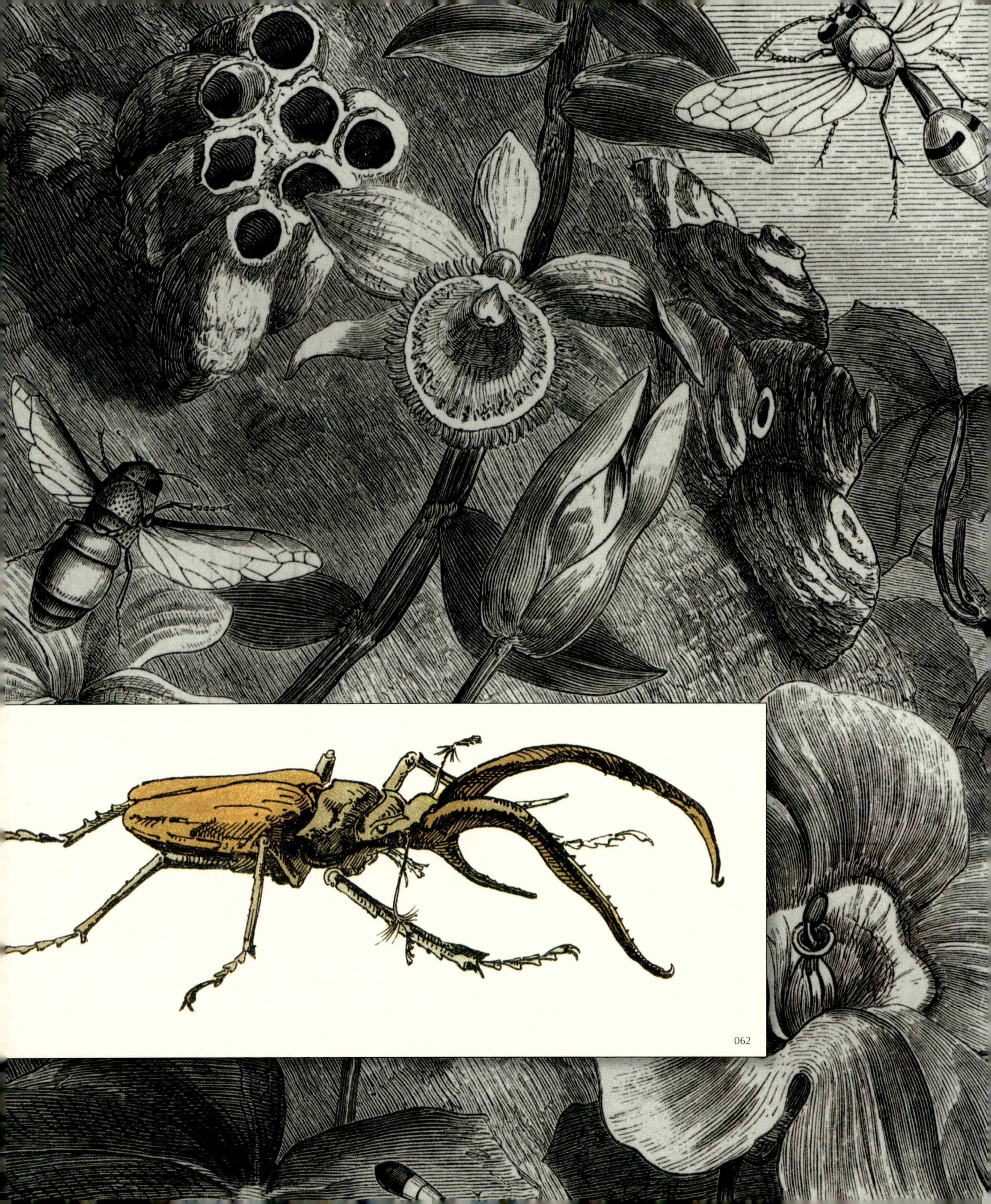

062

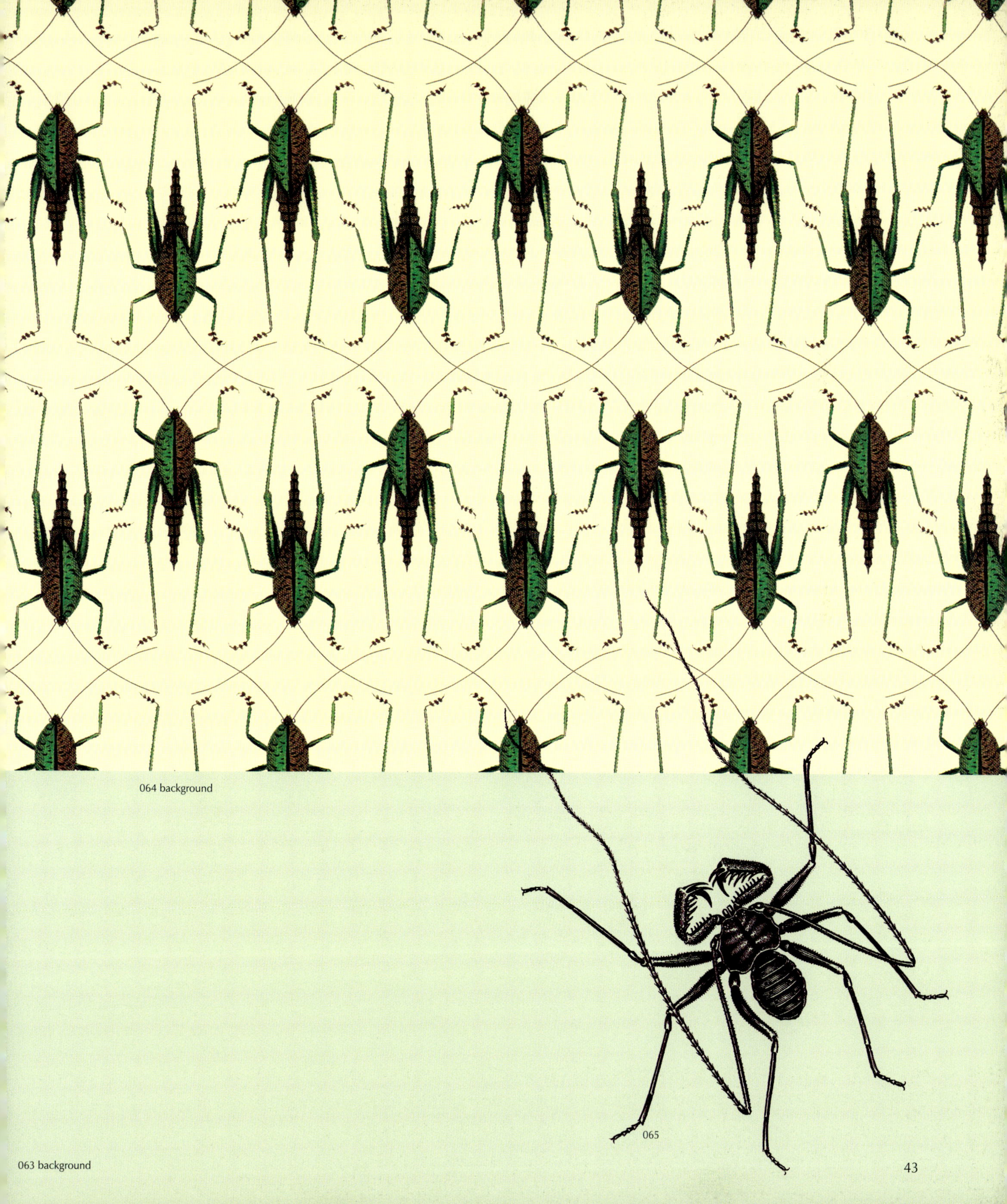
064 background

065

063 background

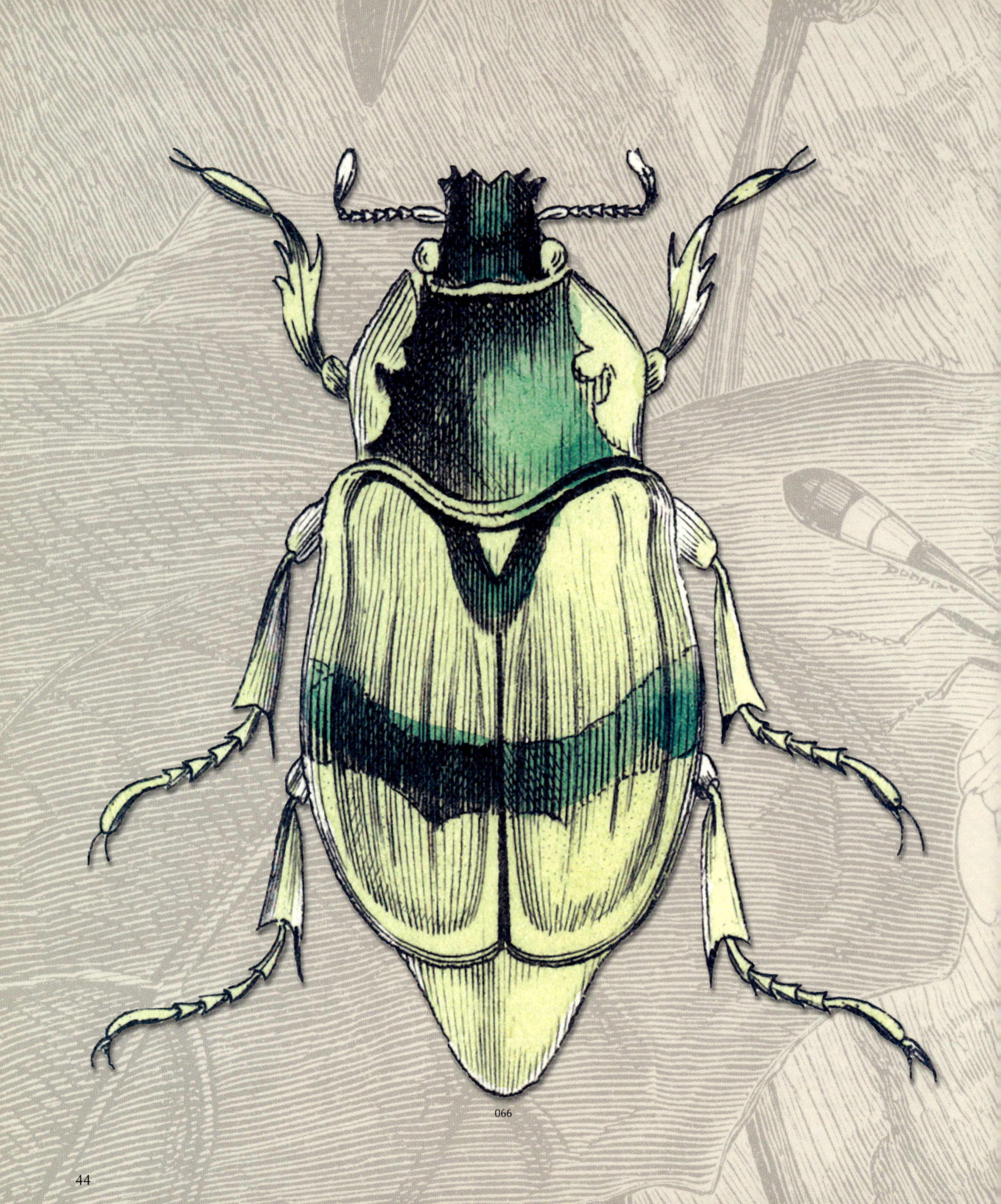
066

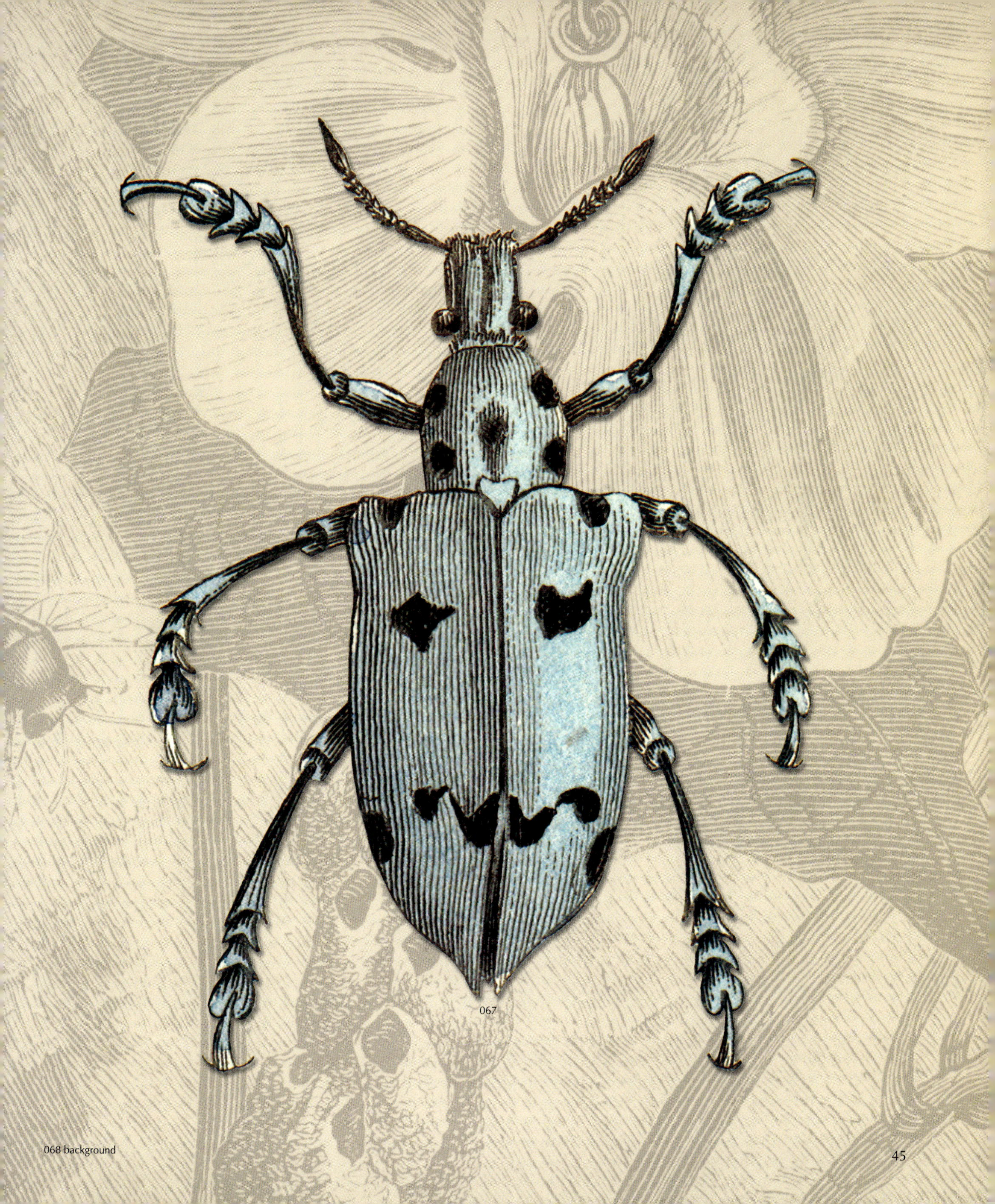

067

068 background

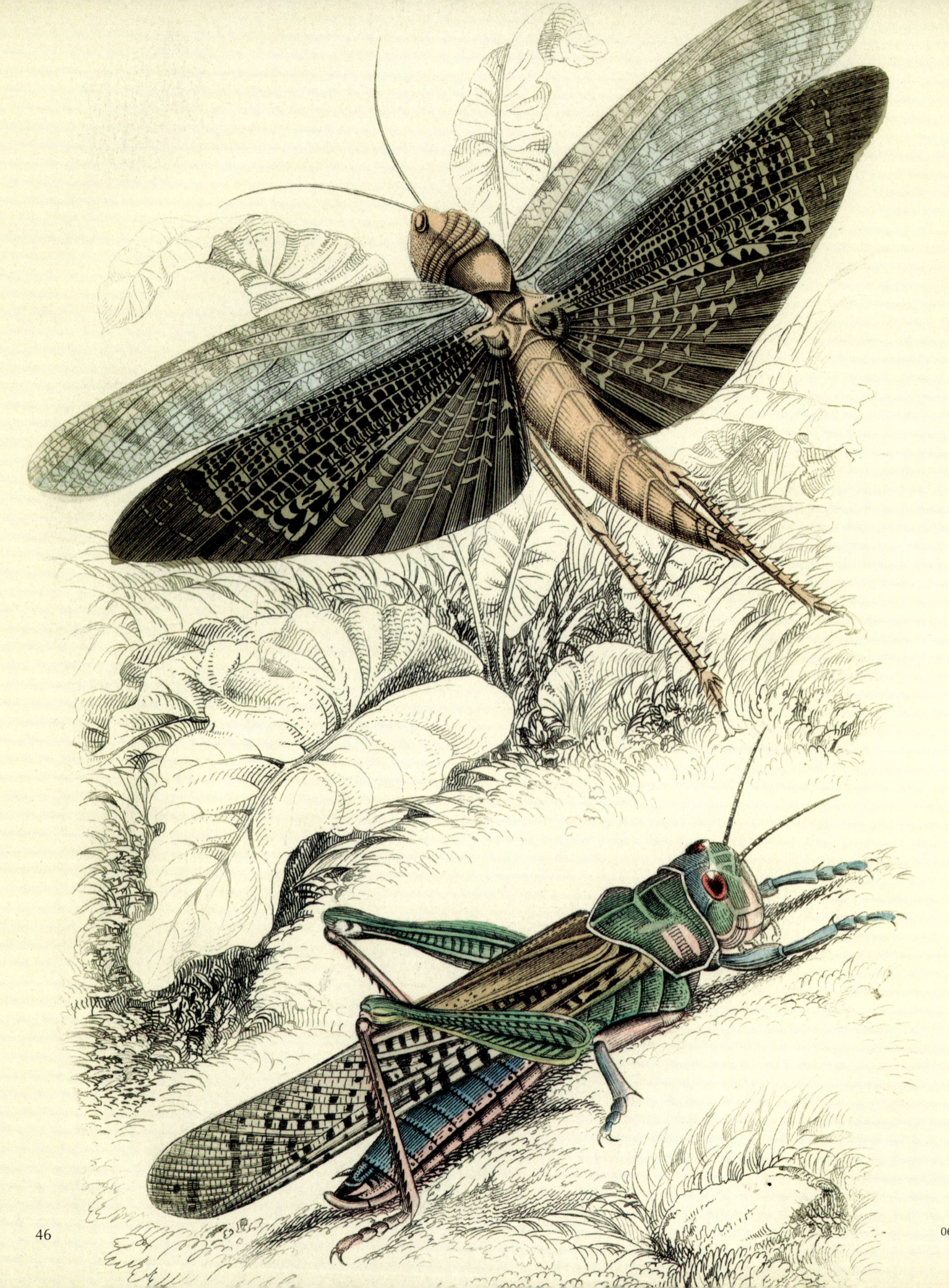

069

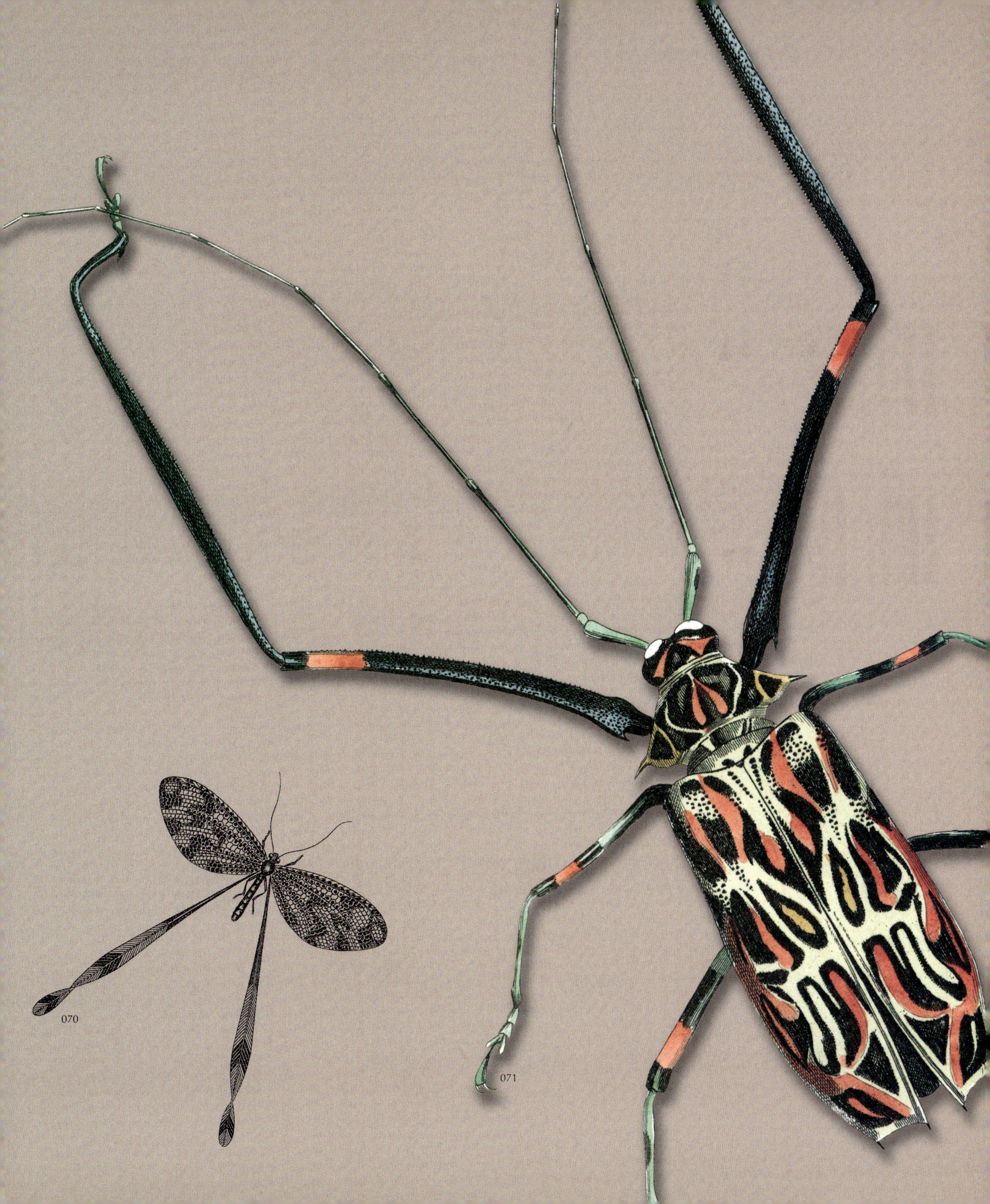

070
071

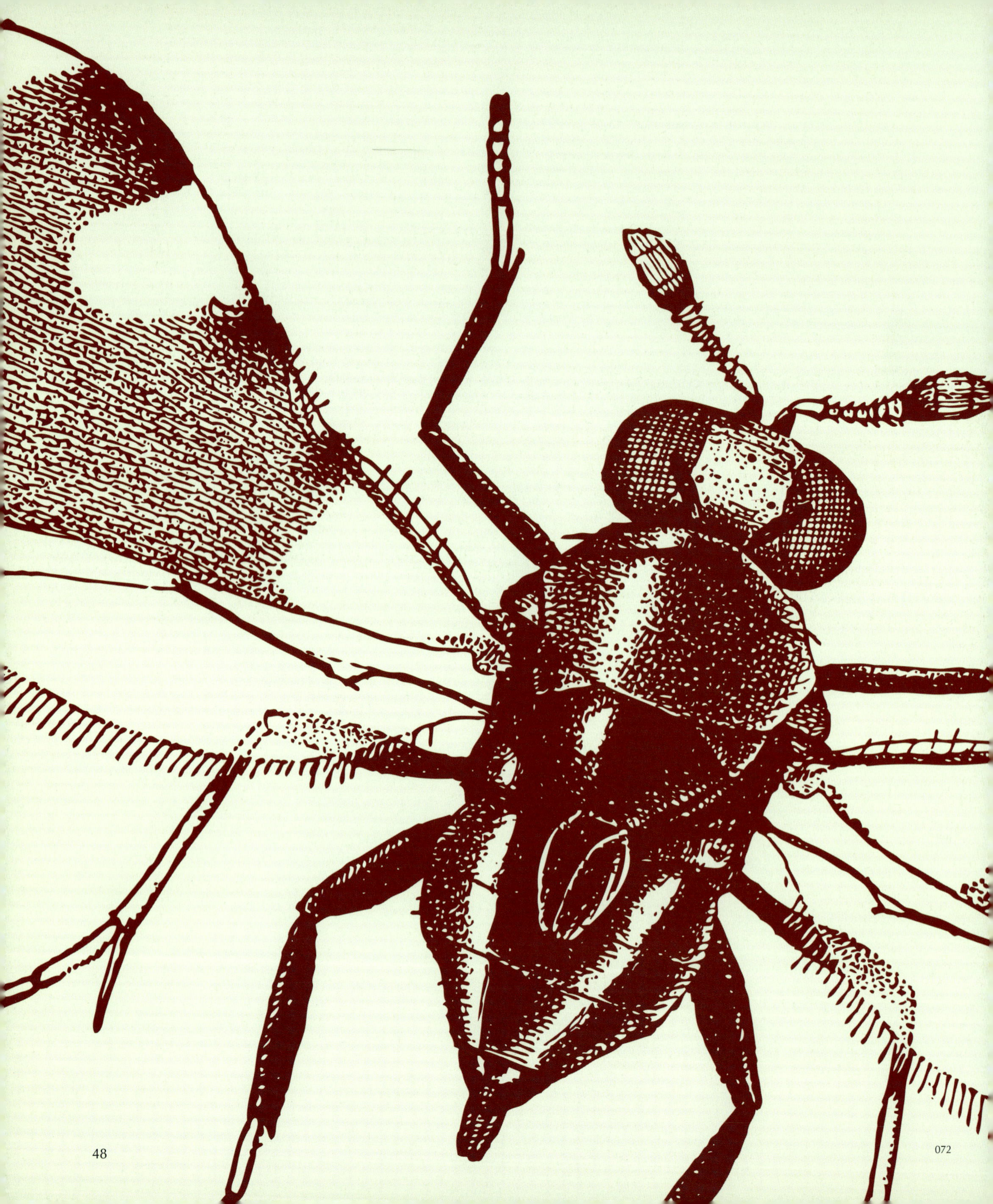

072

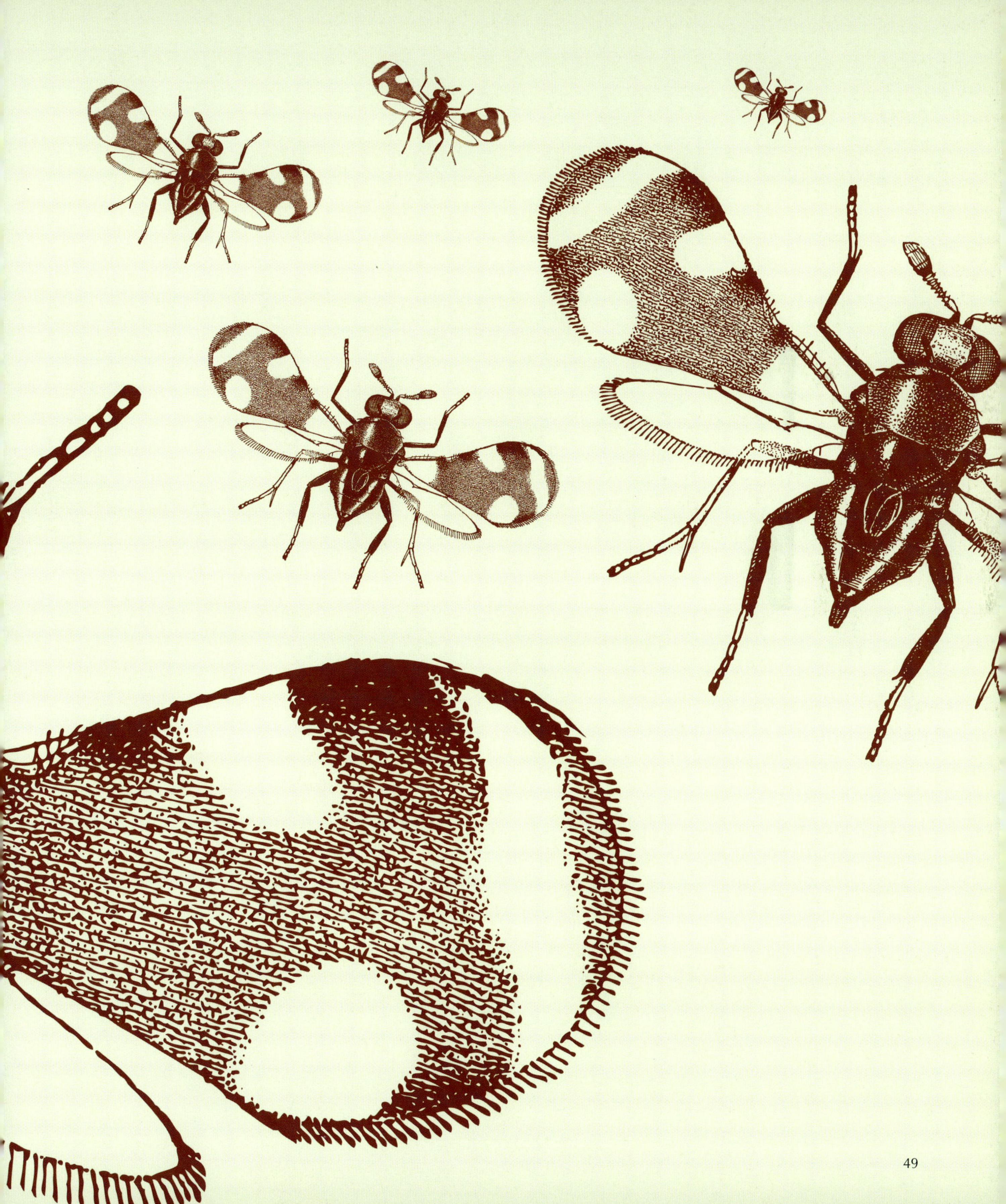

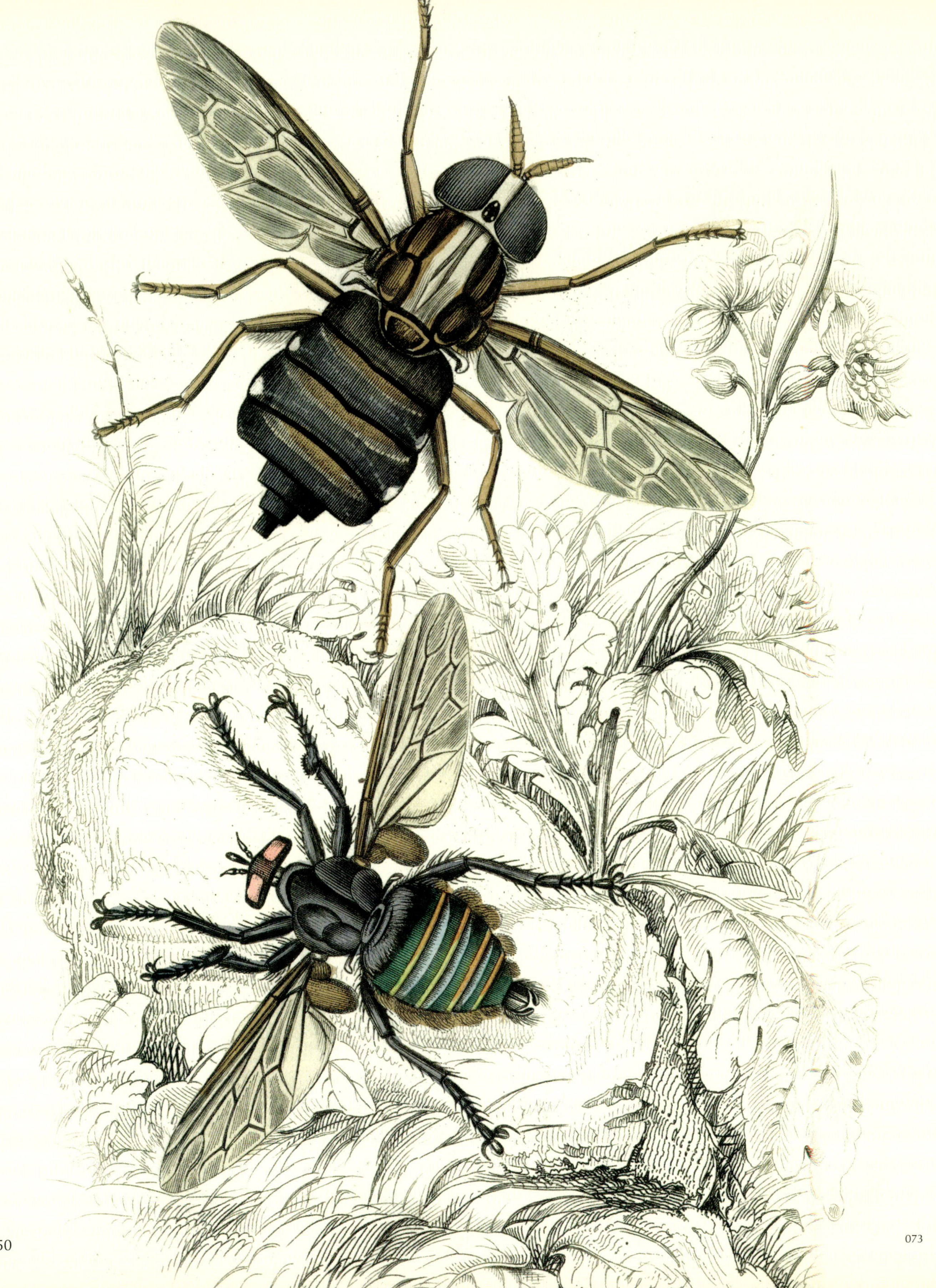

073

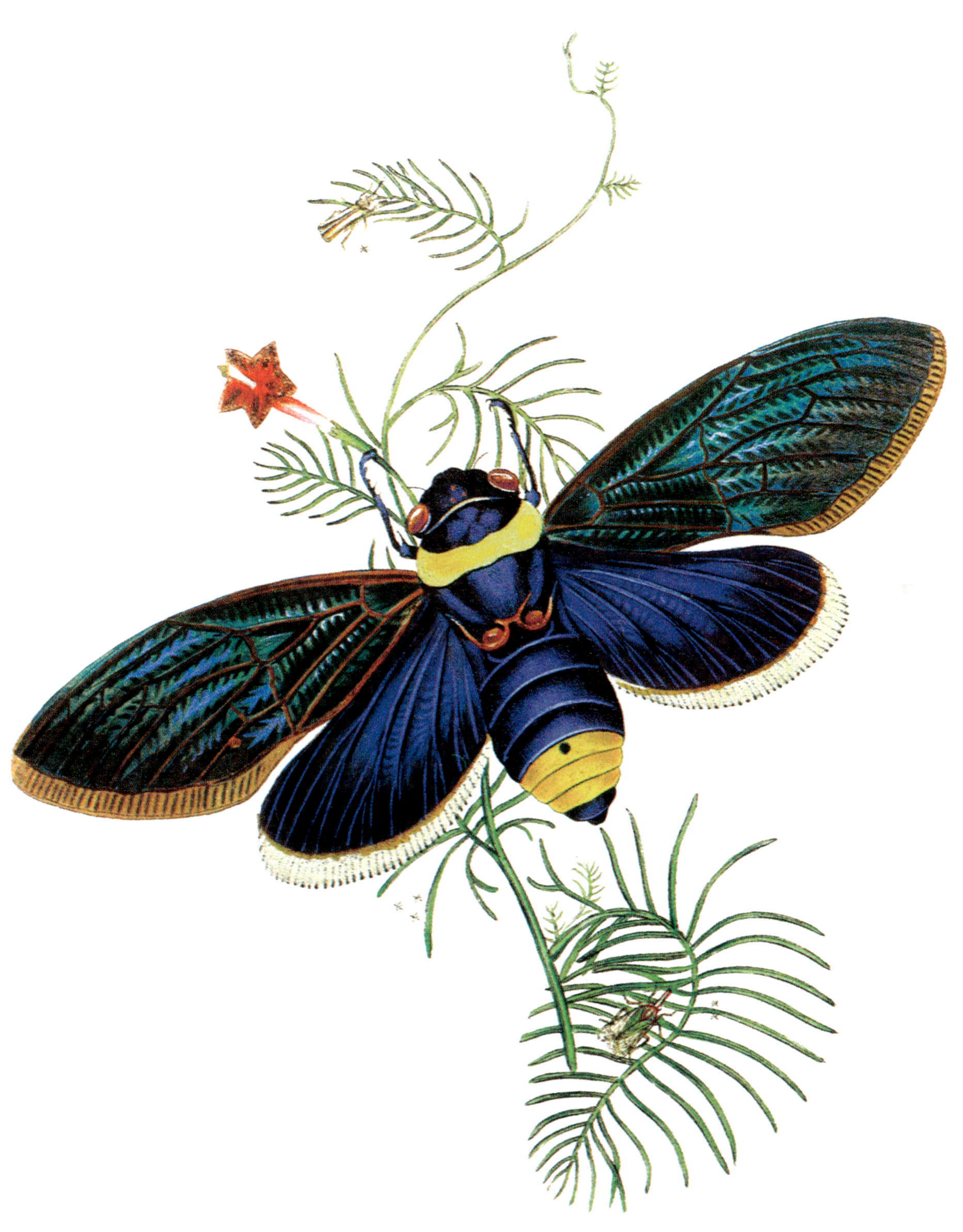

074

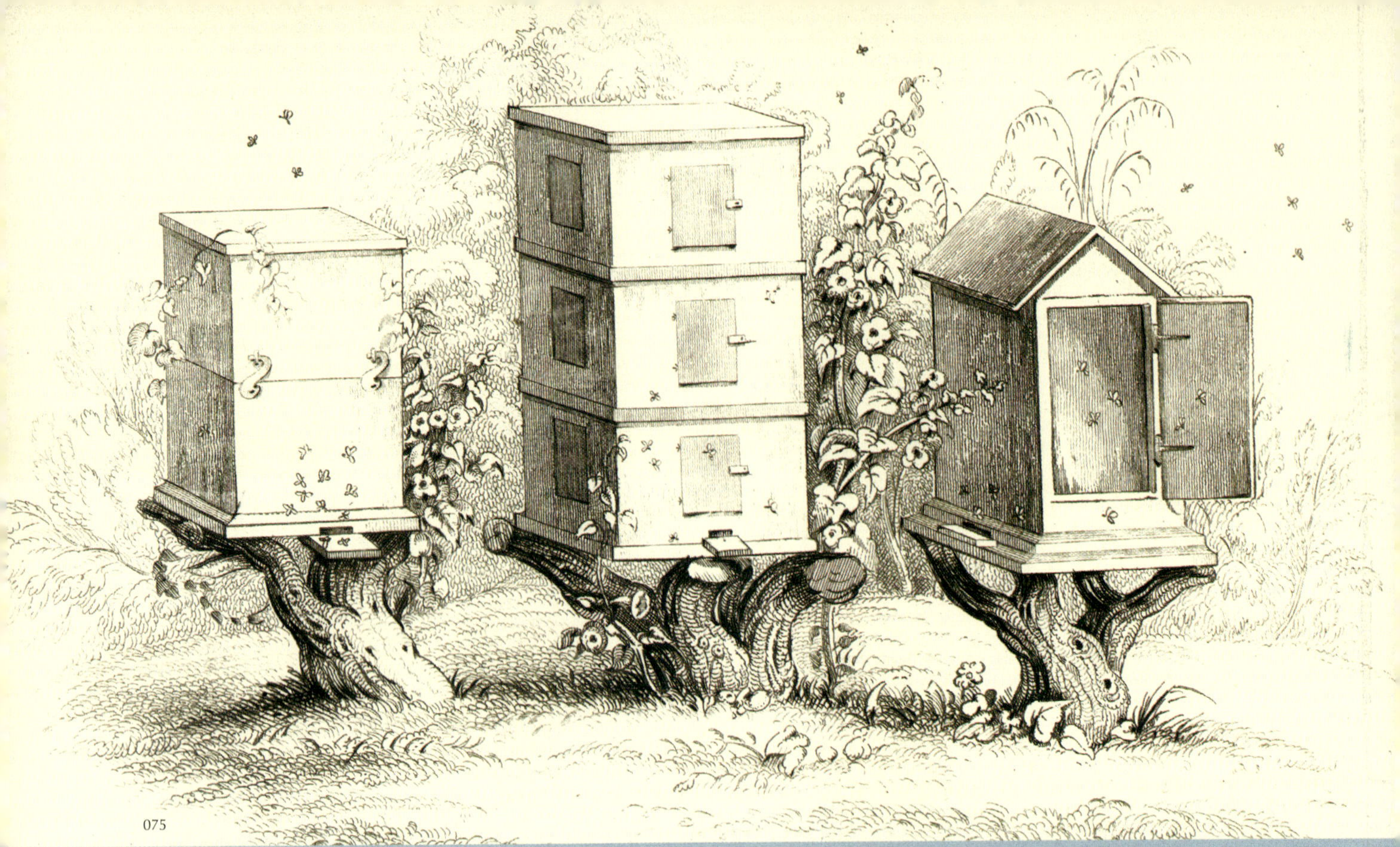

075

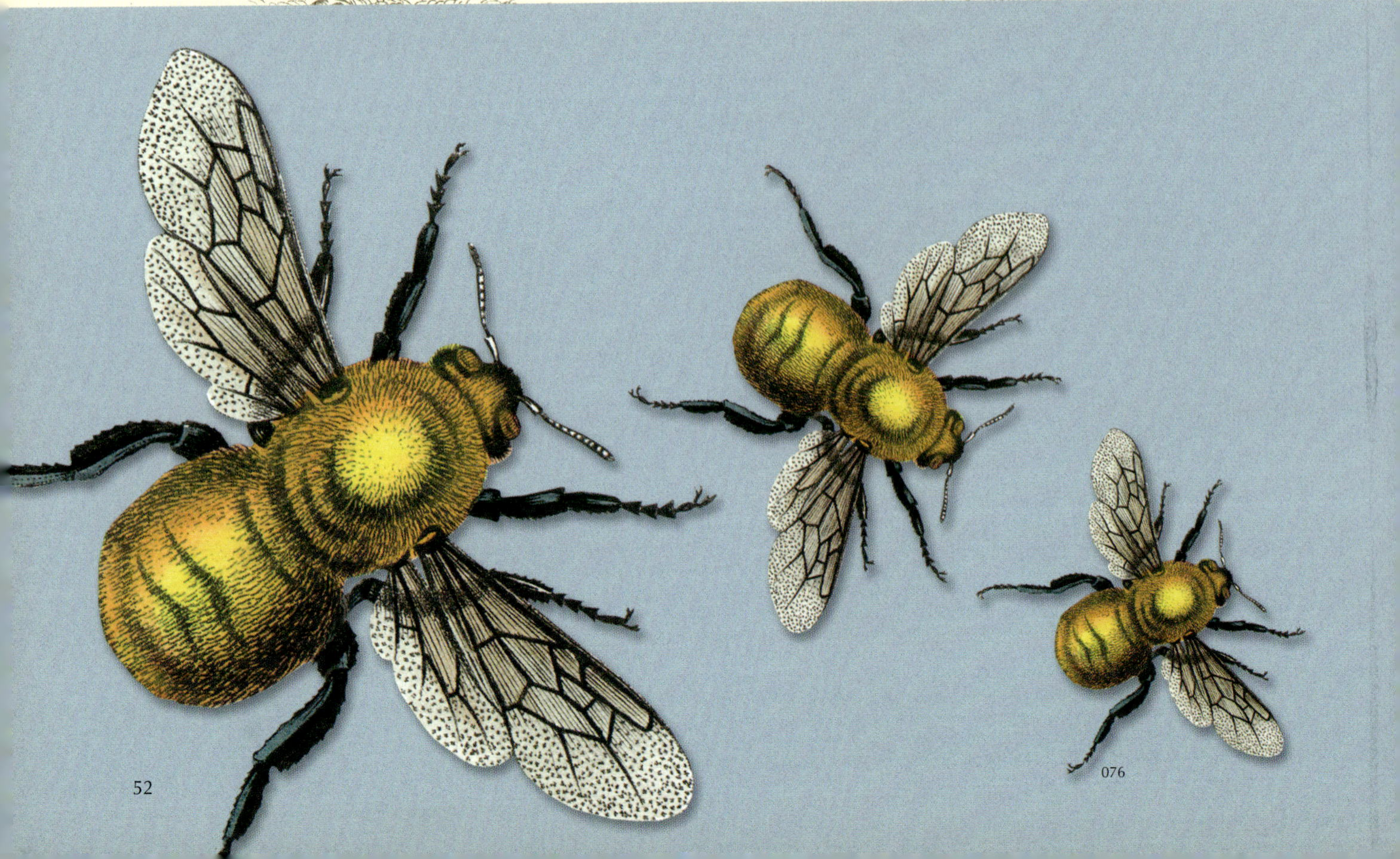

076

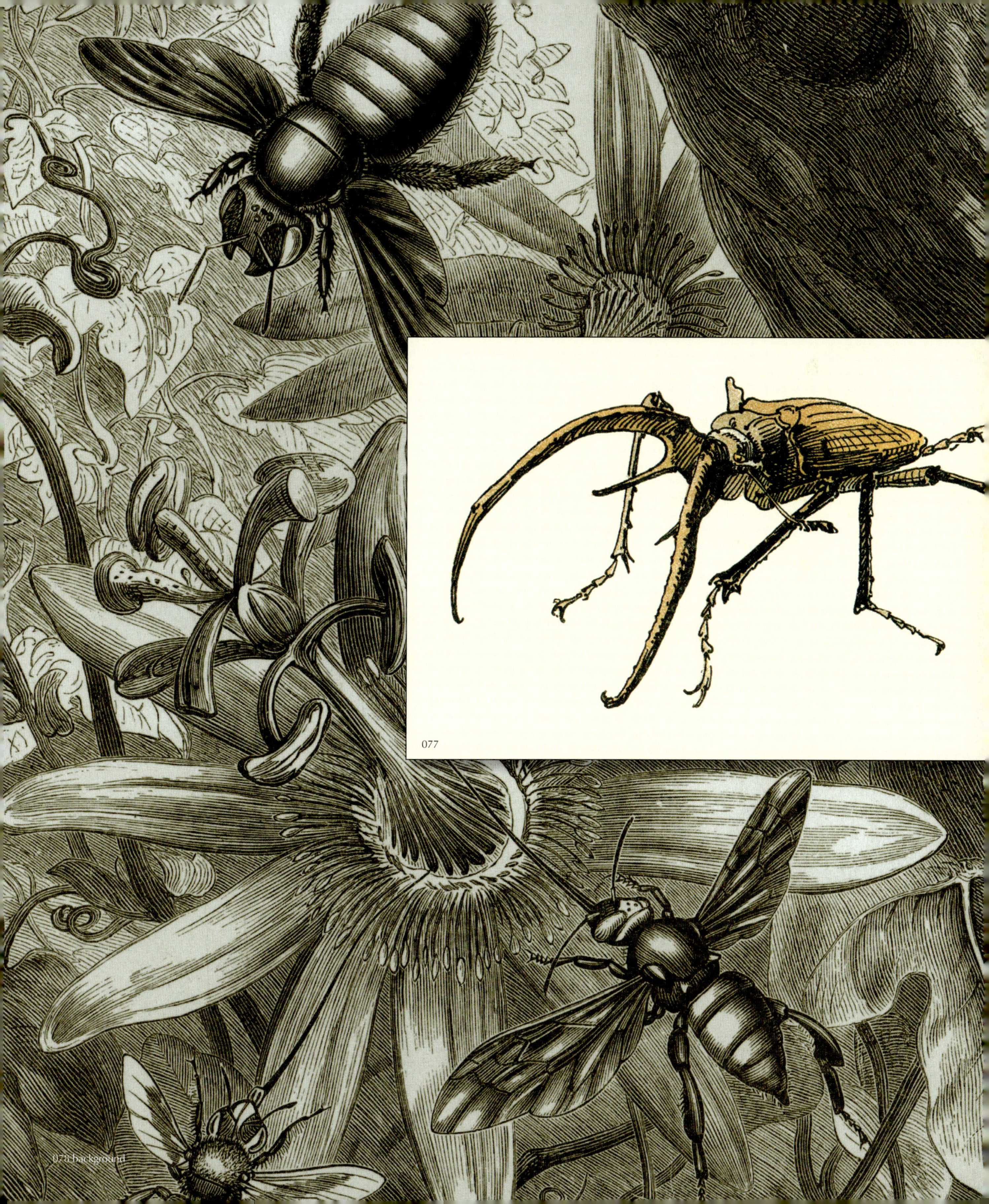
077
070 background

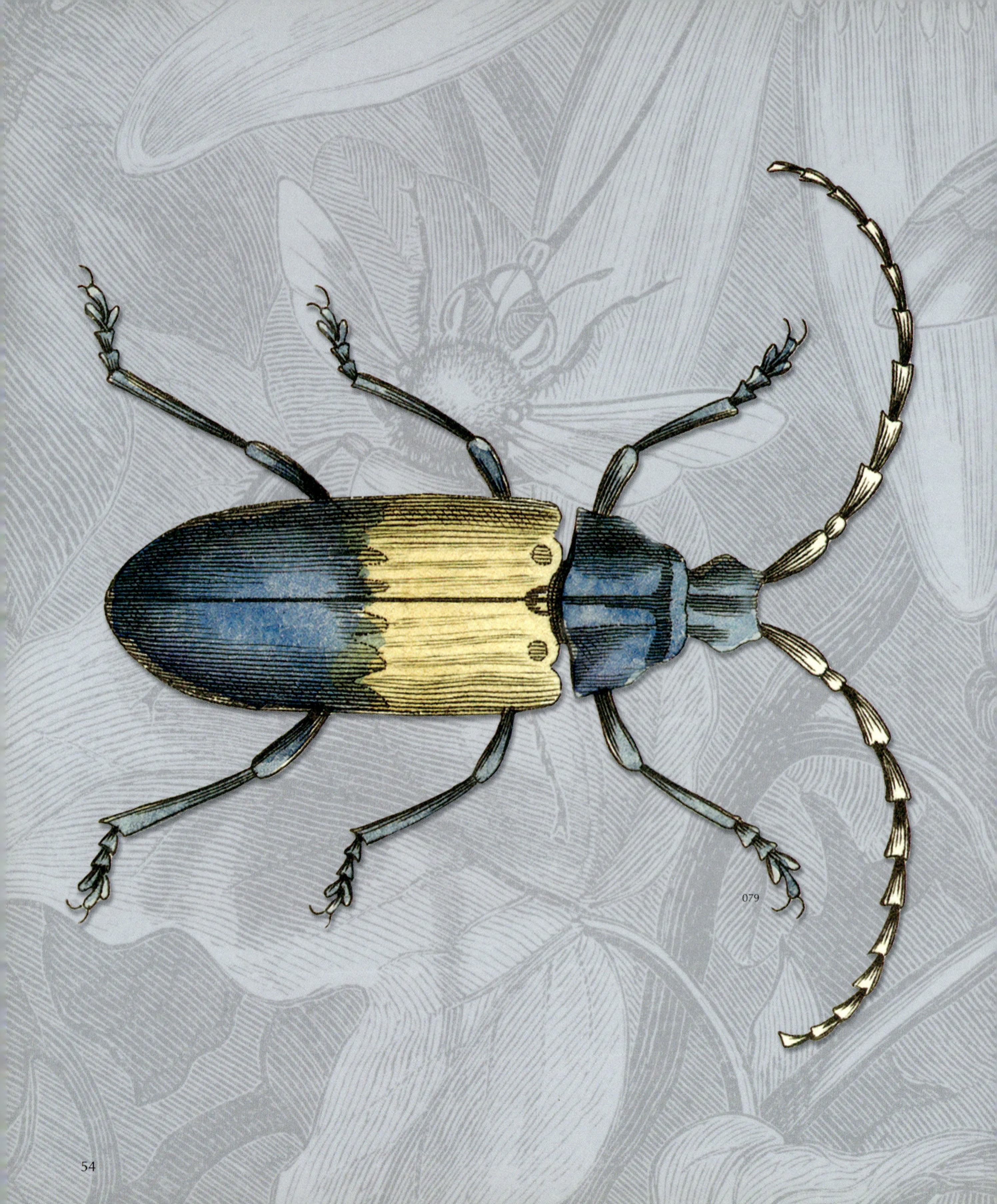

079

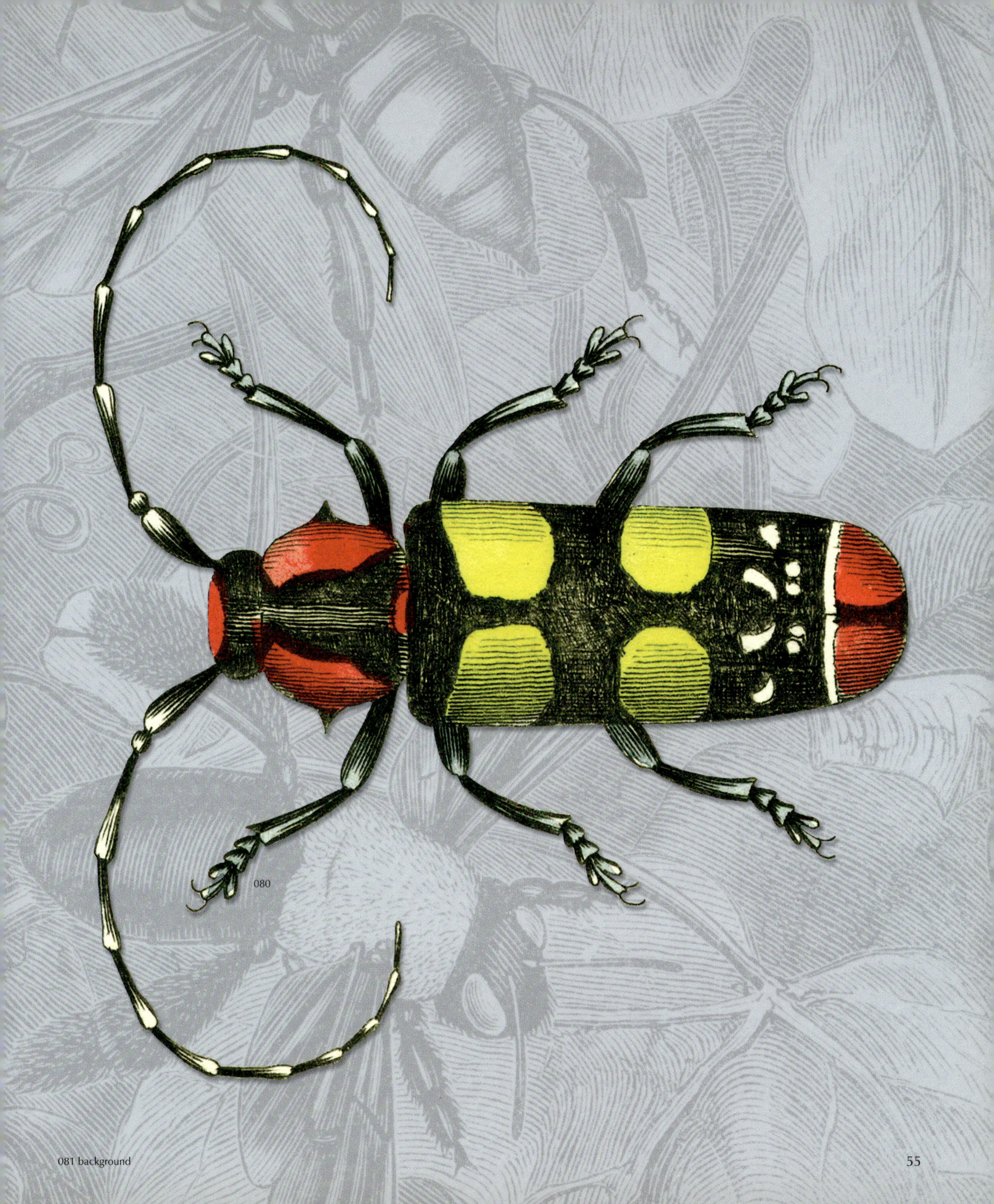

081 background

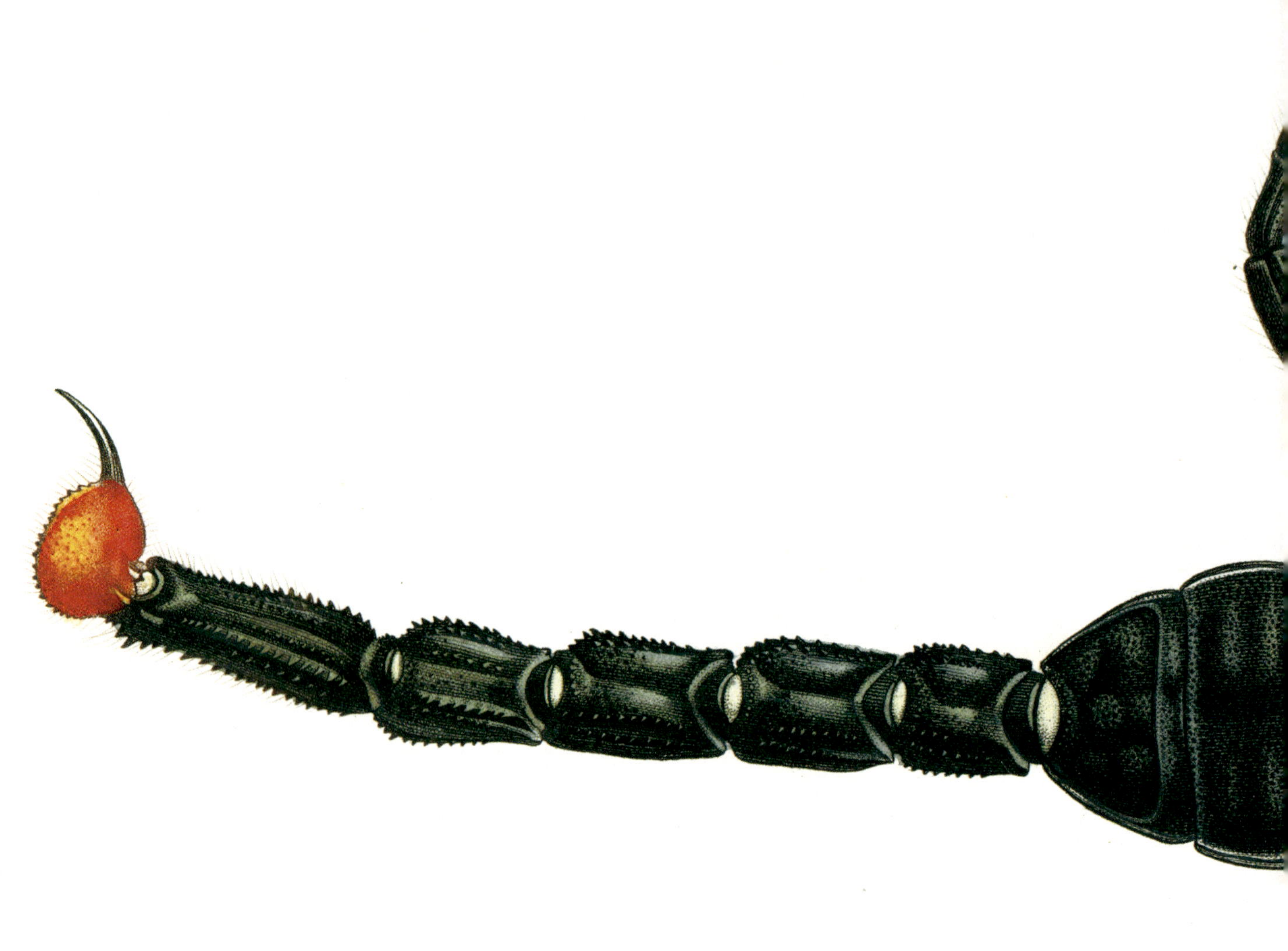

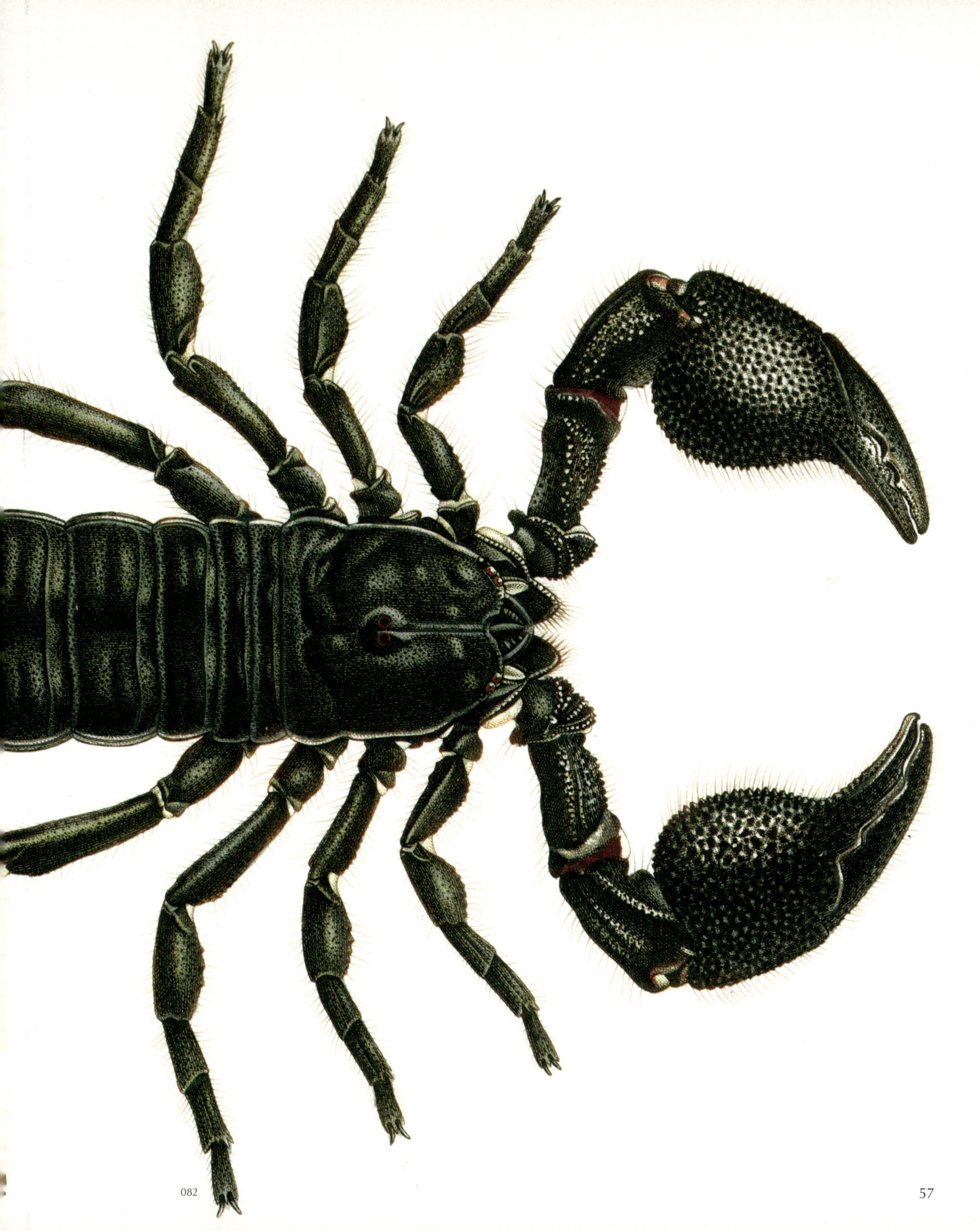

082

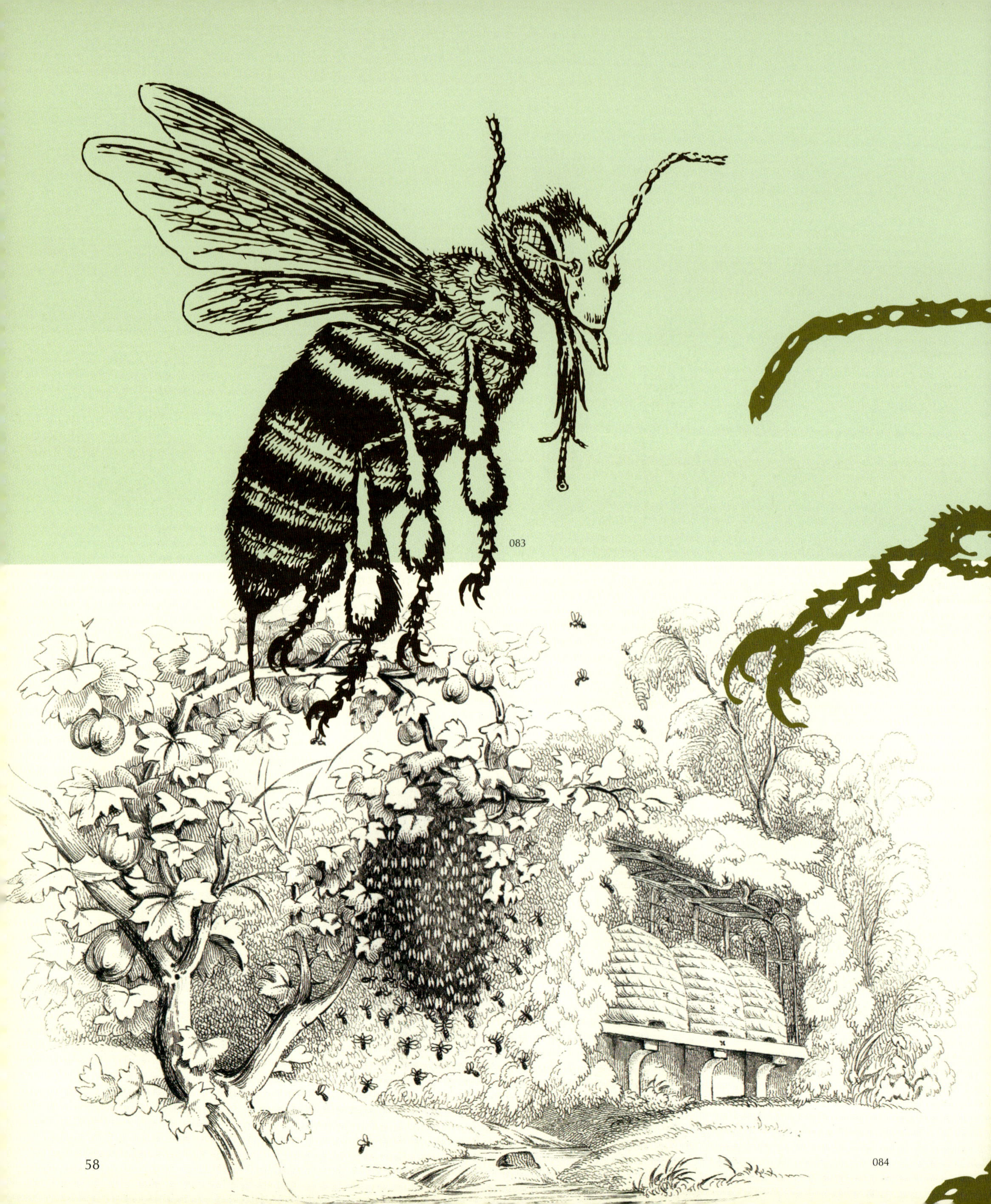
083
084

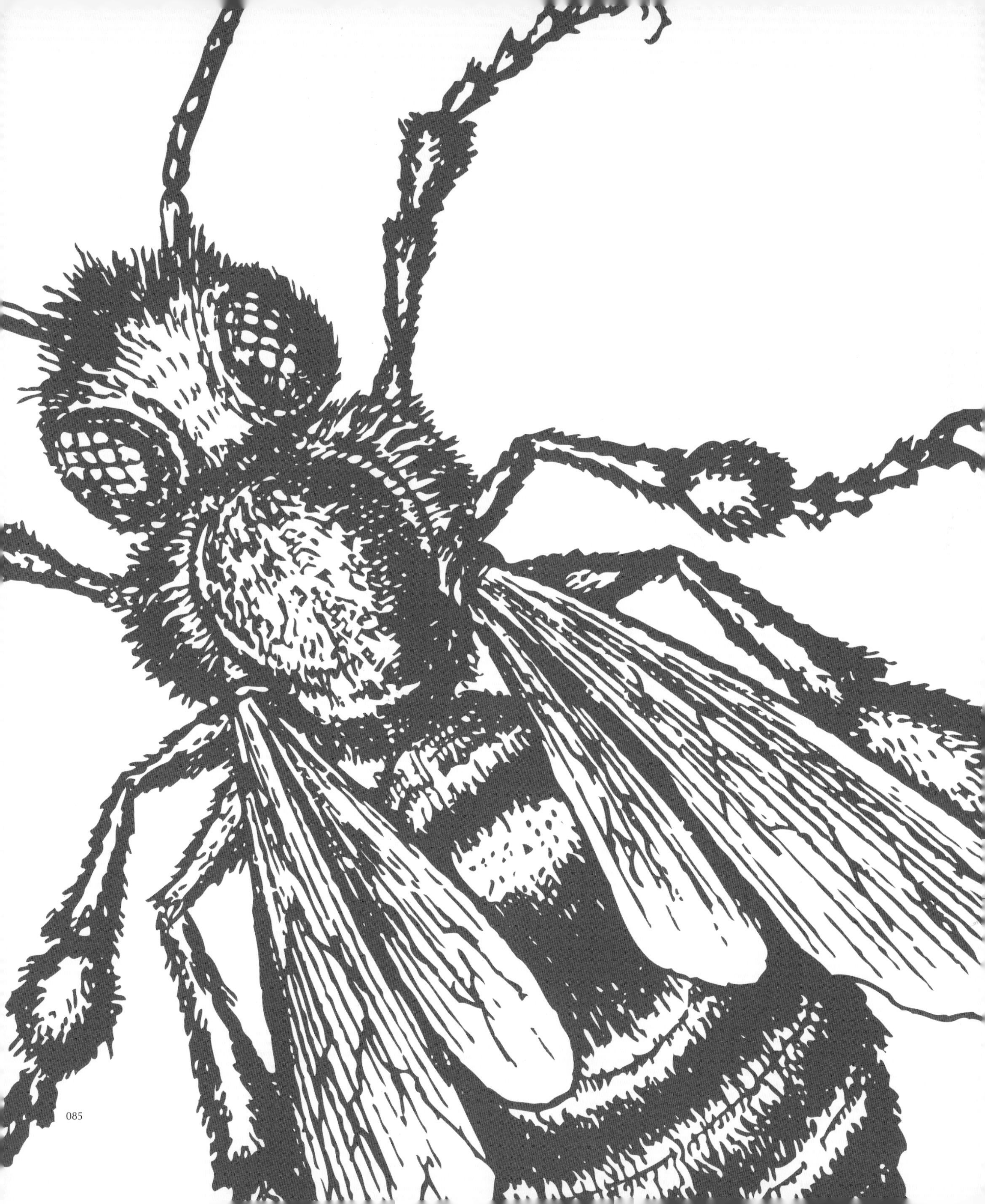

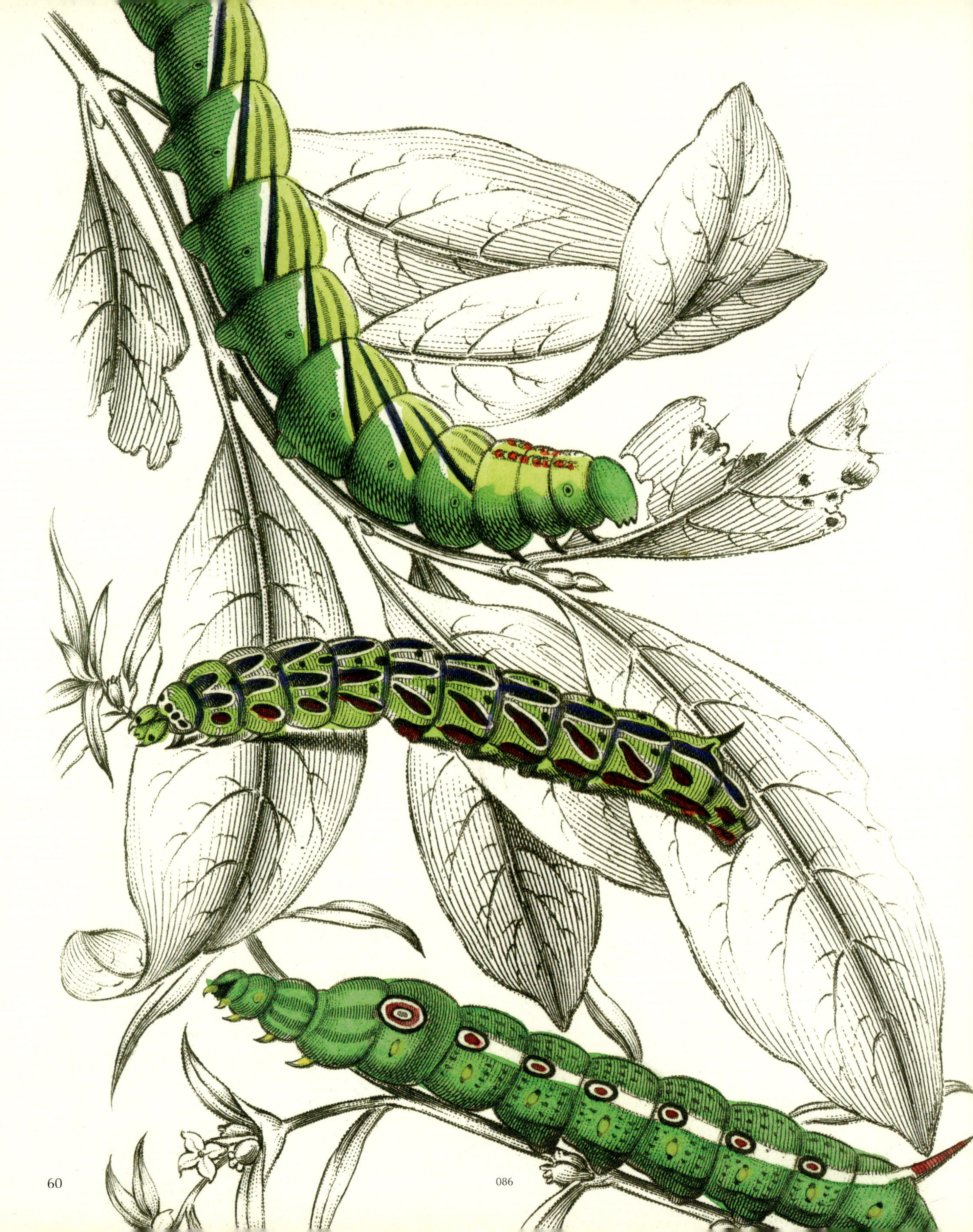

086

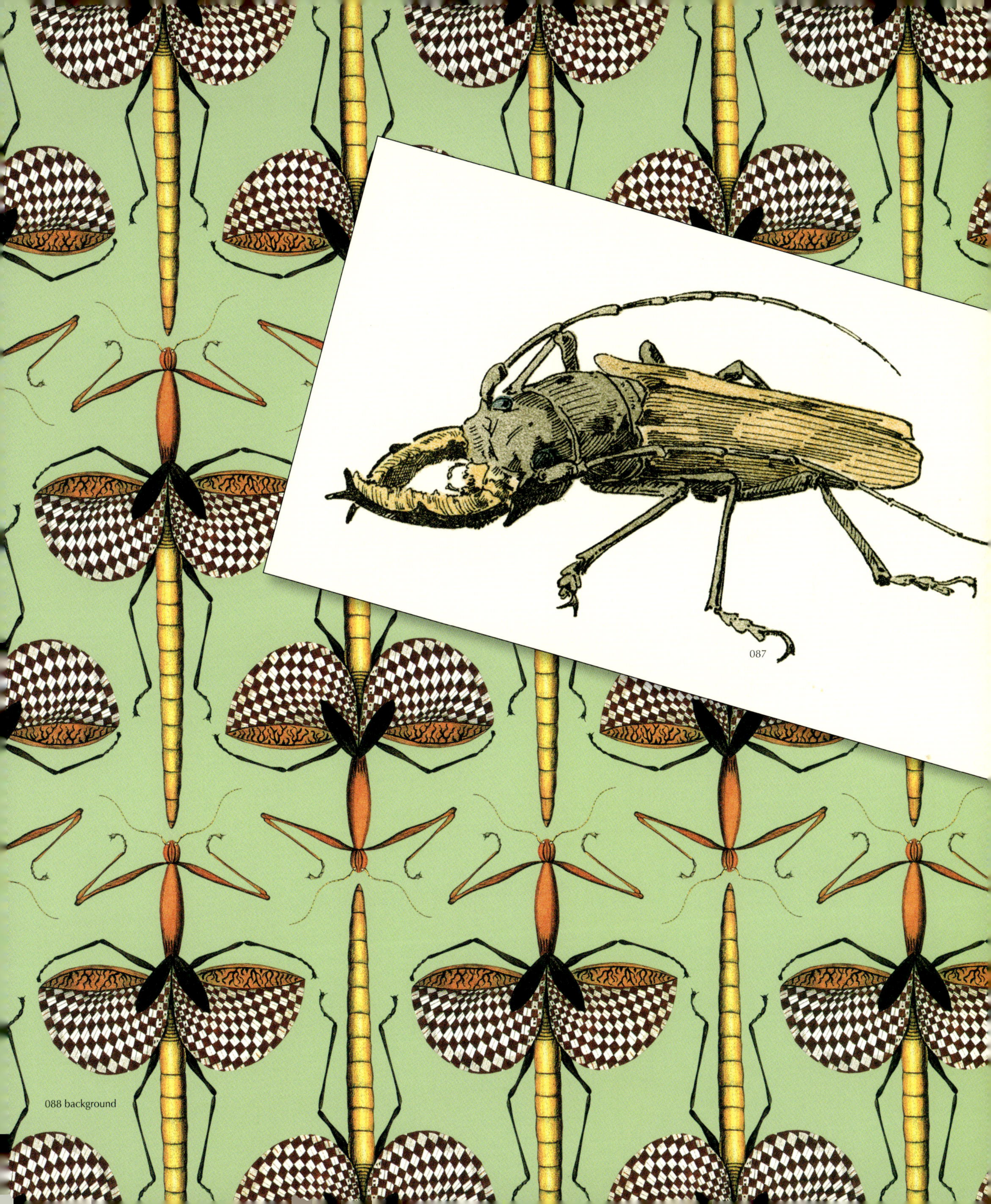

087
088 background

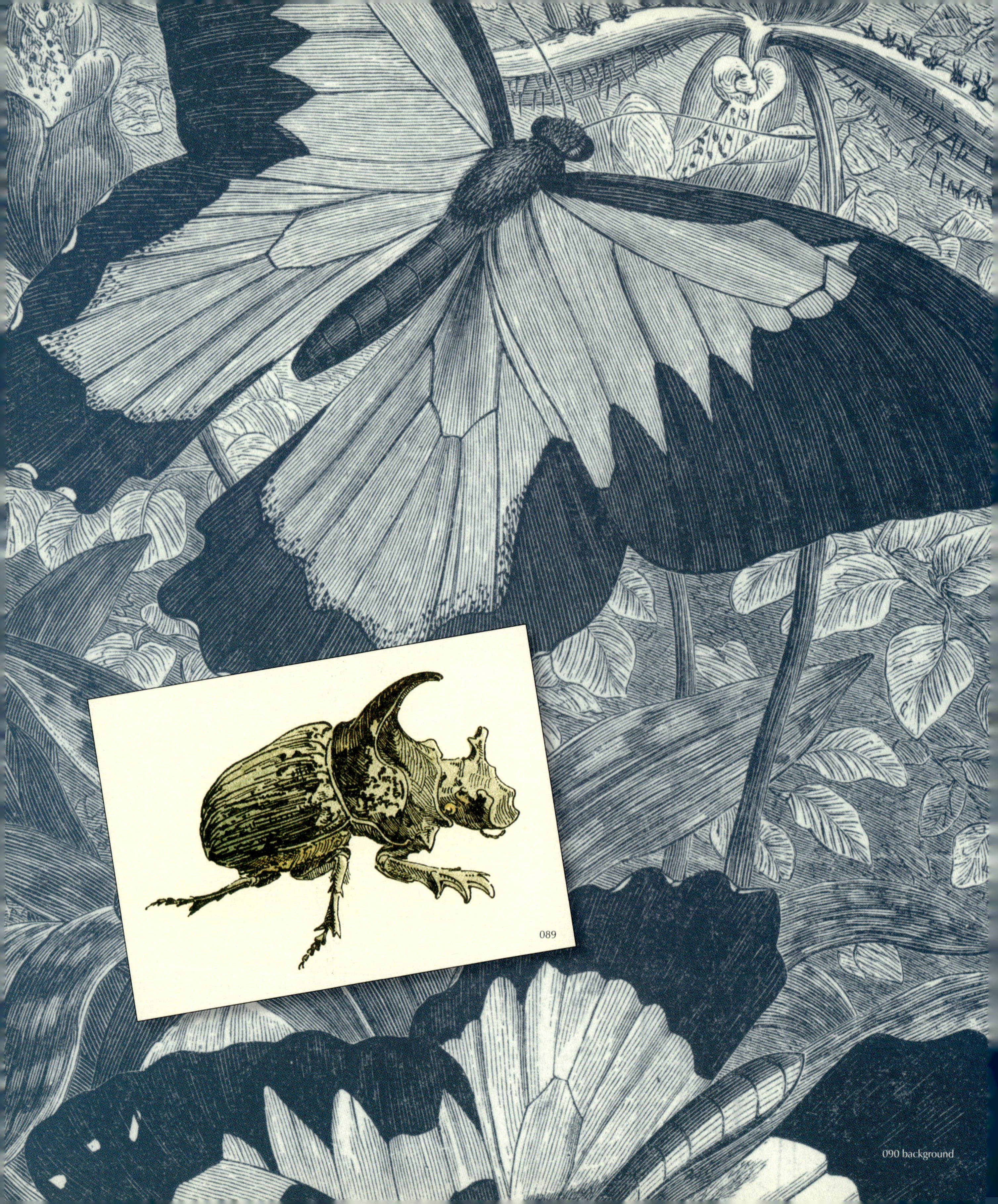
089
090 background

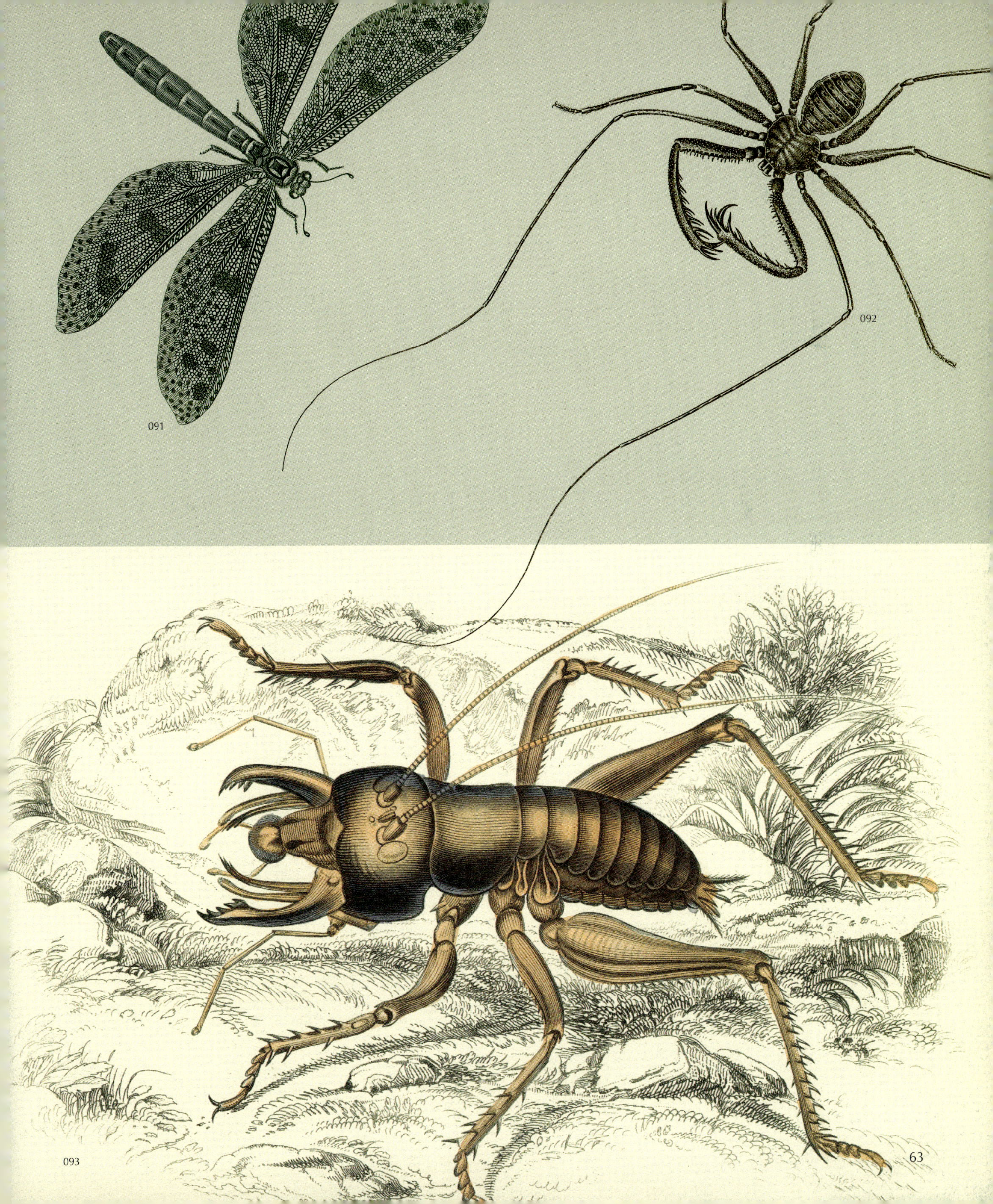
091
092
093

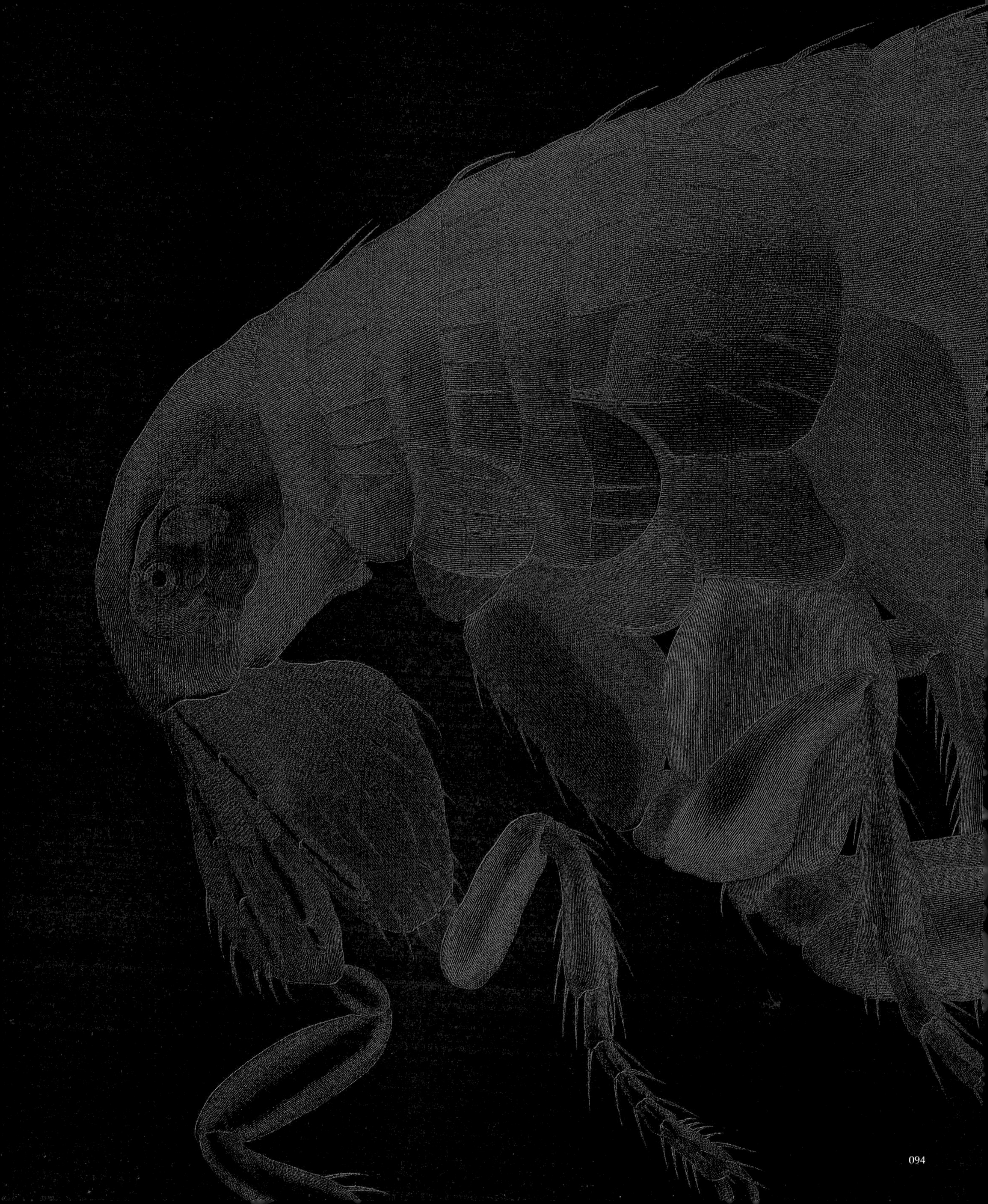

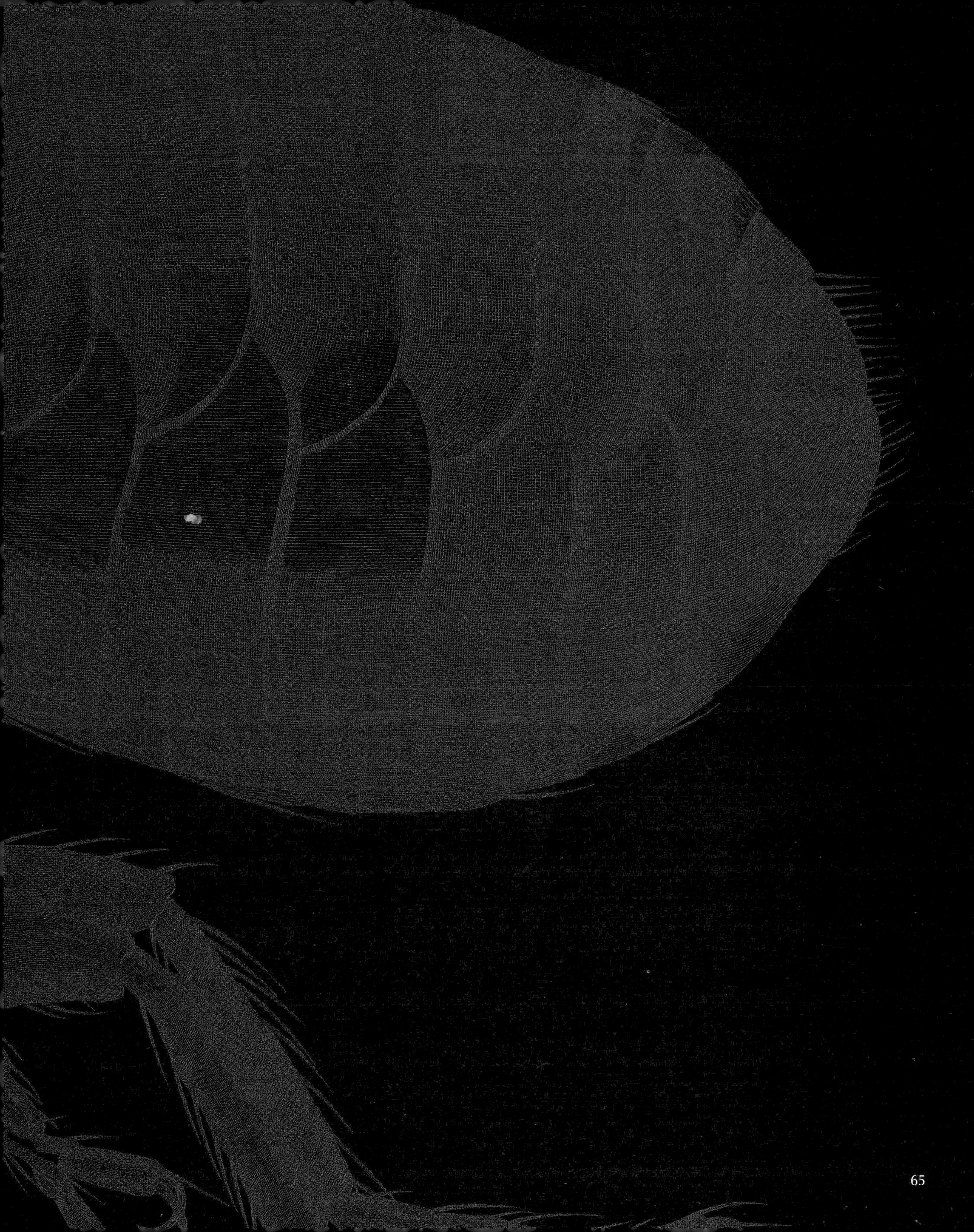

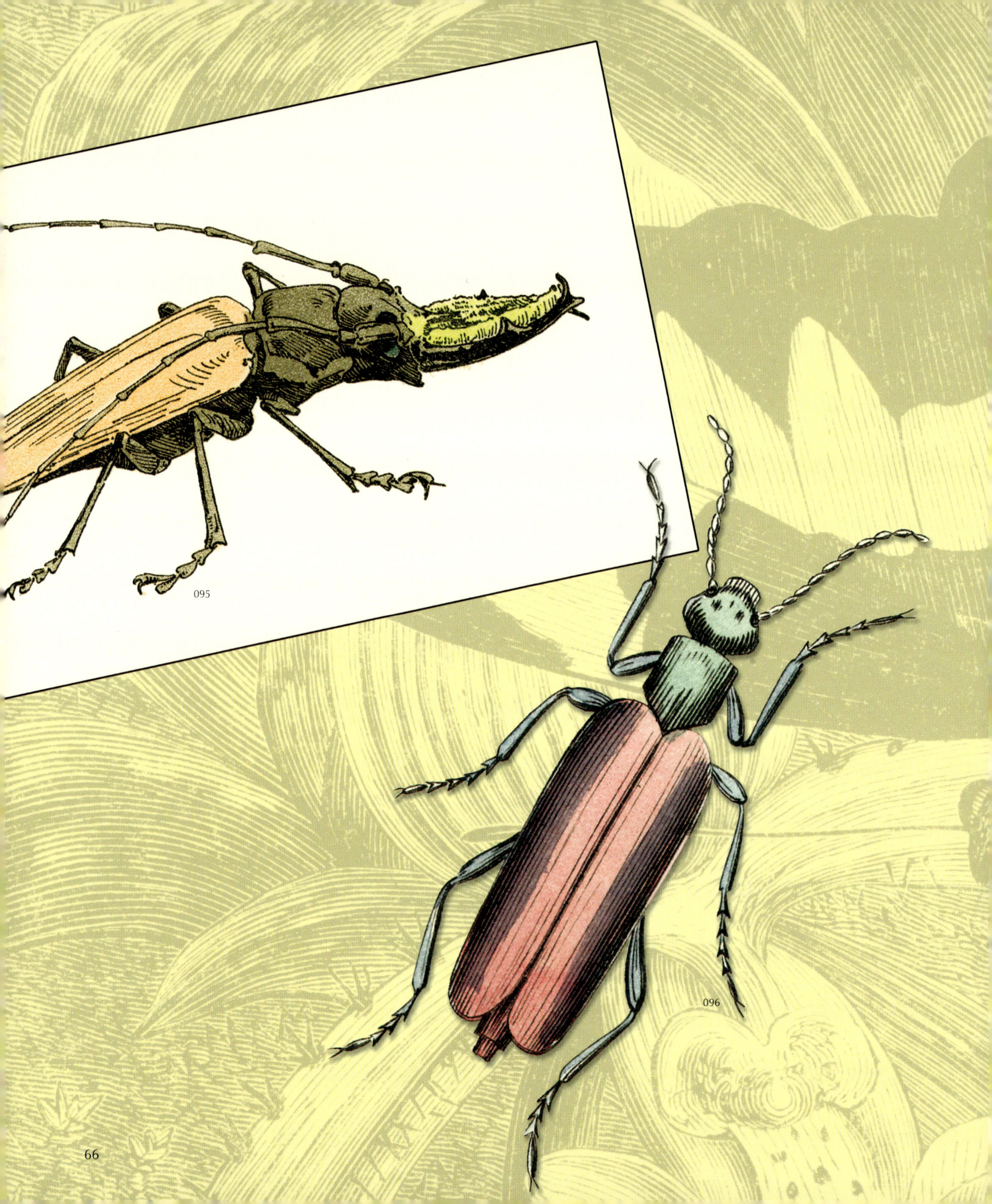
095
096

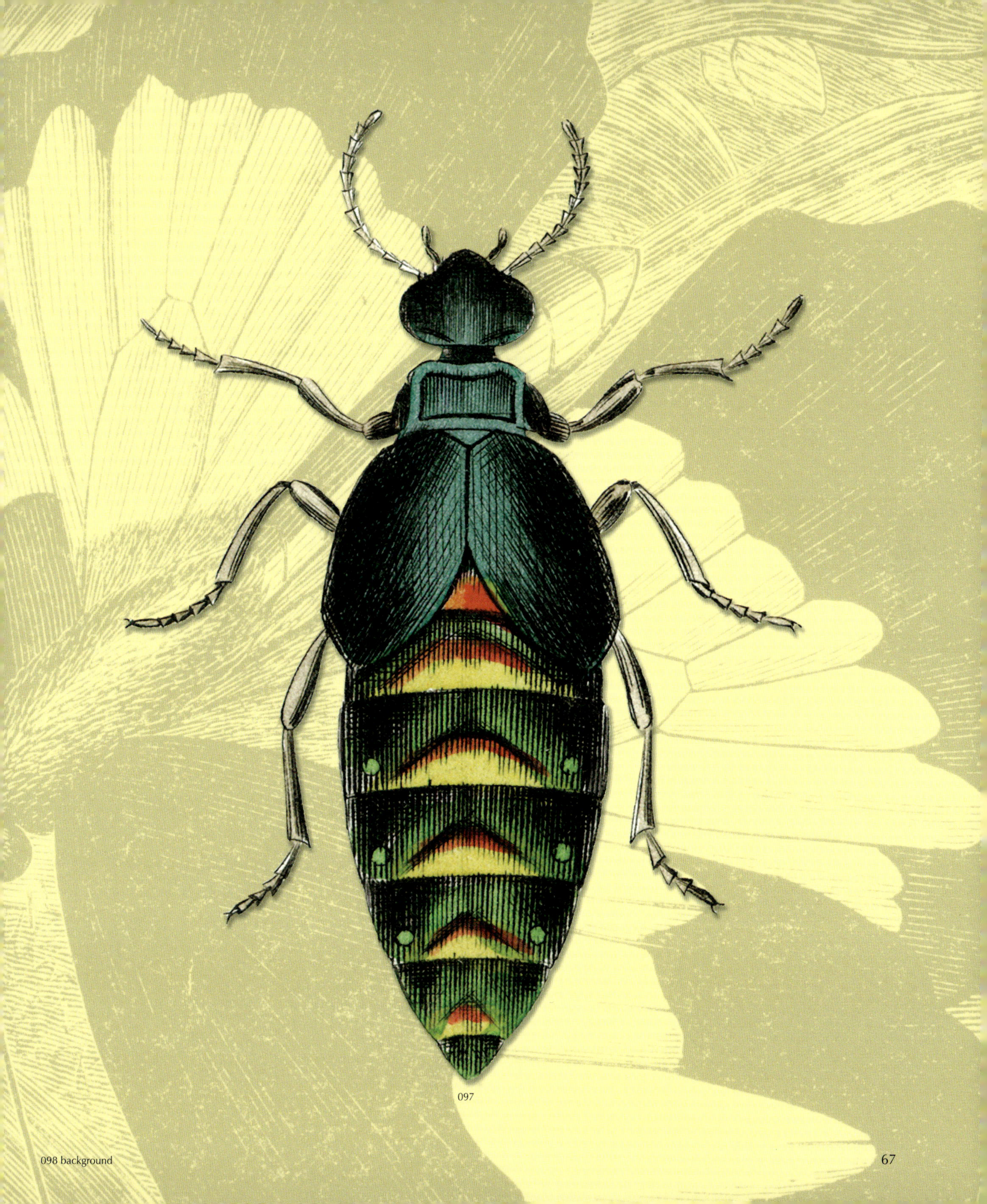
097
098 background

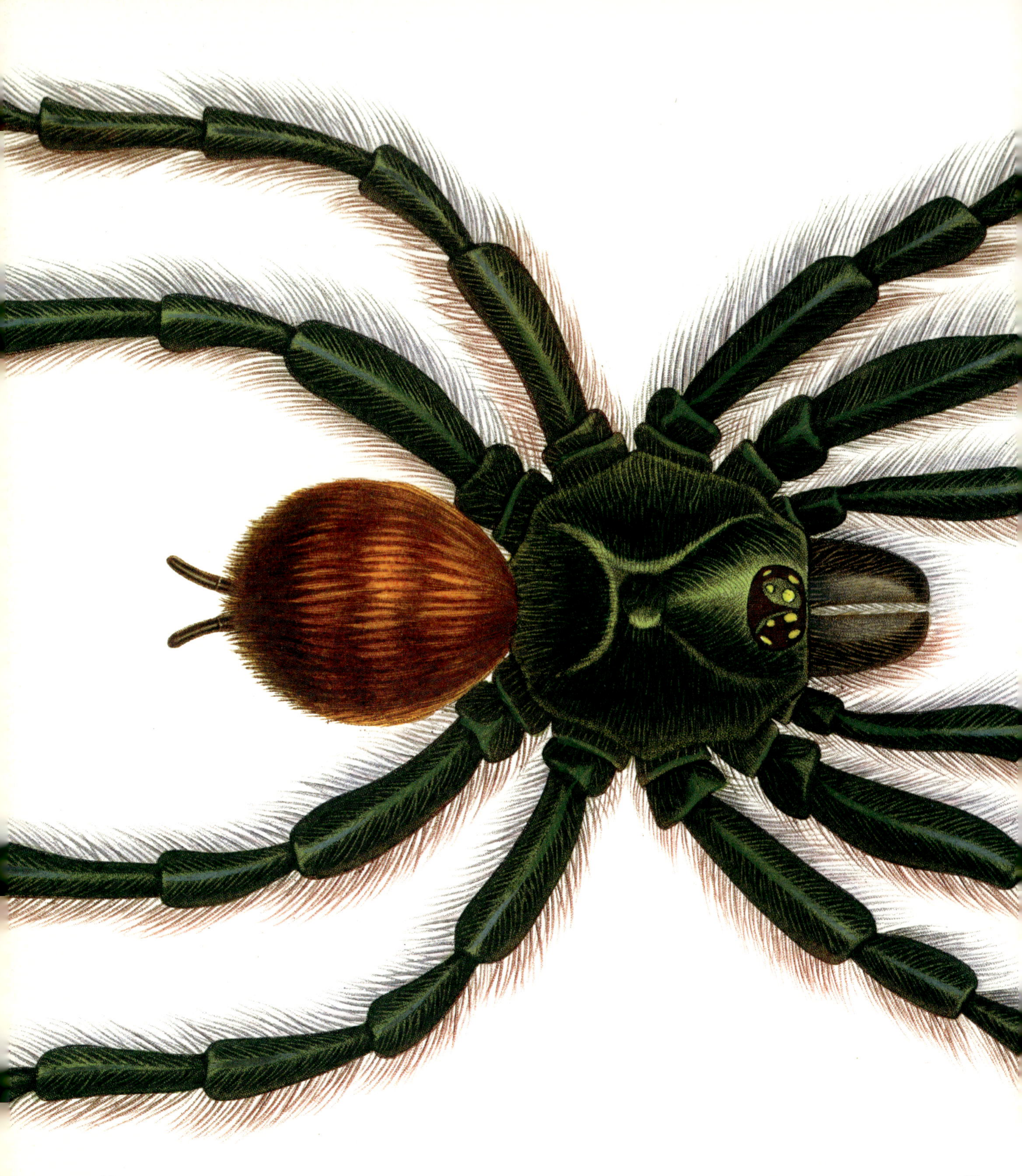

099

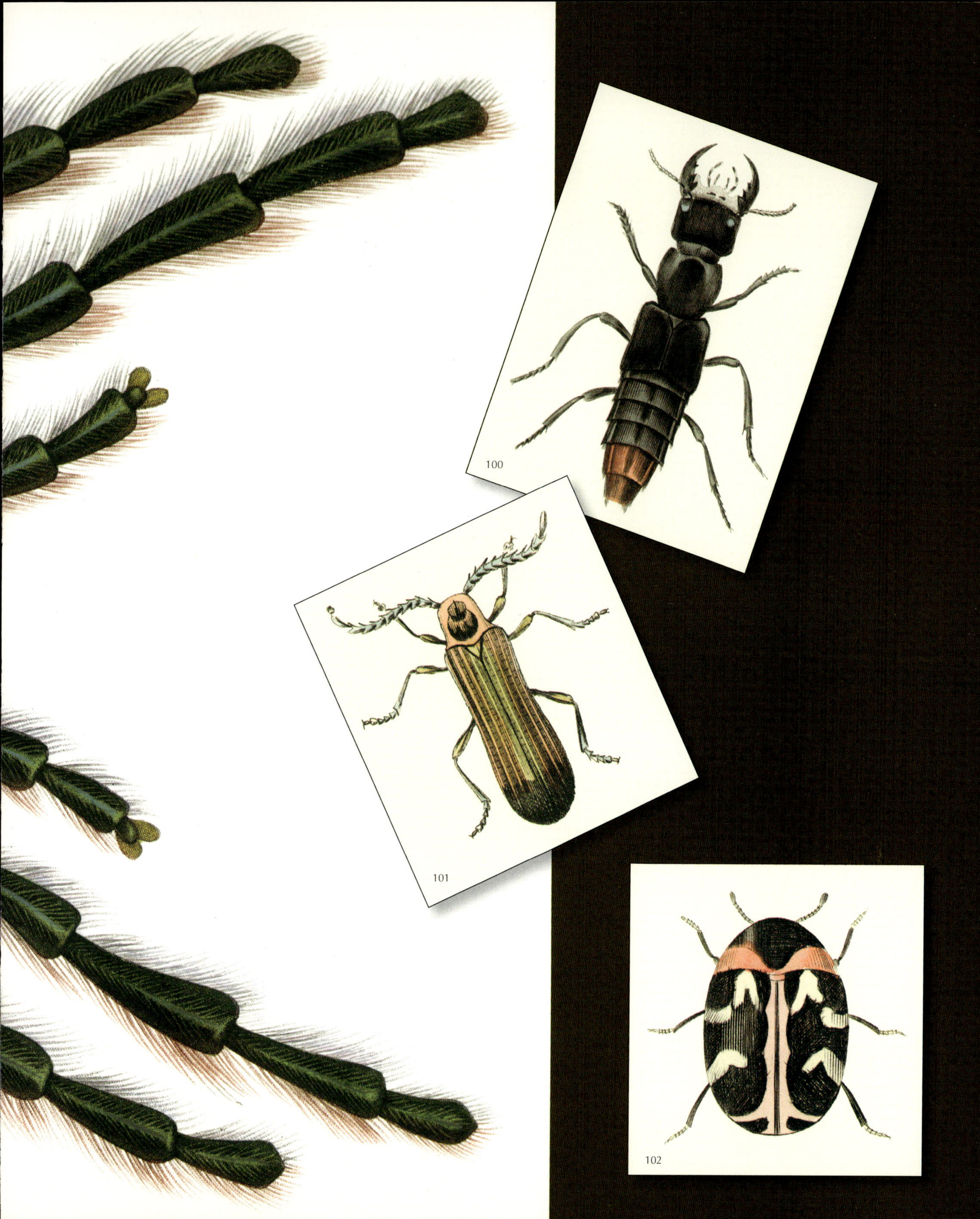
100
101
102

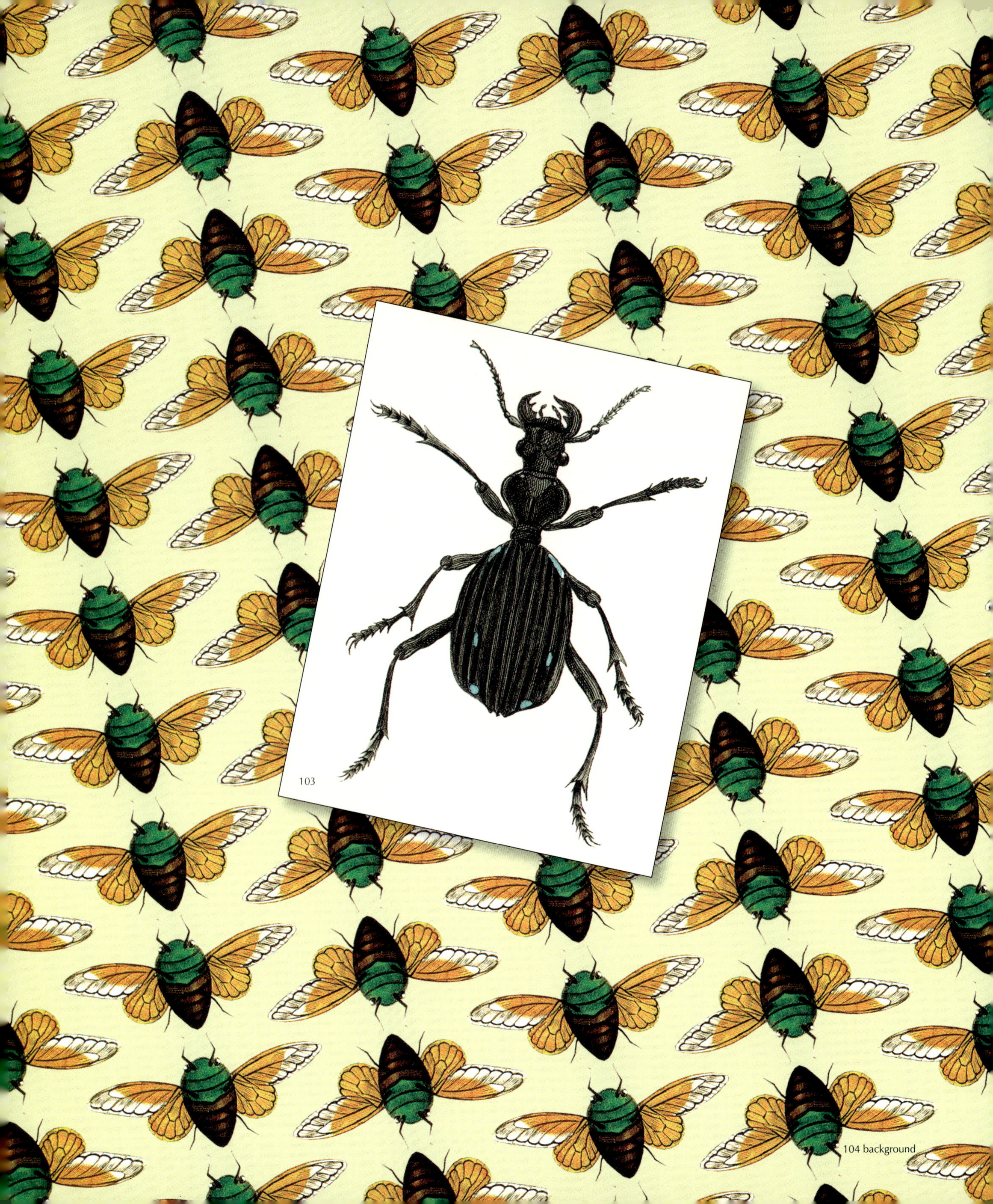
103
104 background

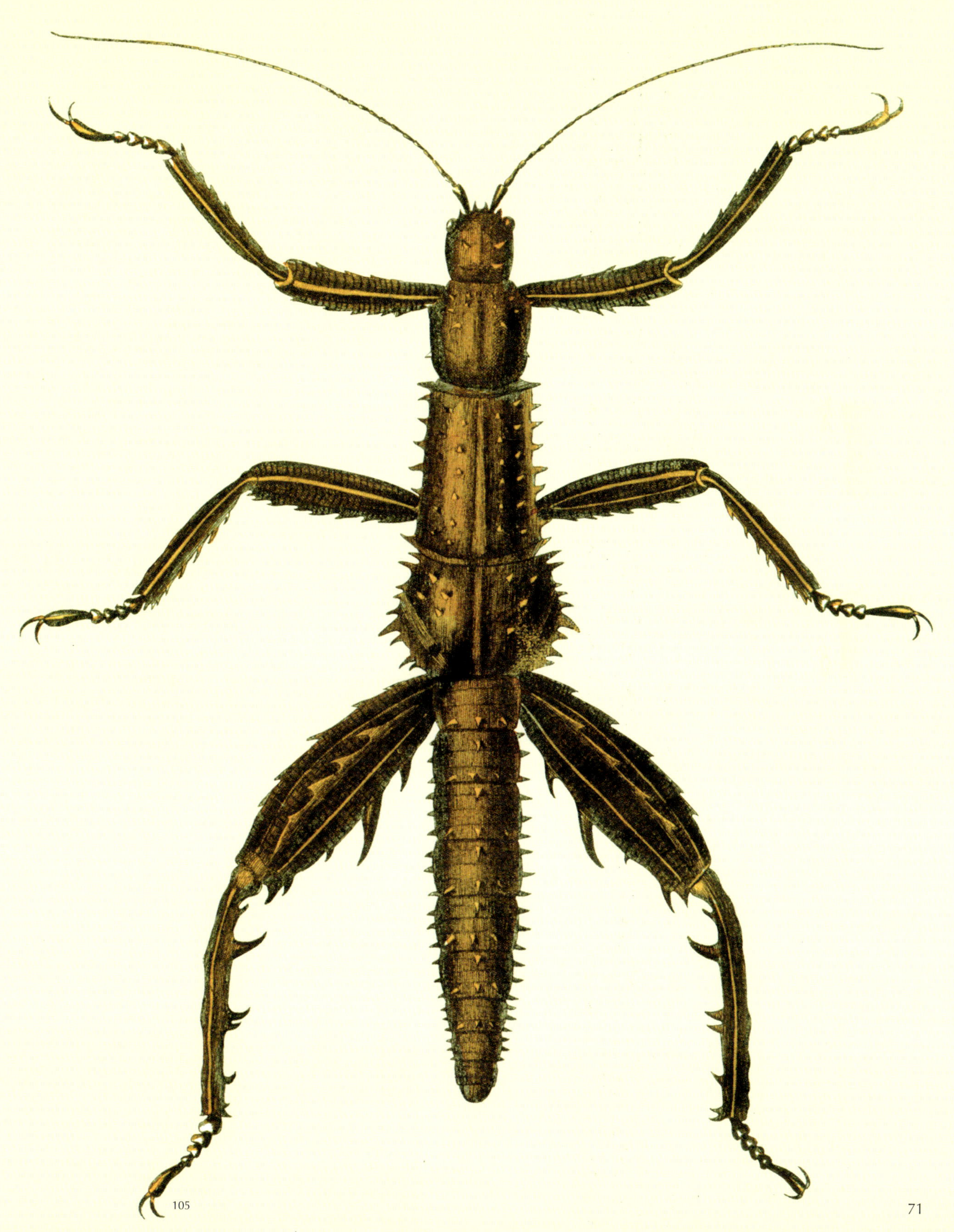

105

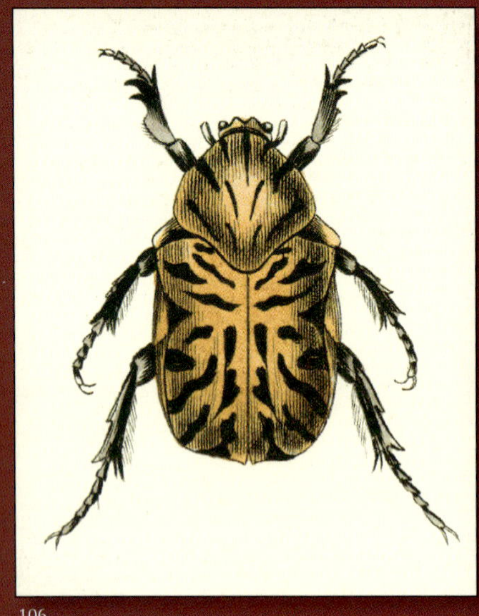

106

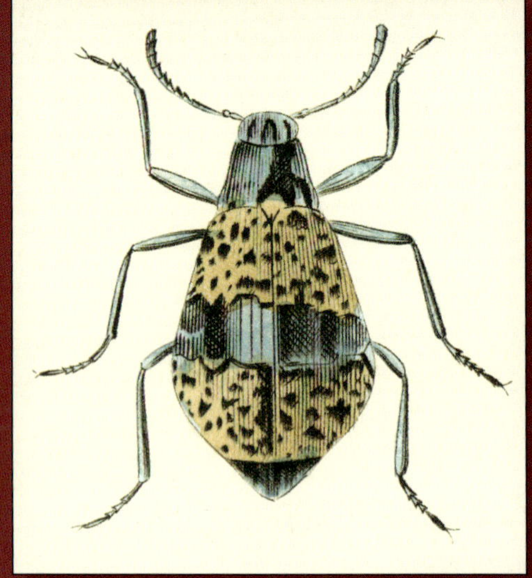

107

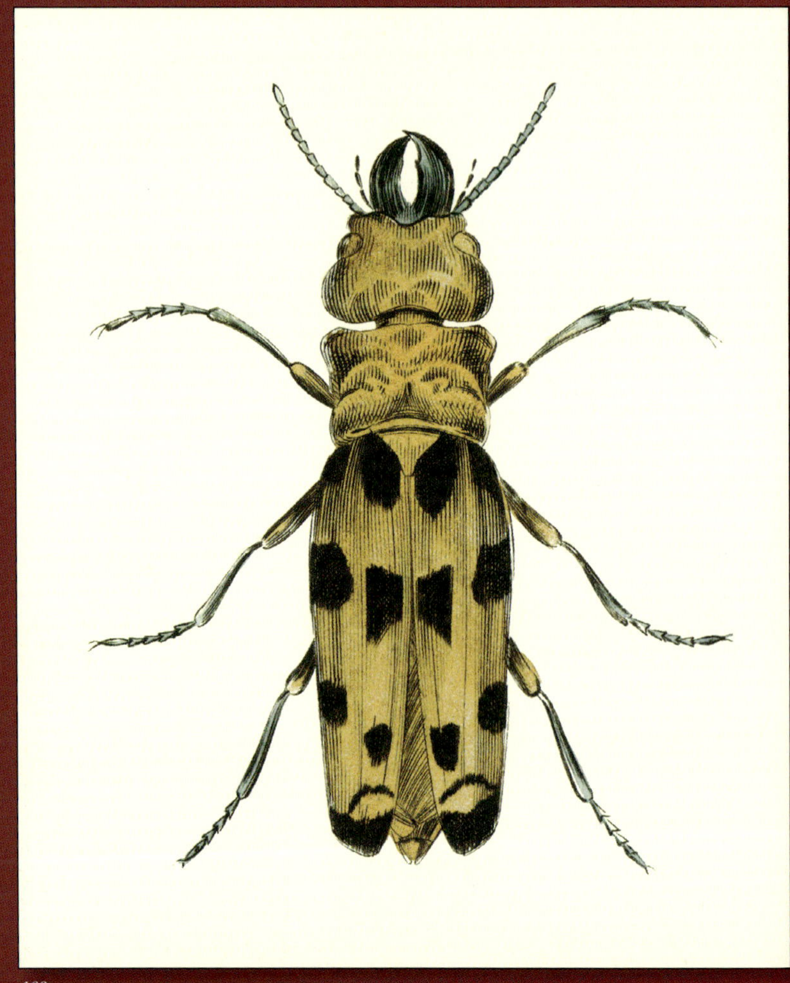

108

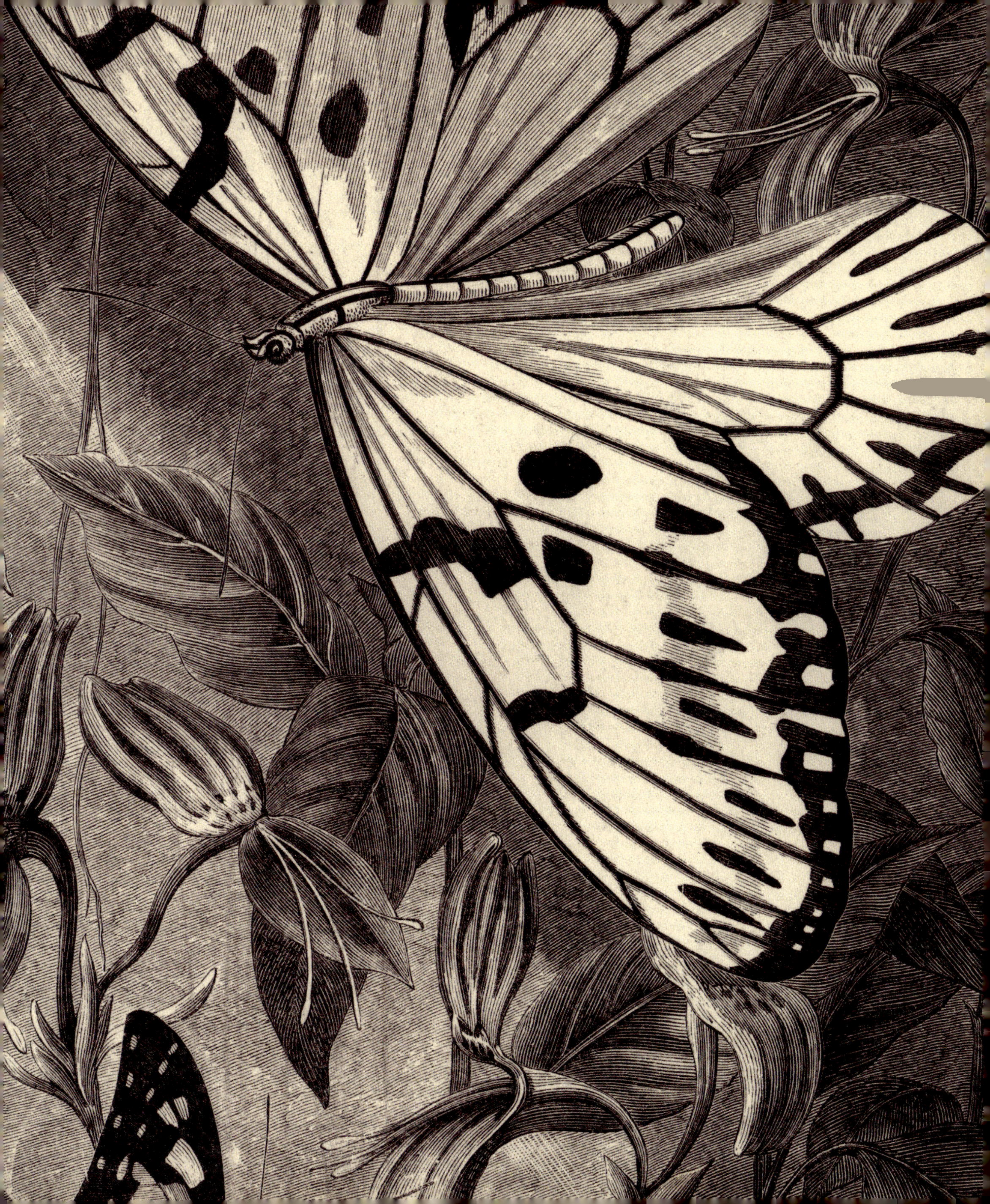

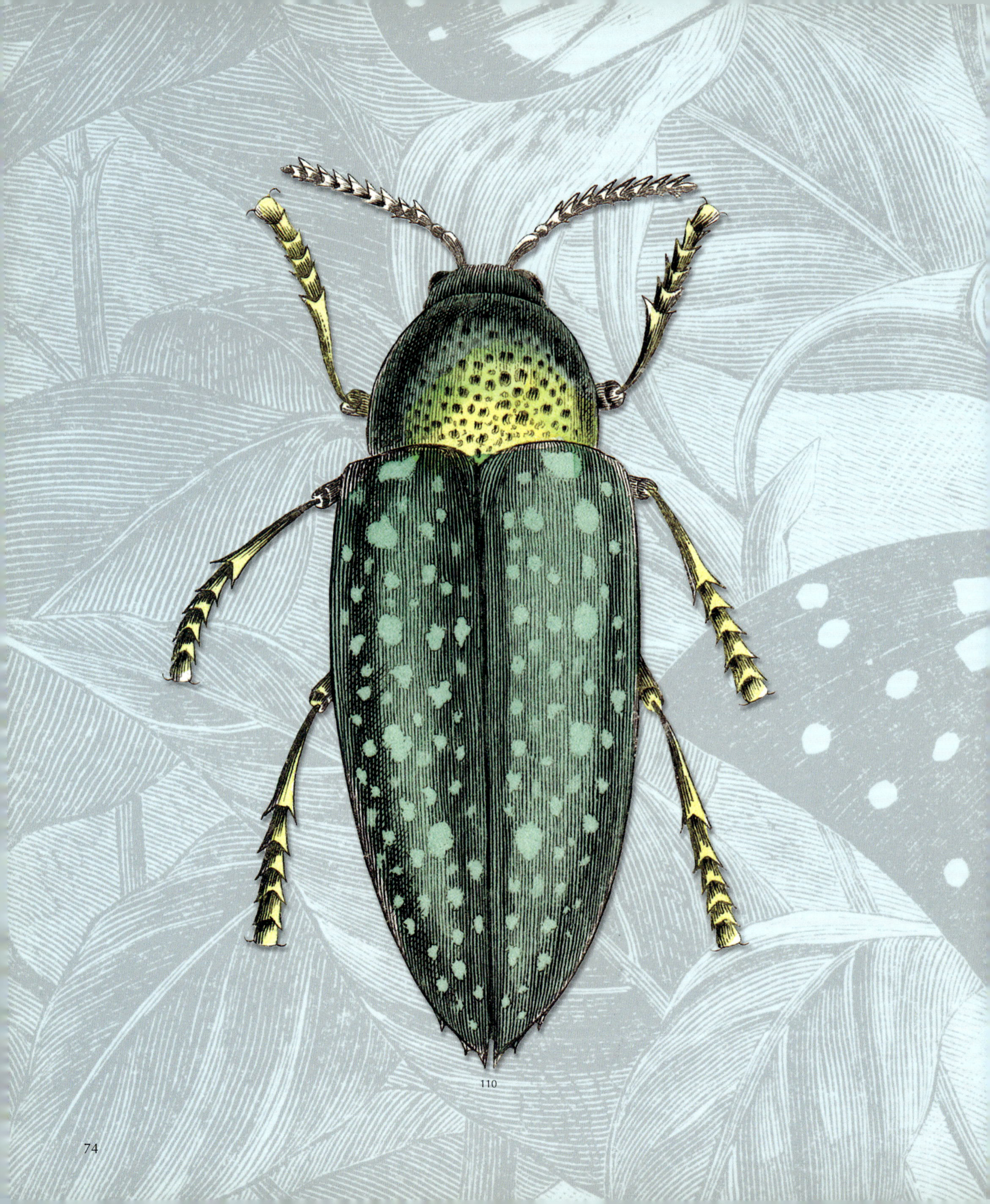
110

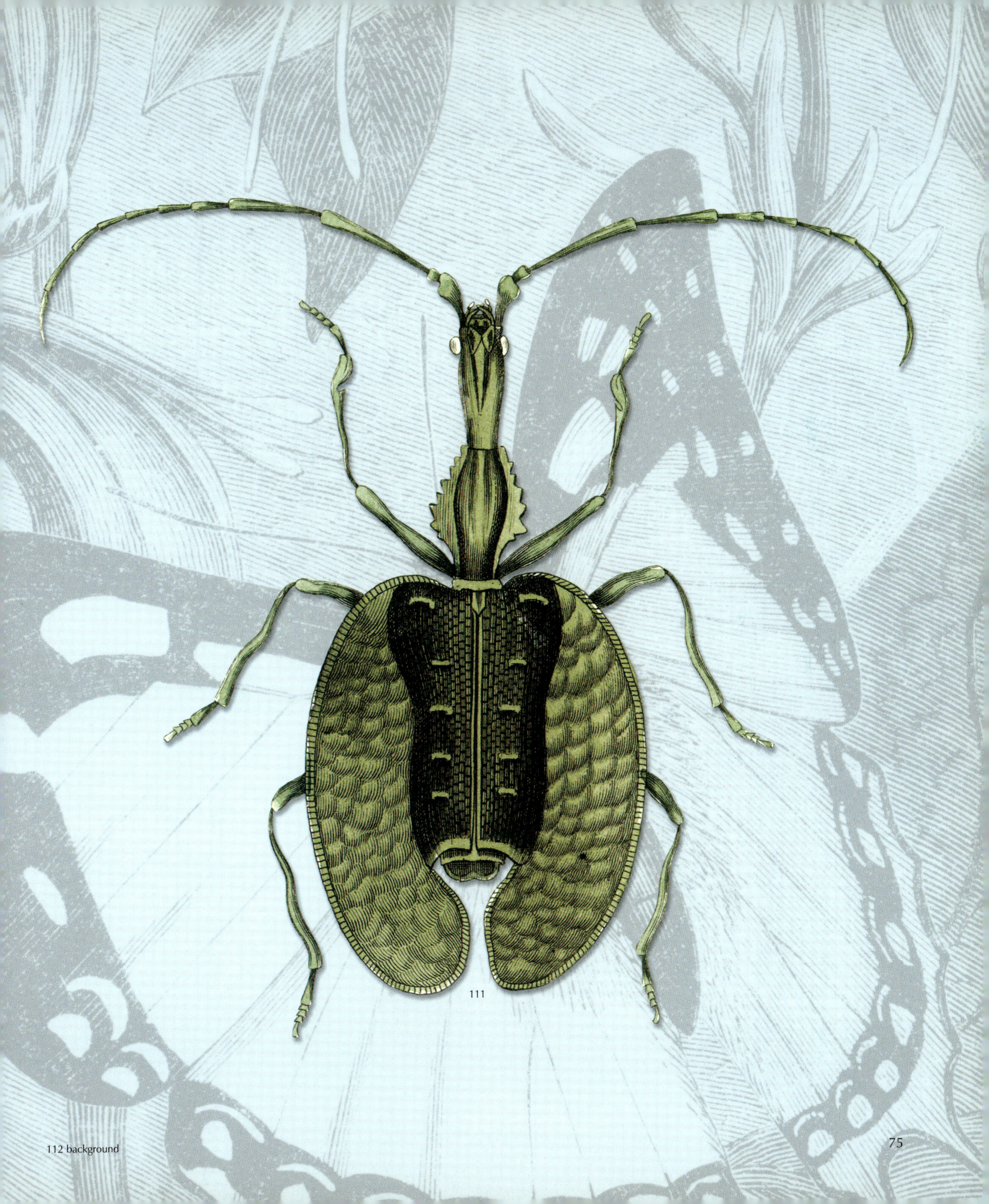

111

112 background

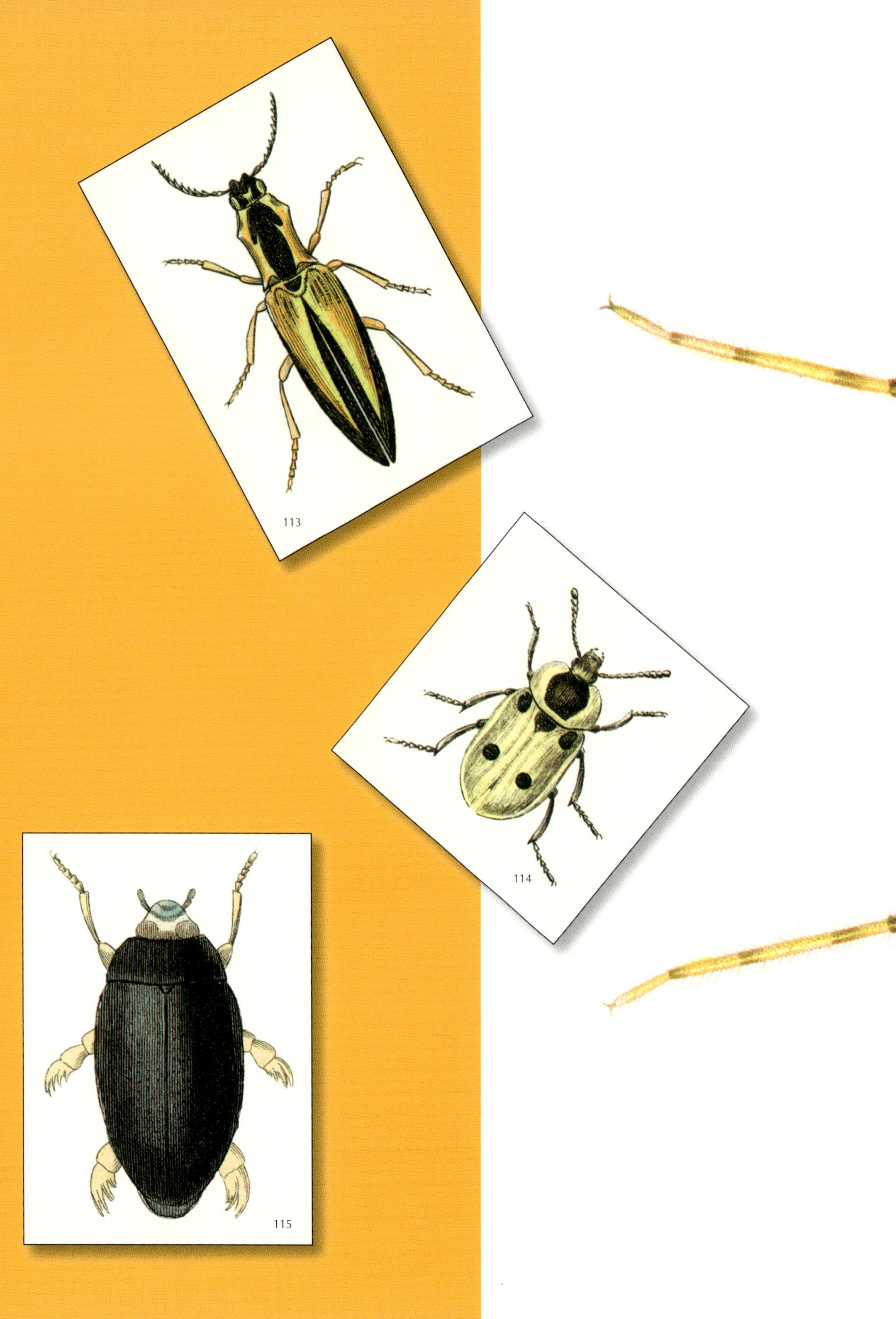

113
114
115

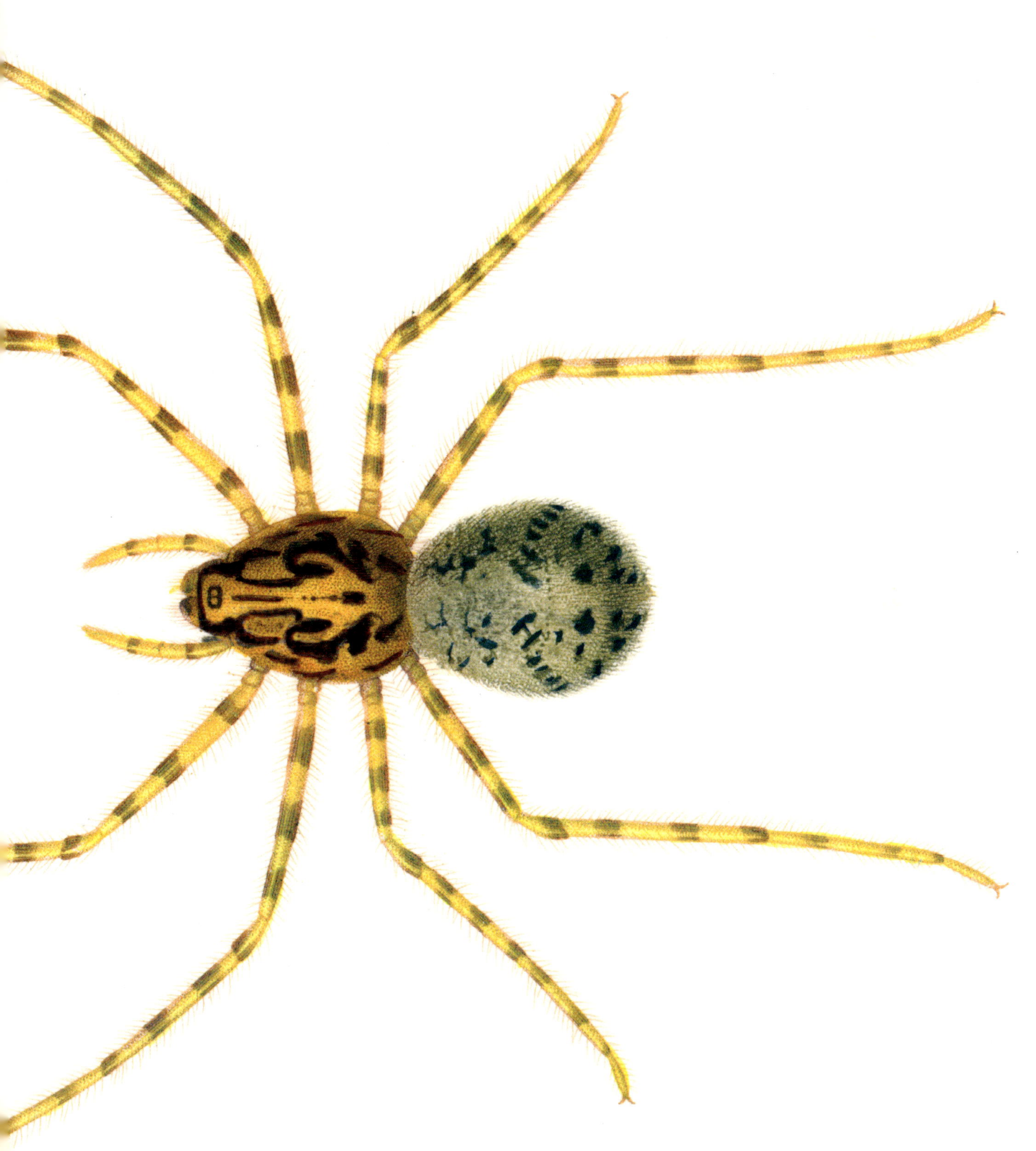

116

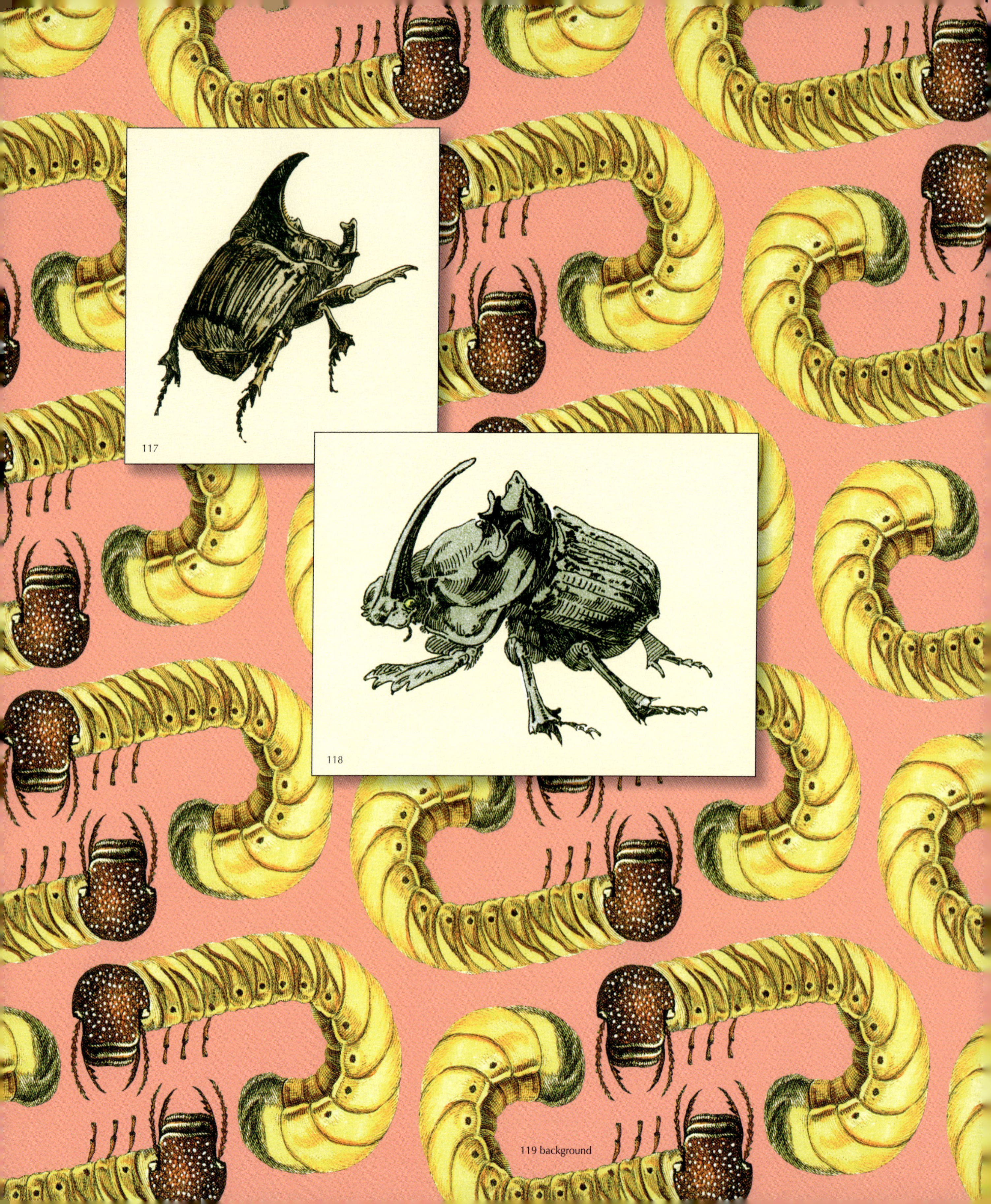

117

118

119 background

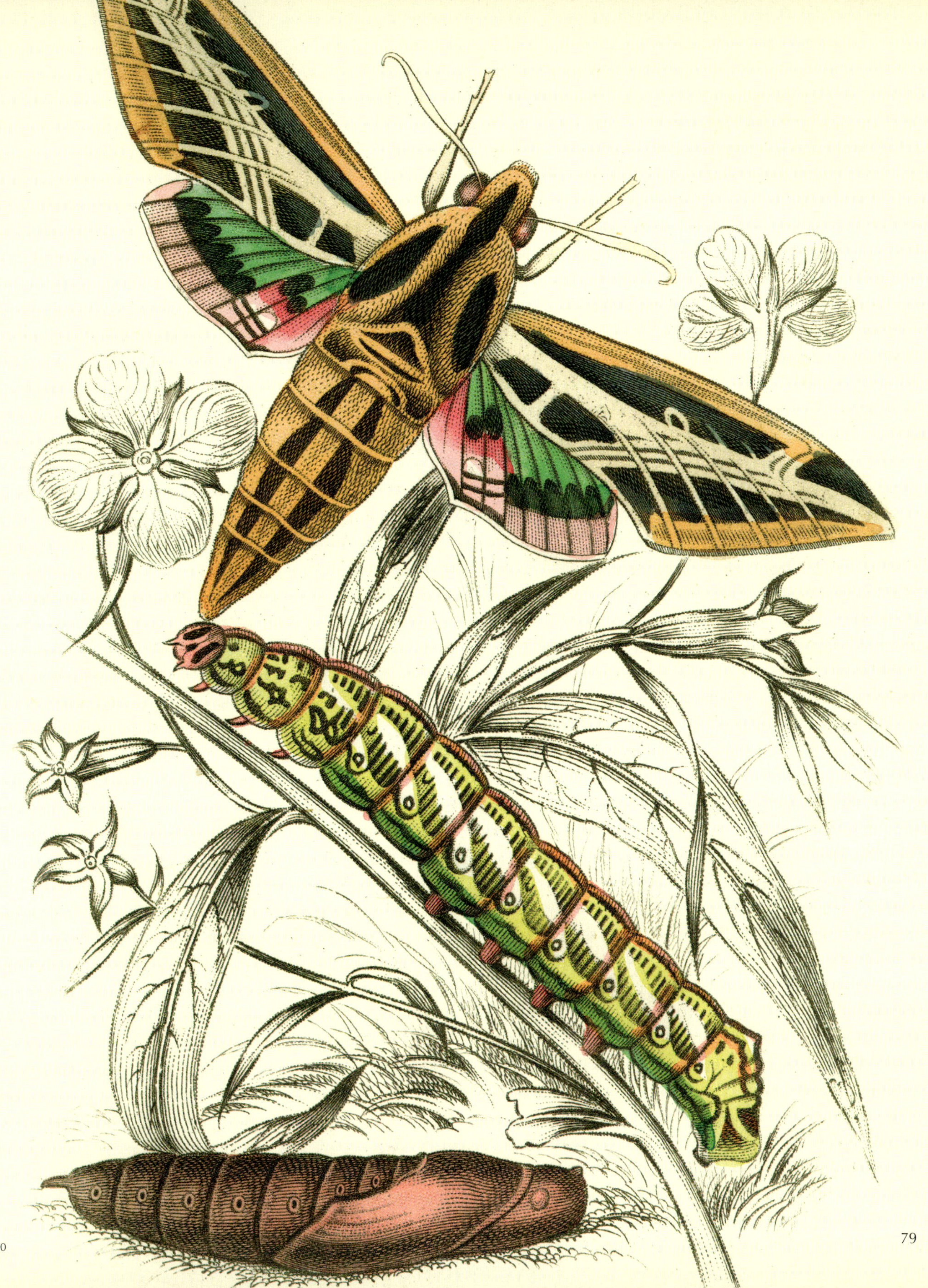

120

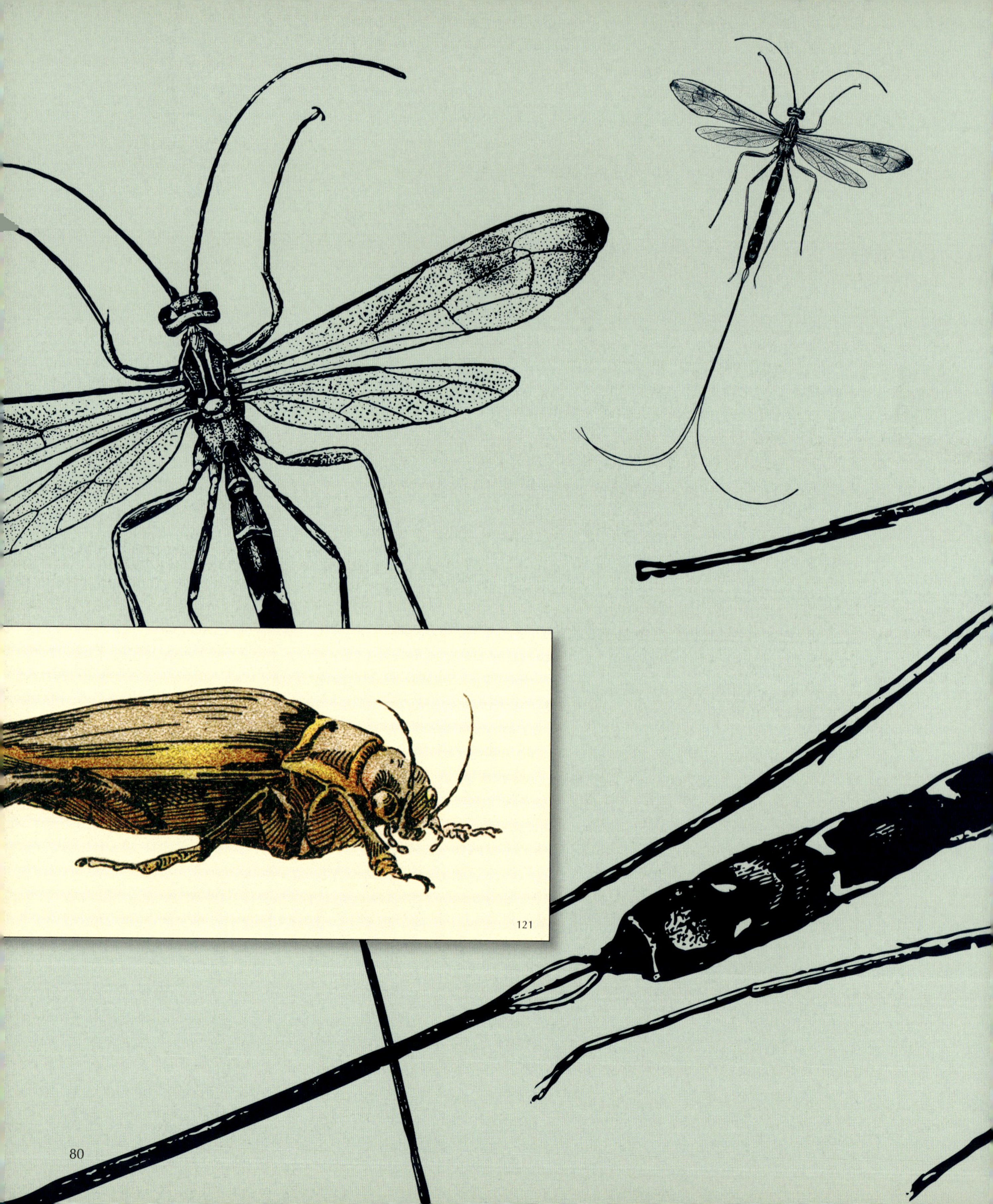

121

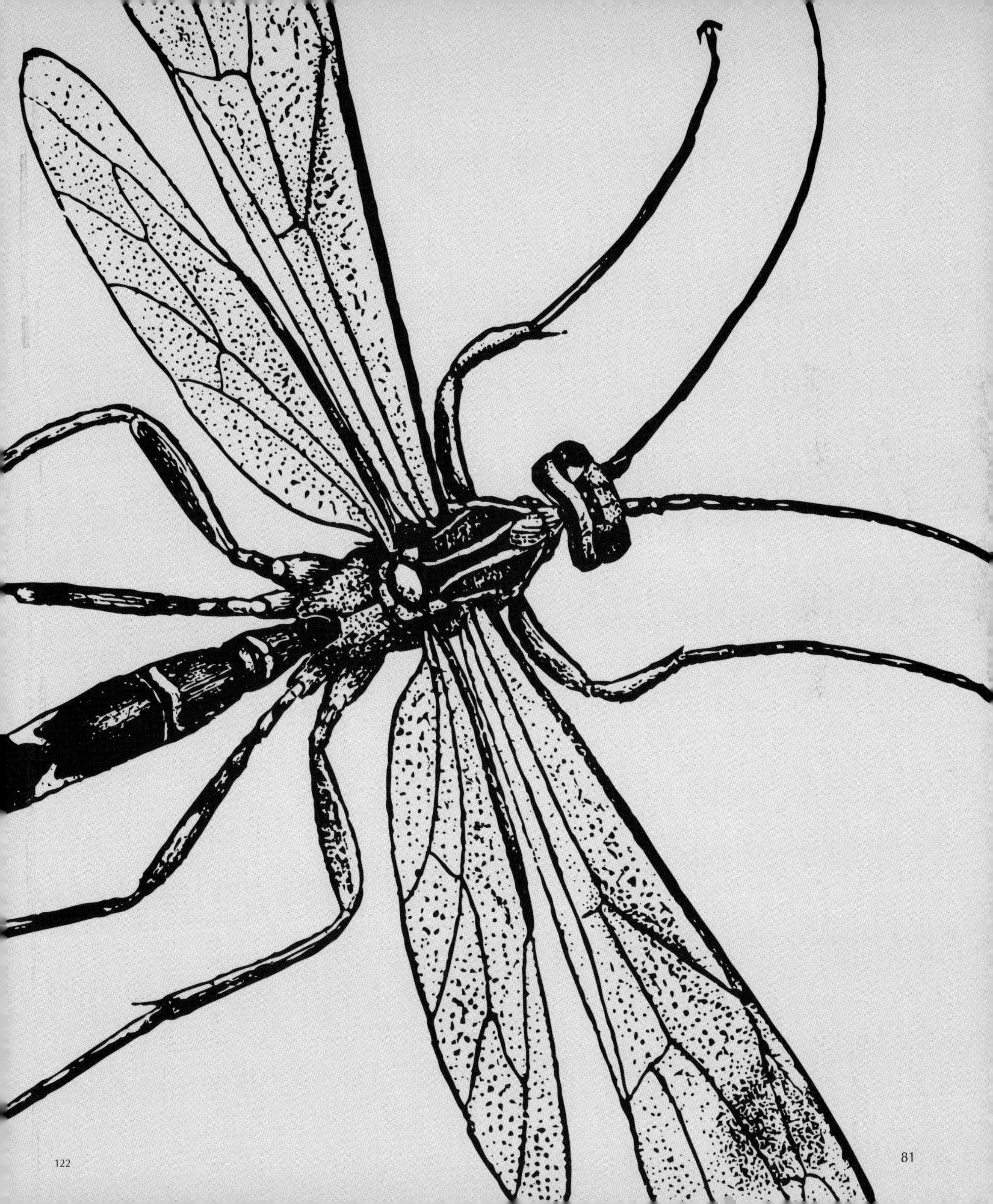

122

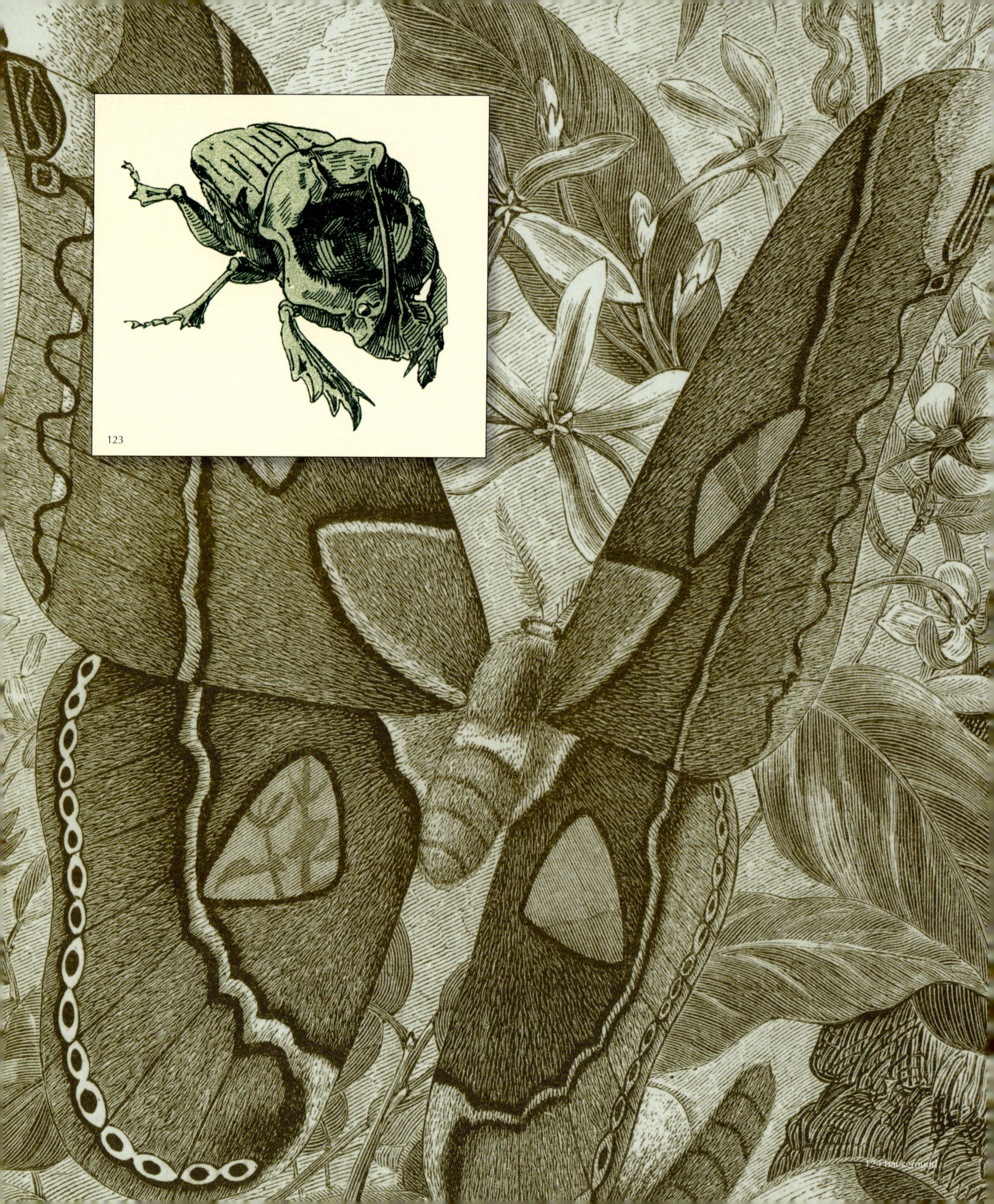

123

124 background

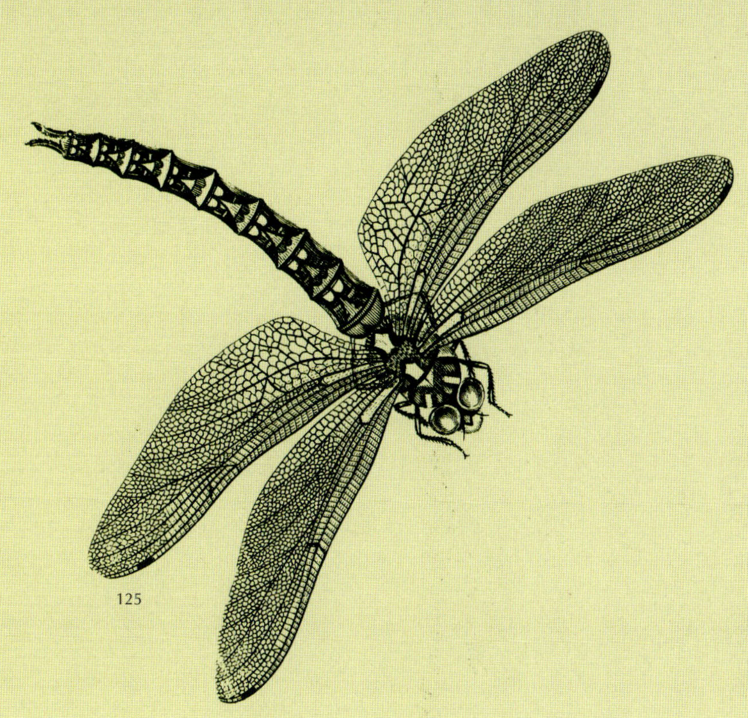
125

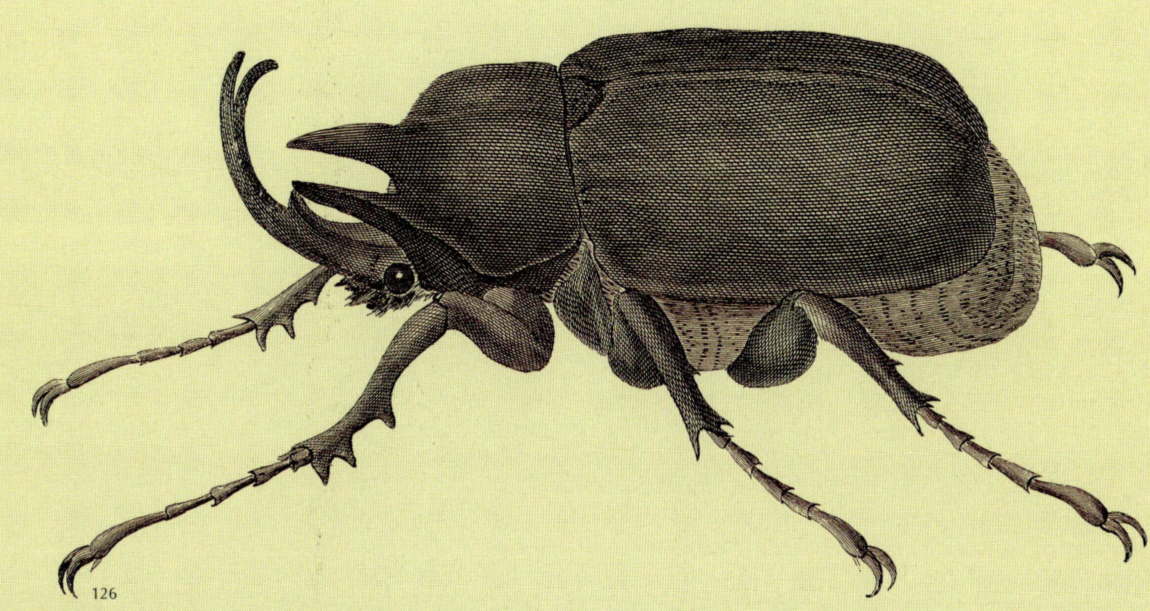
126

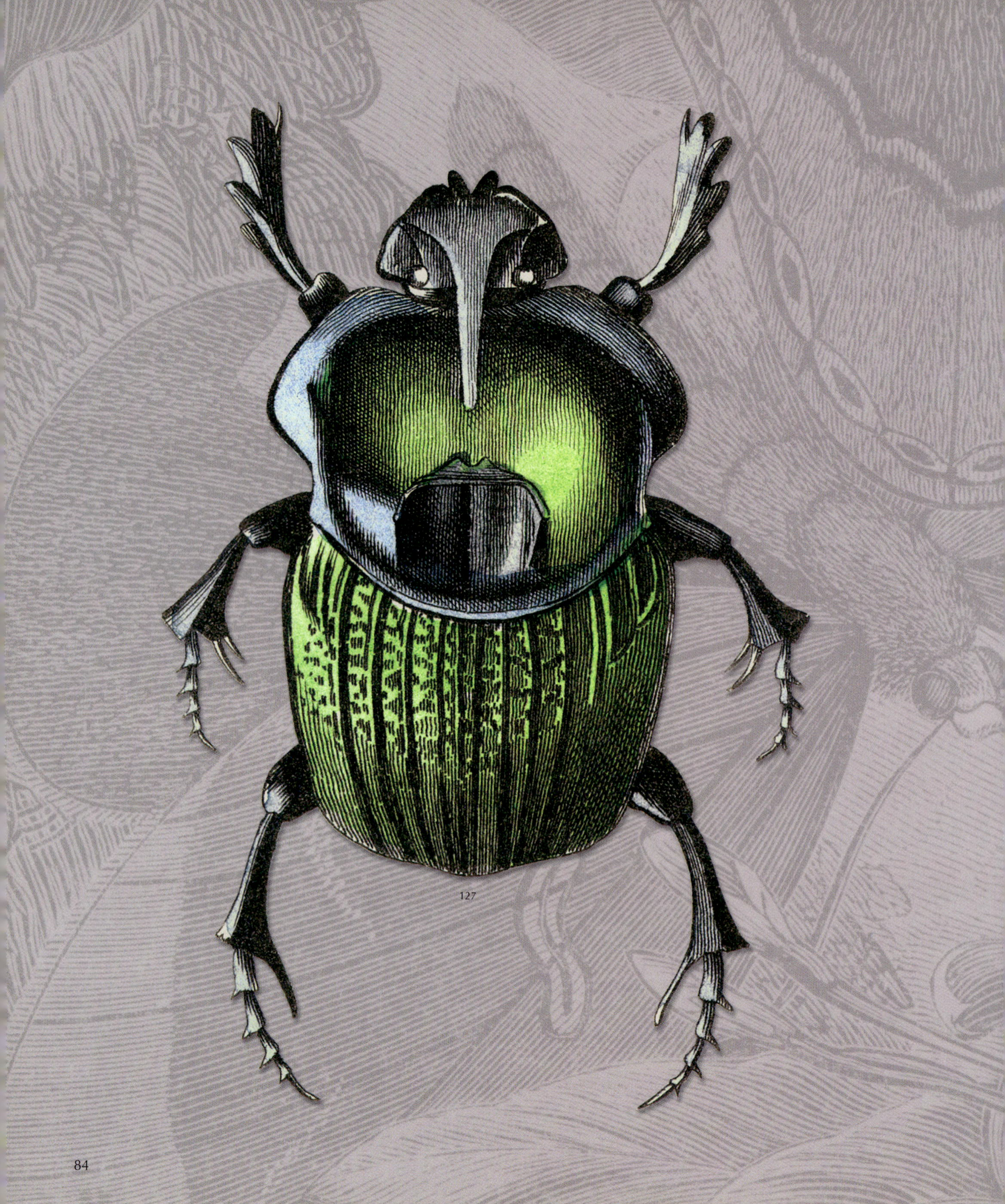
127

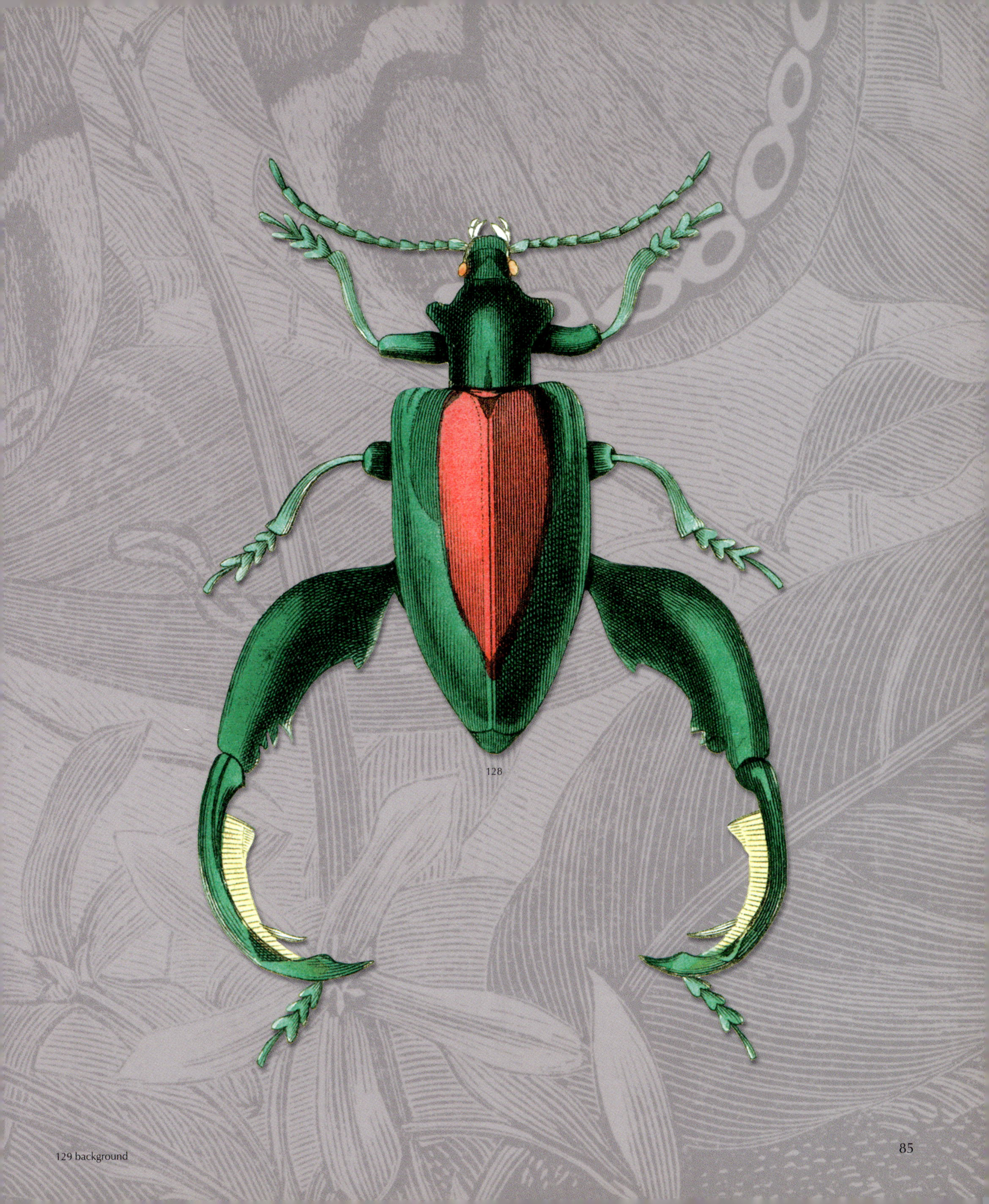
128

129 background

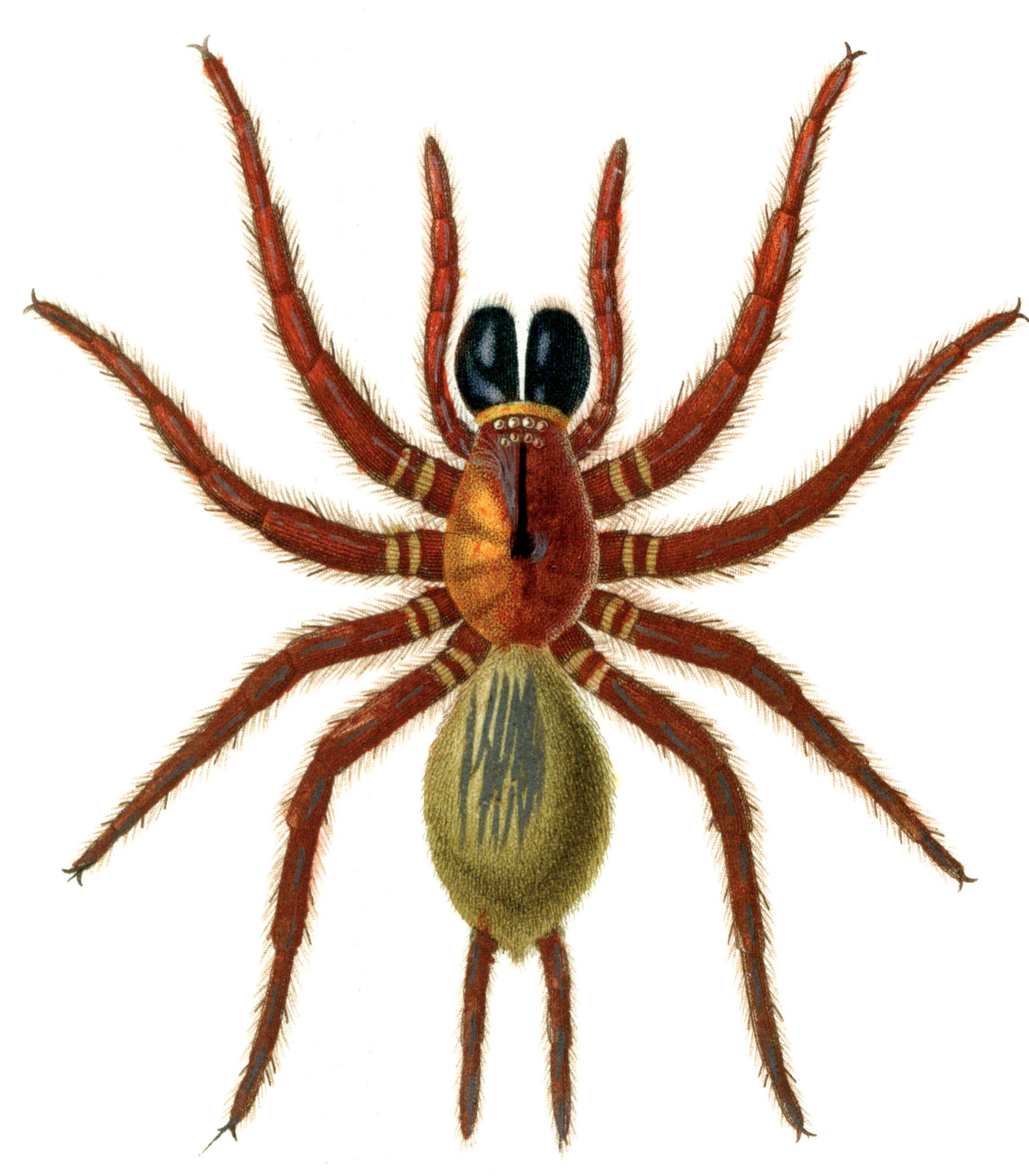

130

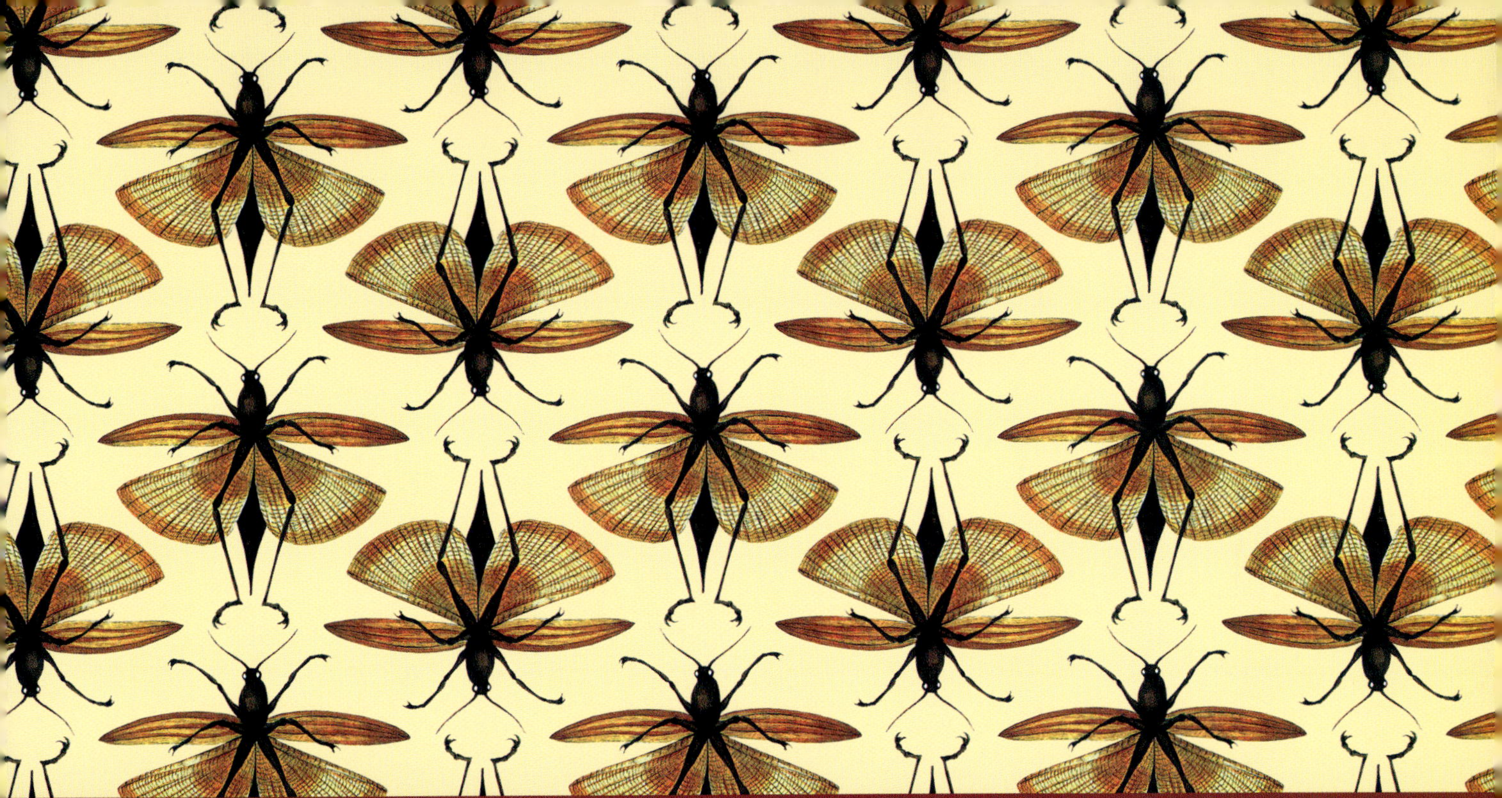

131 background

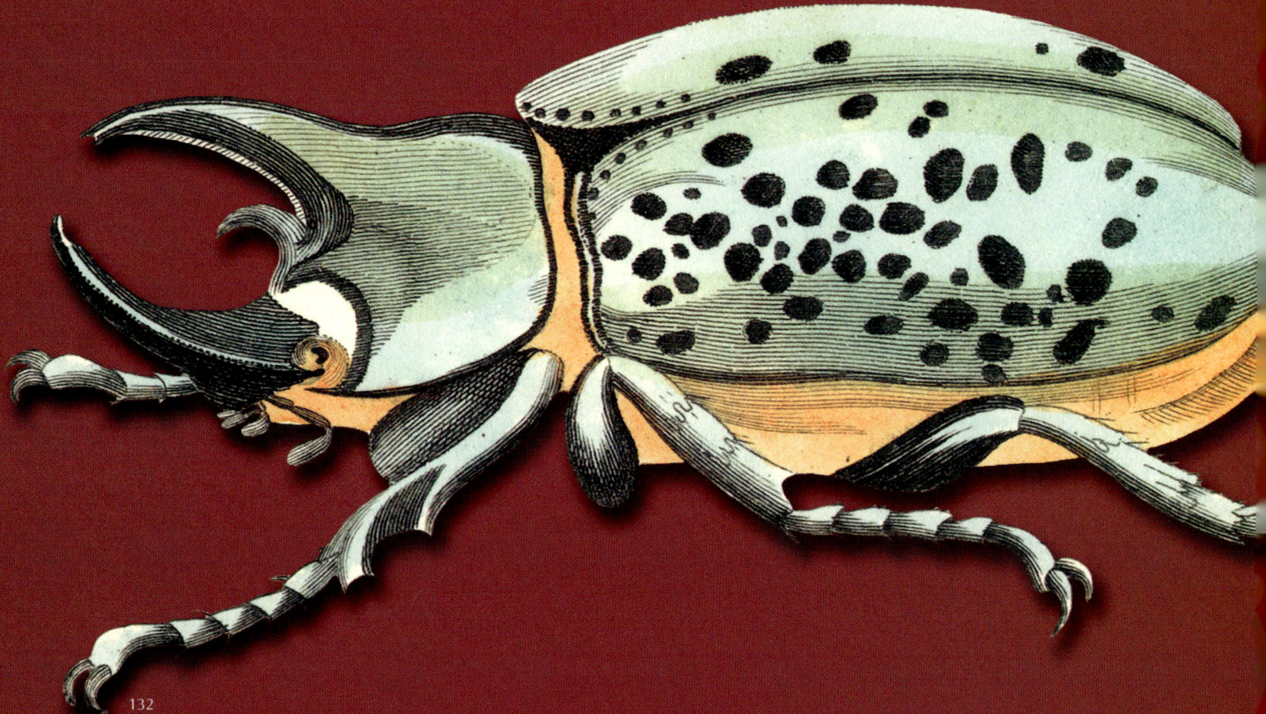

132

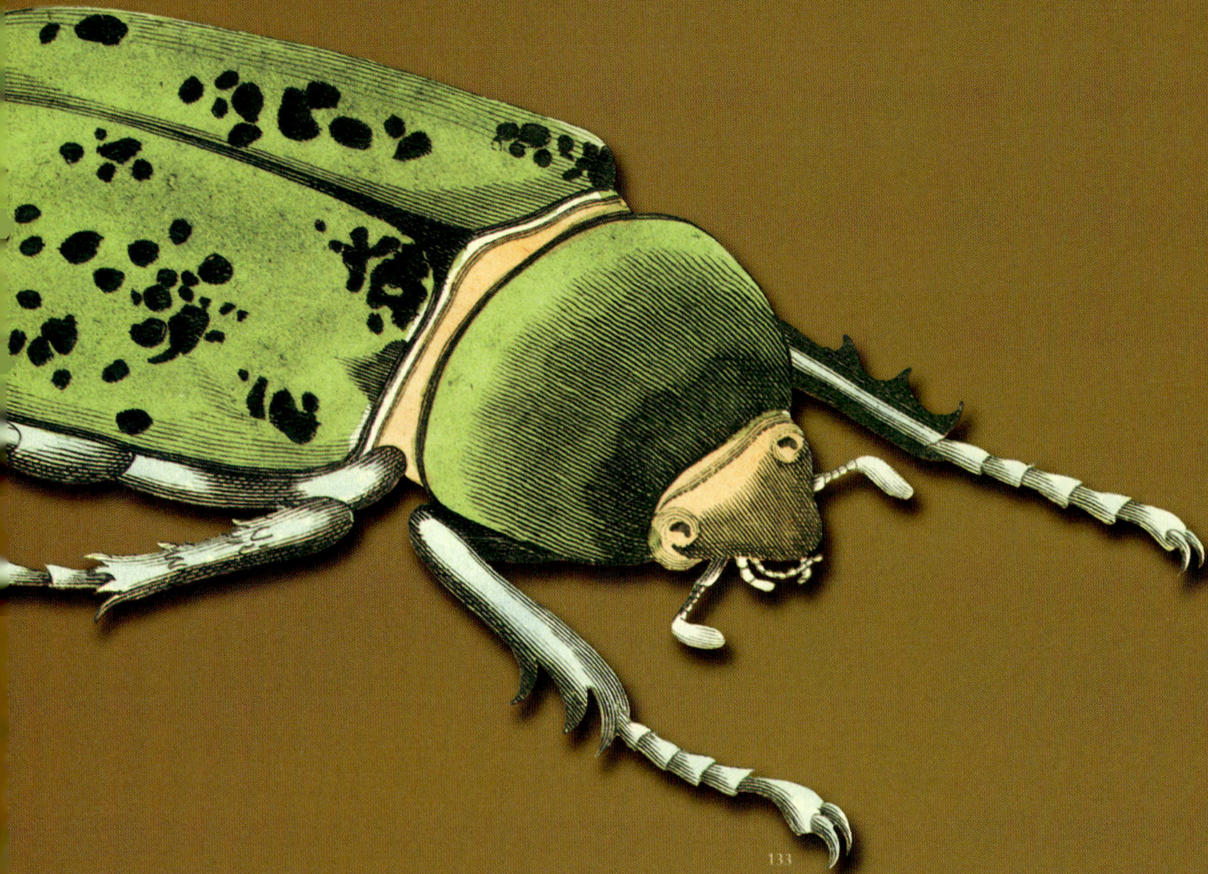

133

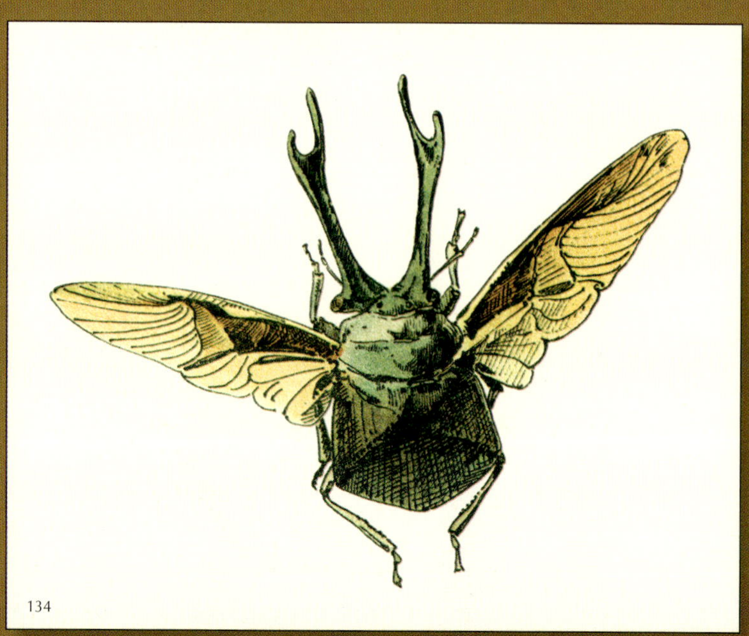

134

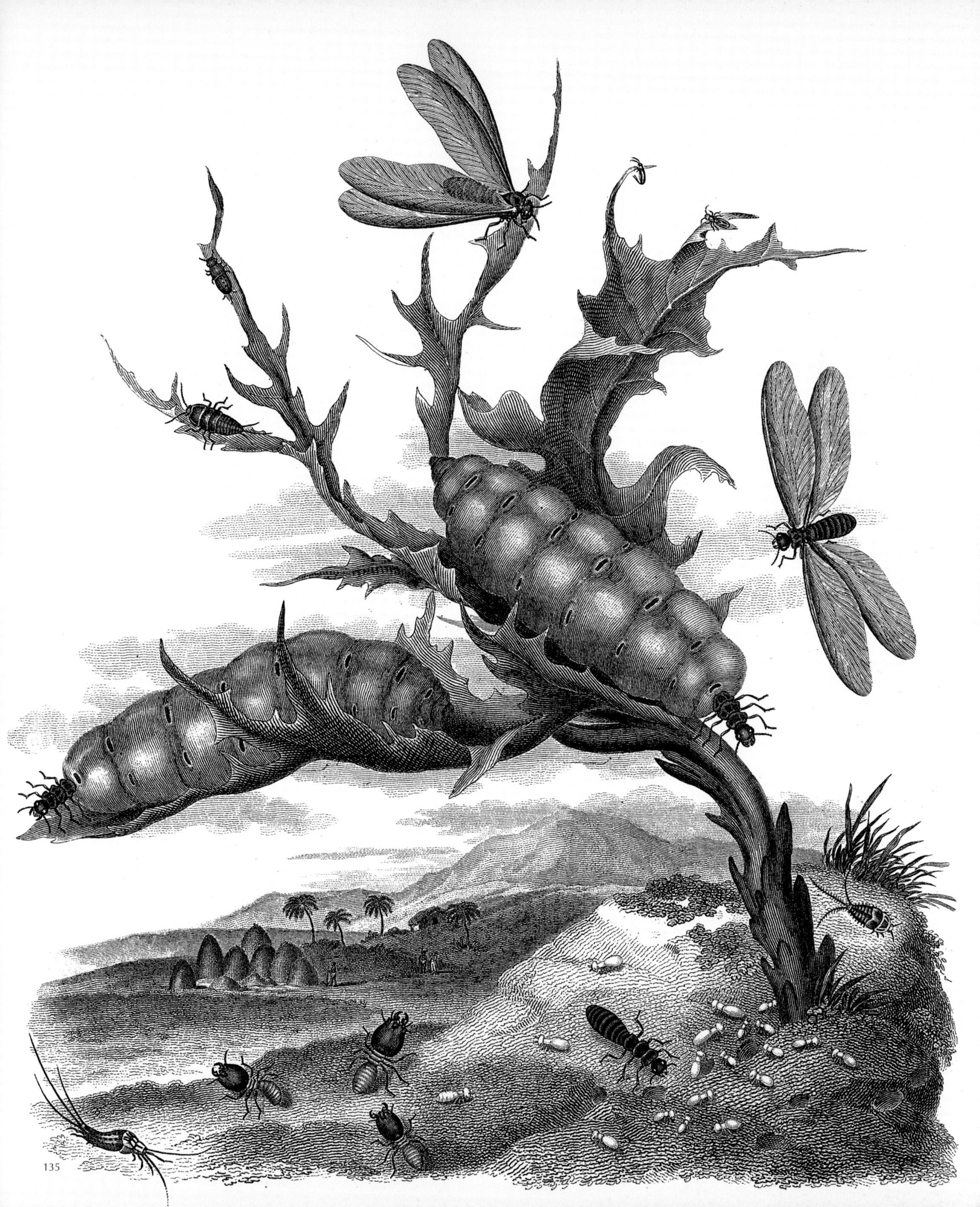

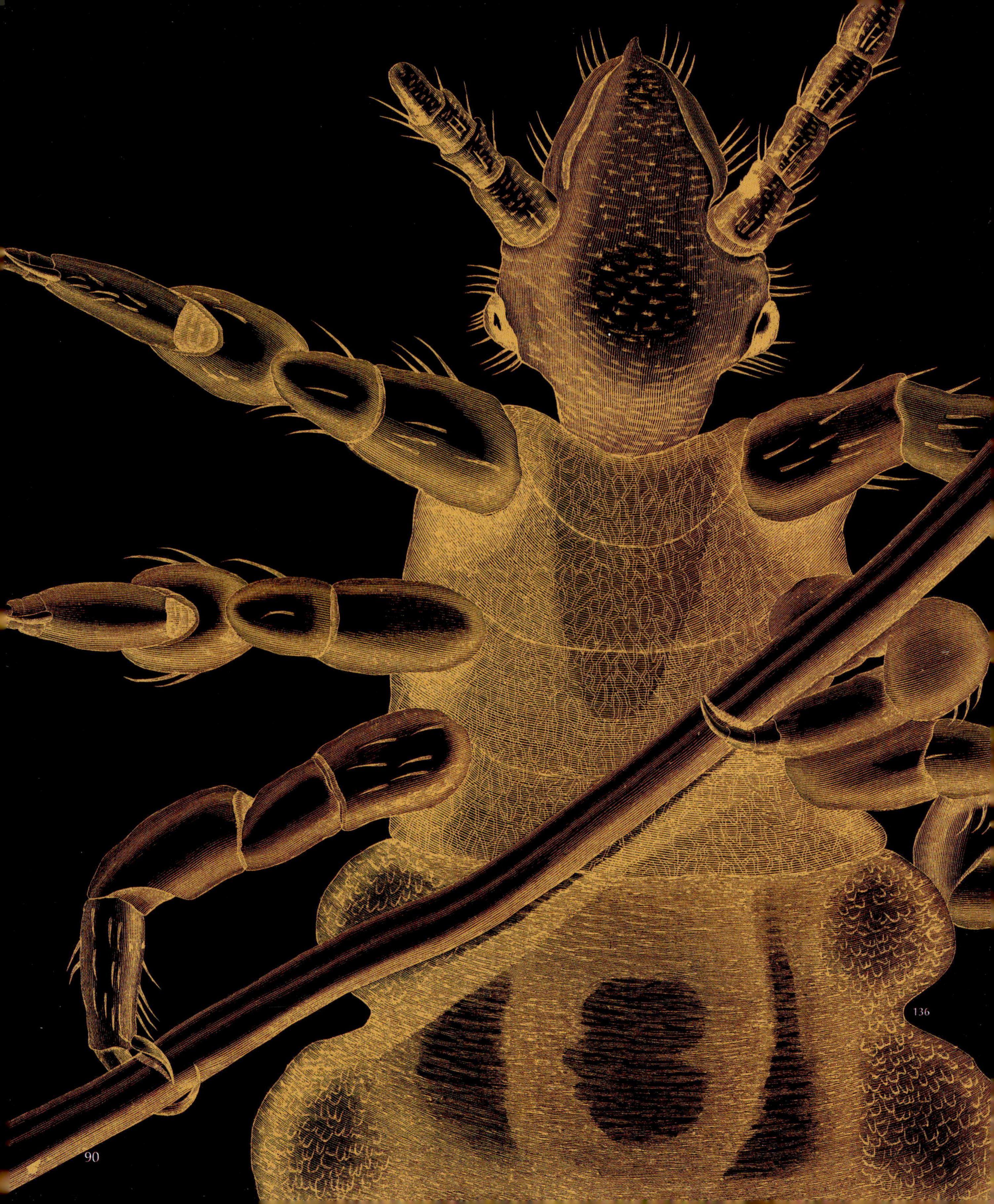

136

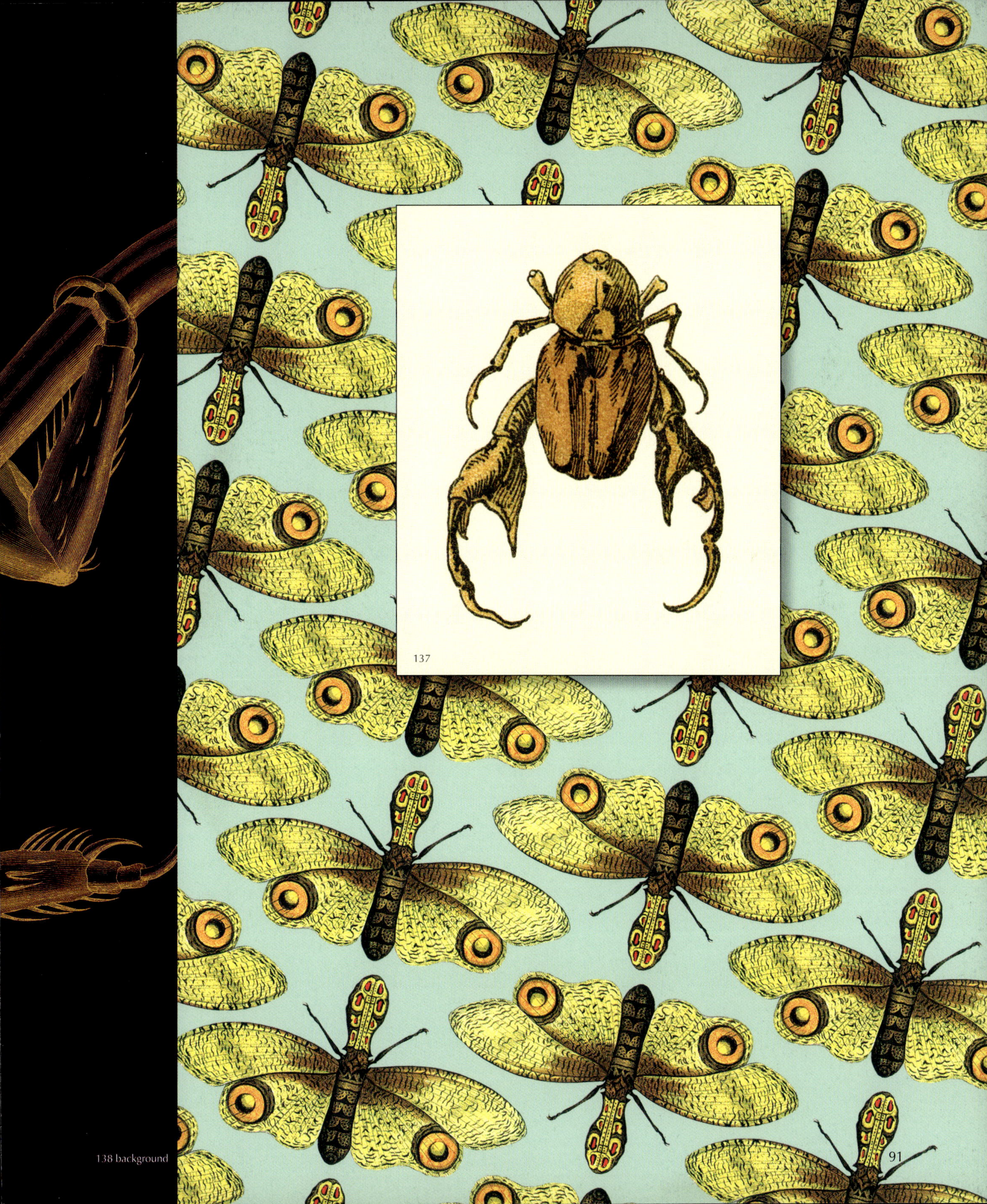
137
138 background

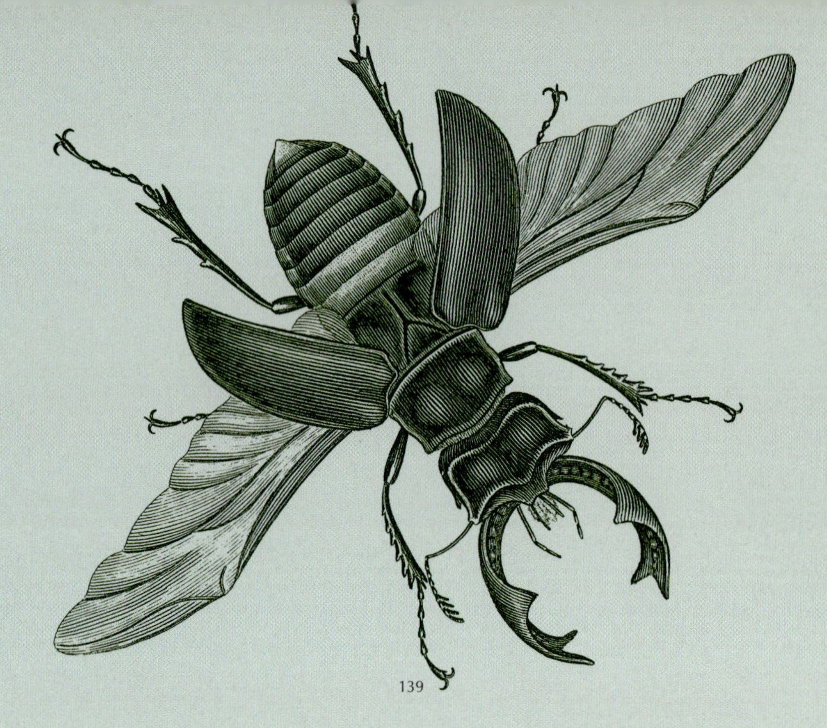

139

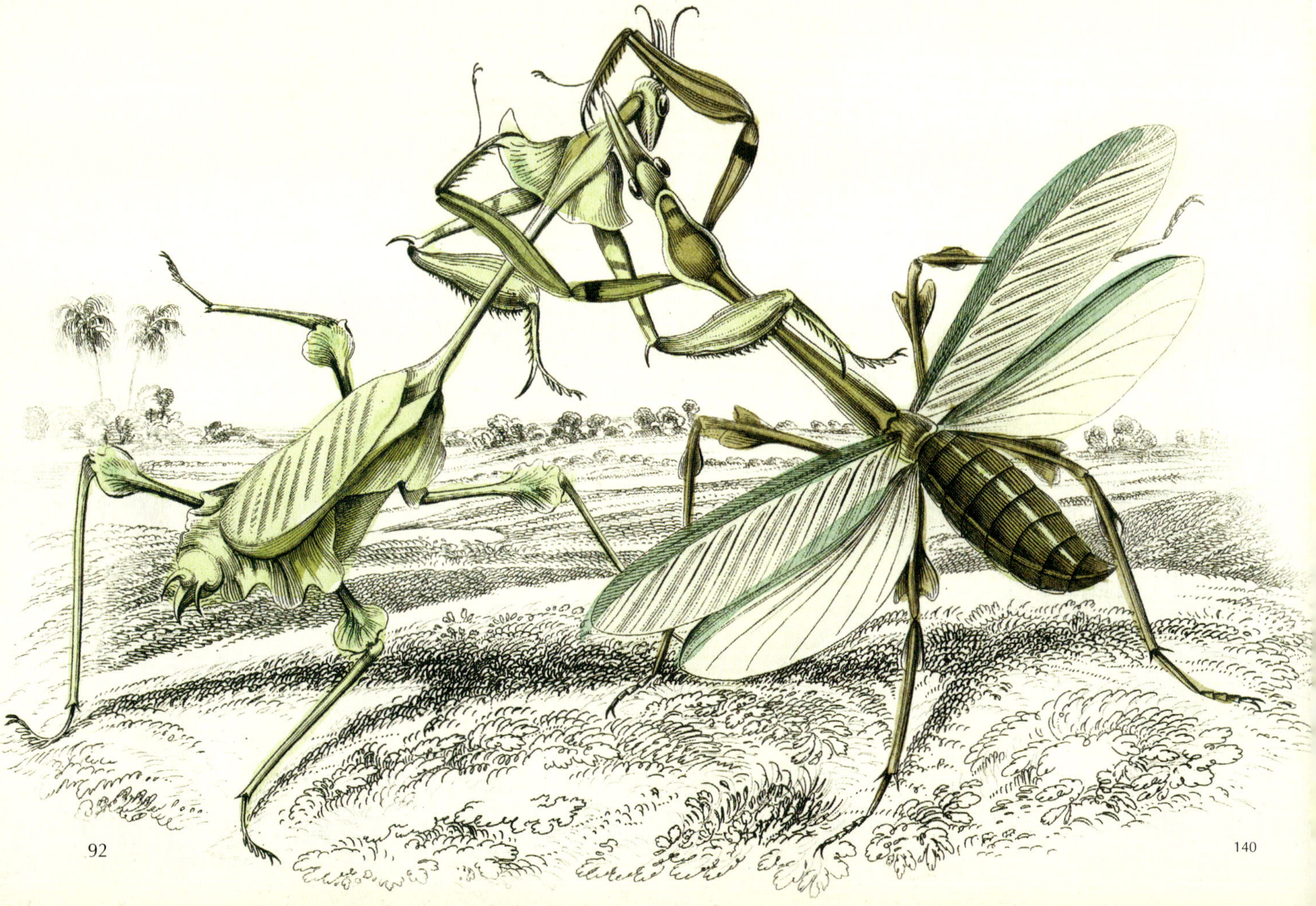

140

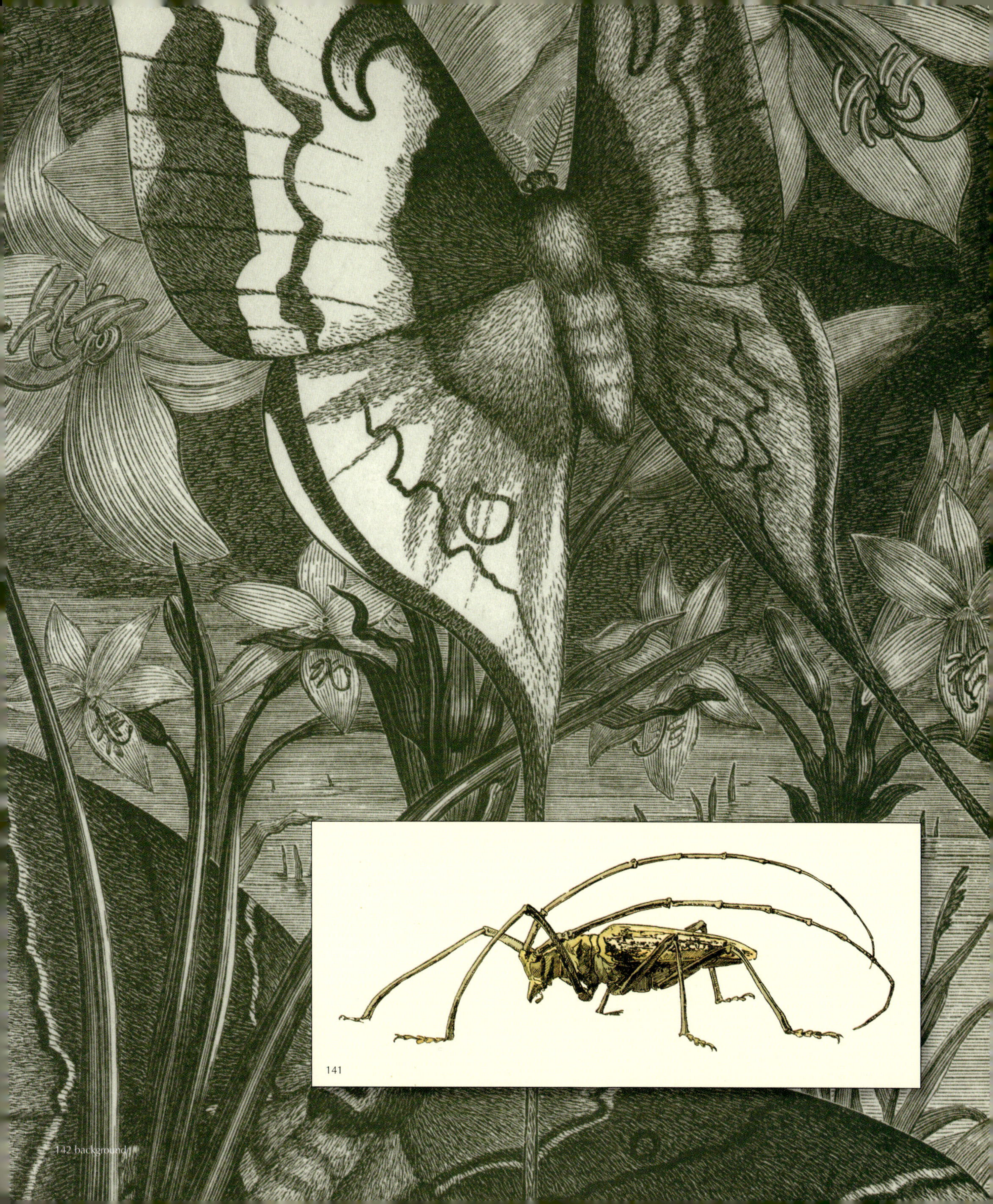

141

142 background

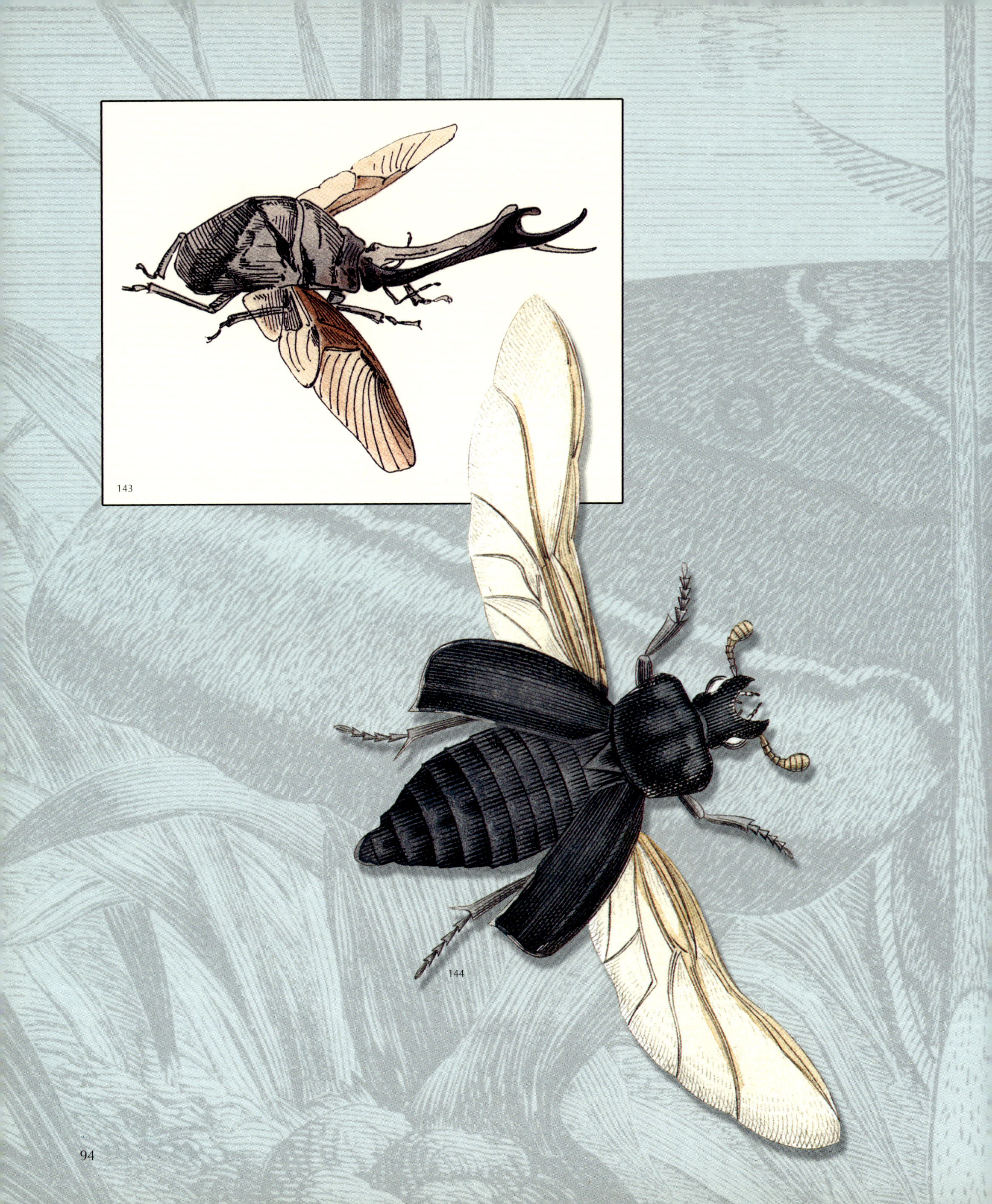
143
144

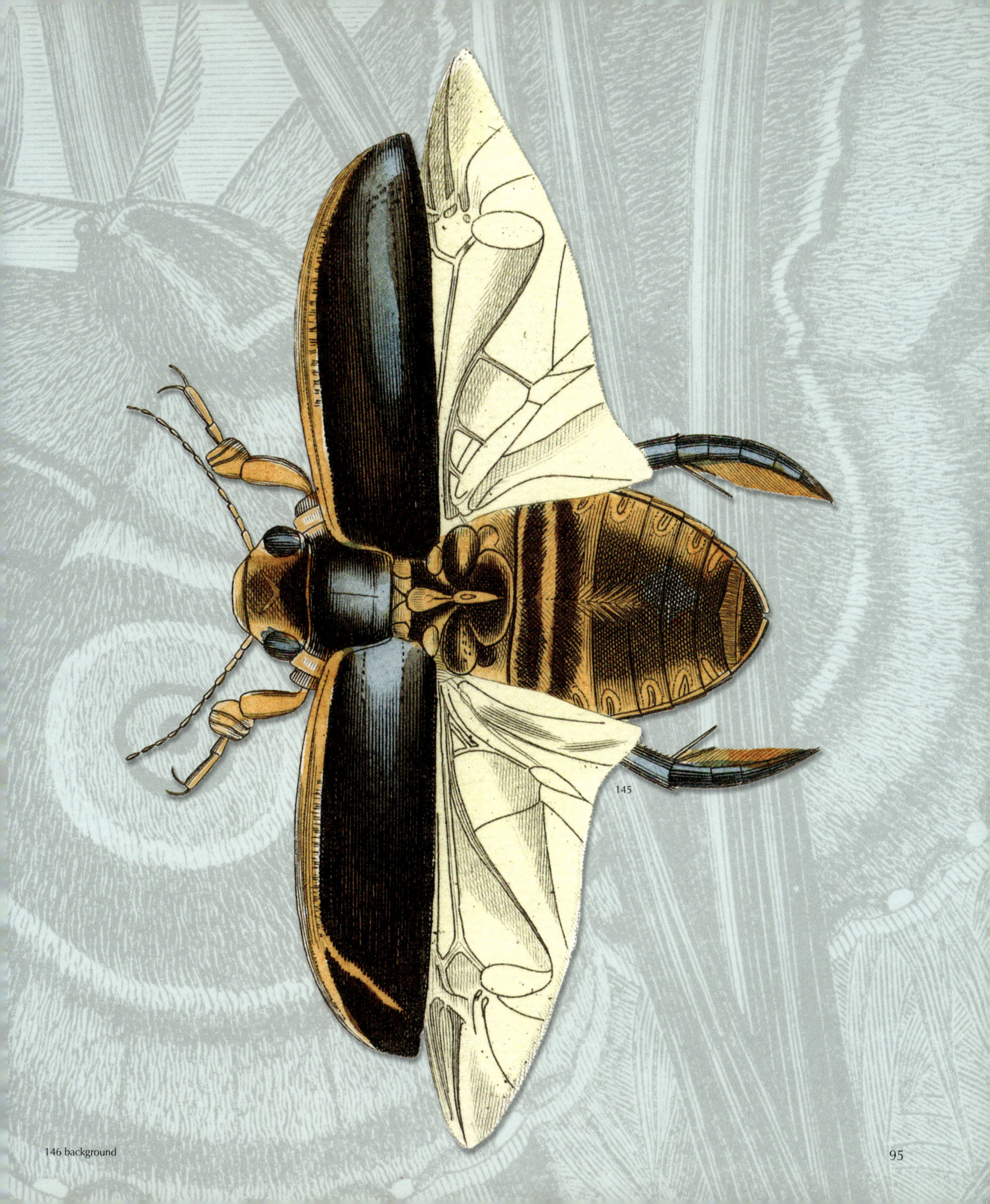

146 background

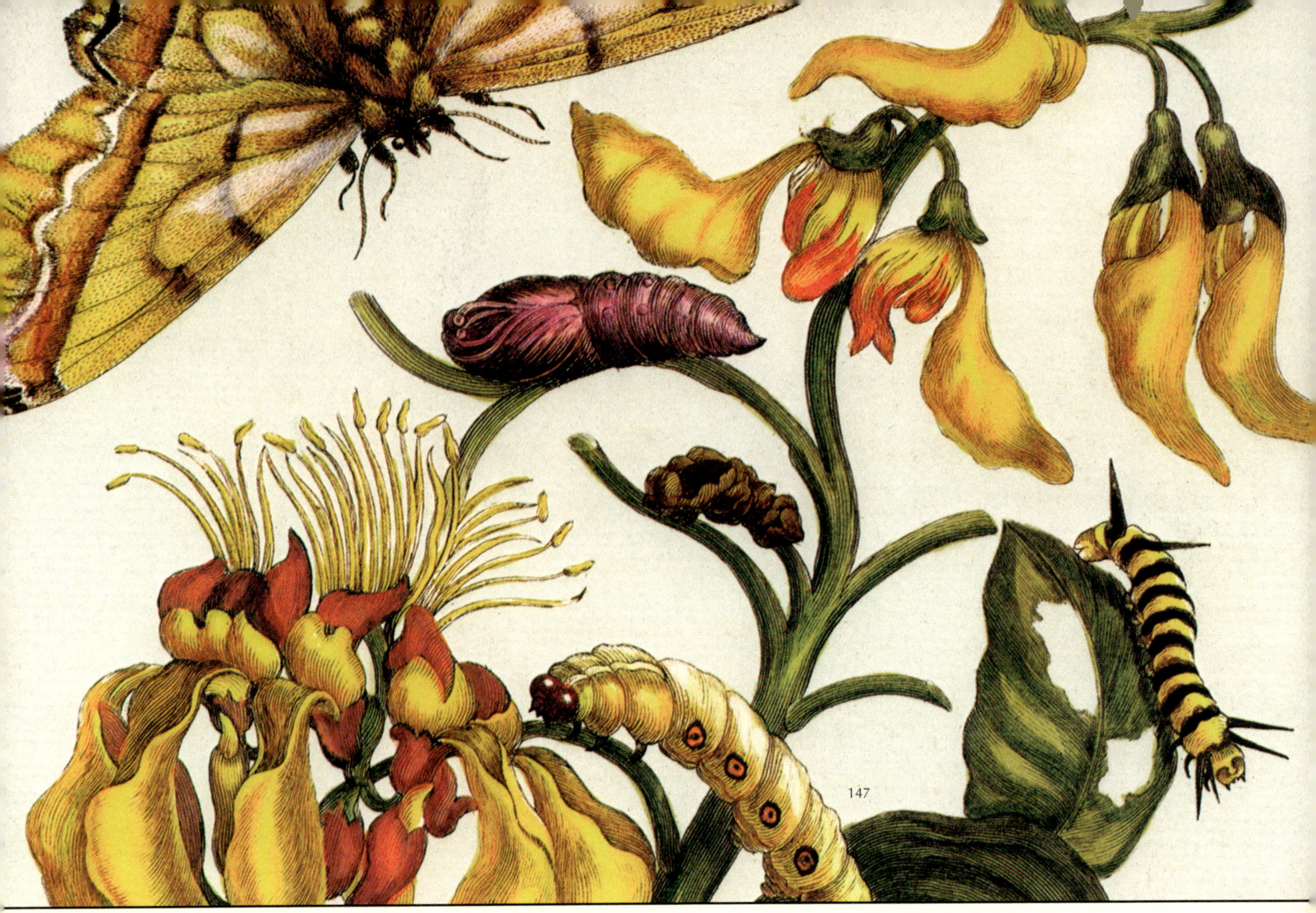

147

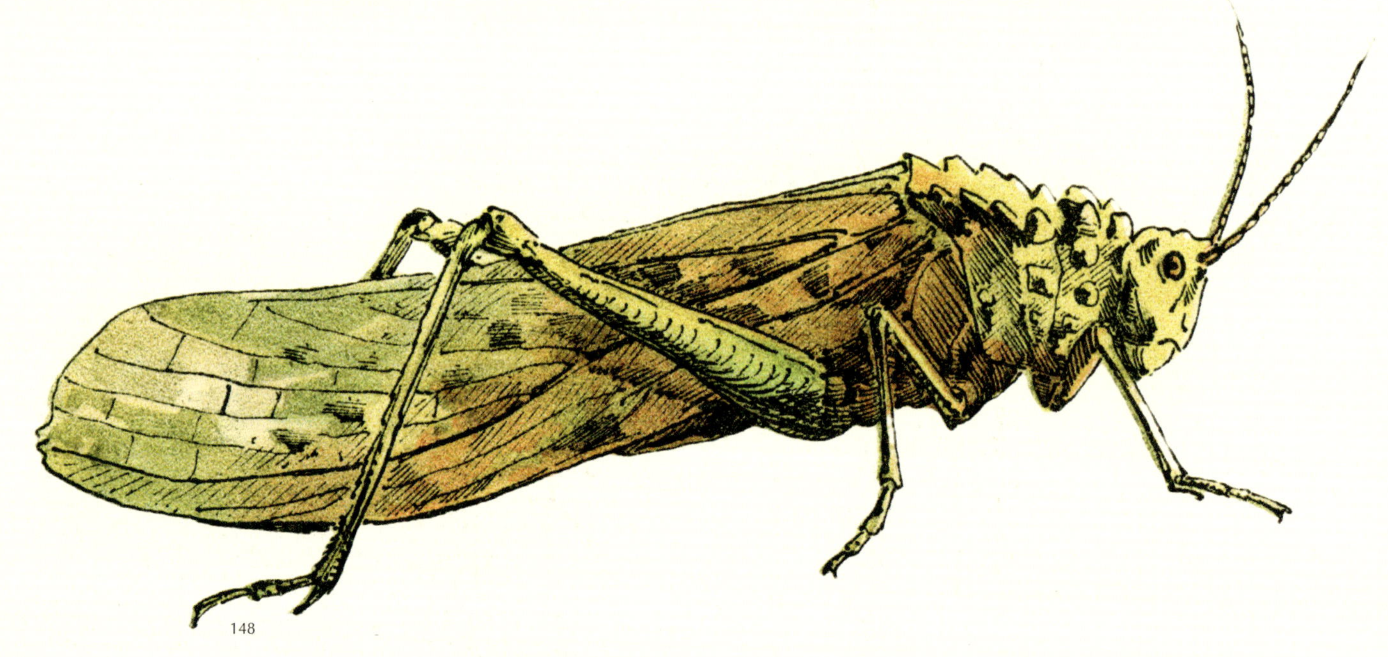

148

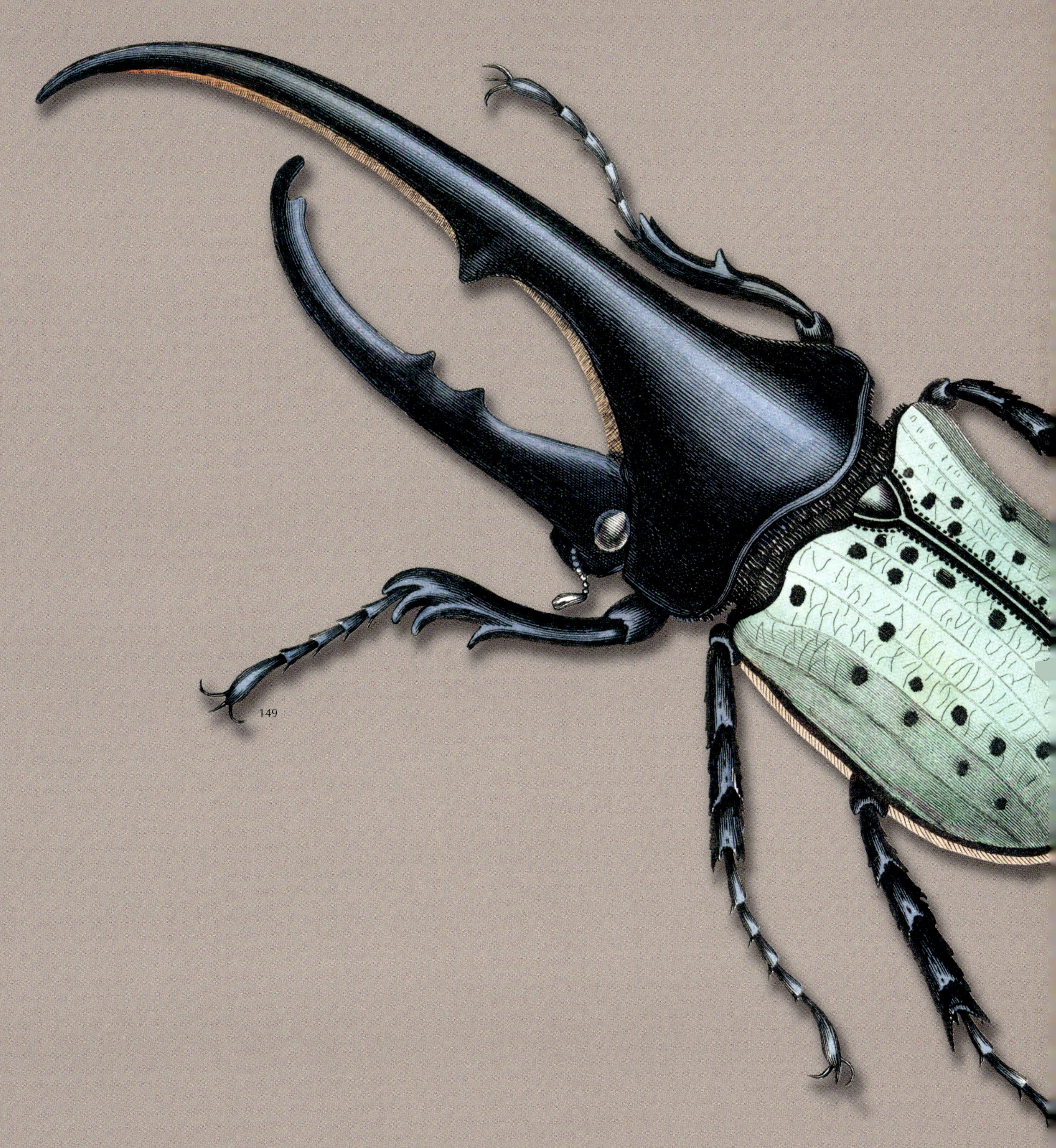
149

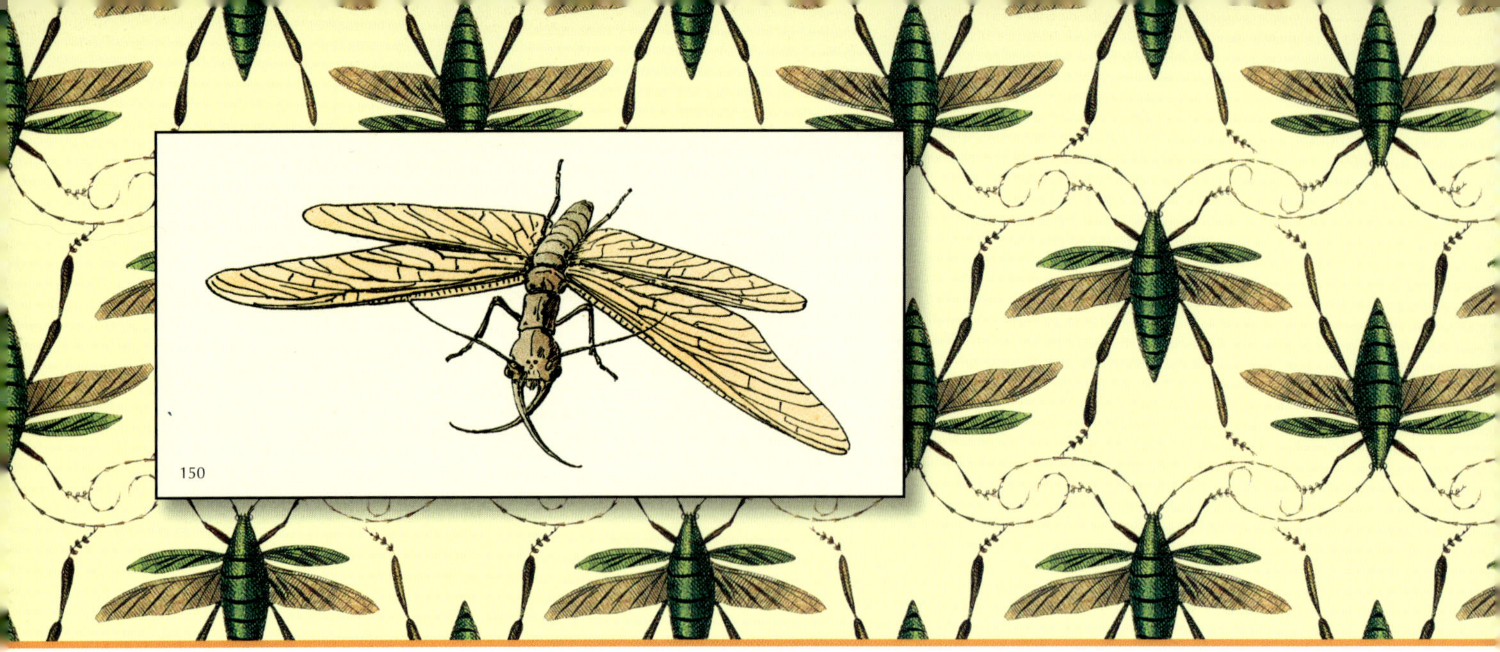

150

151 background

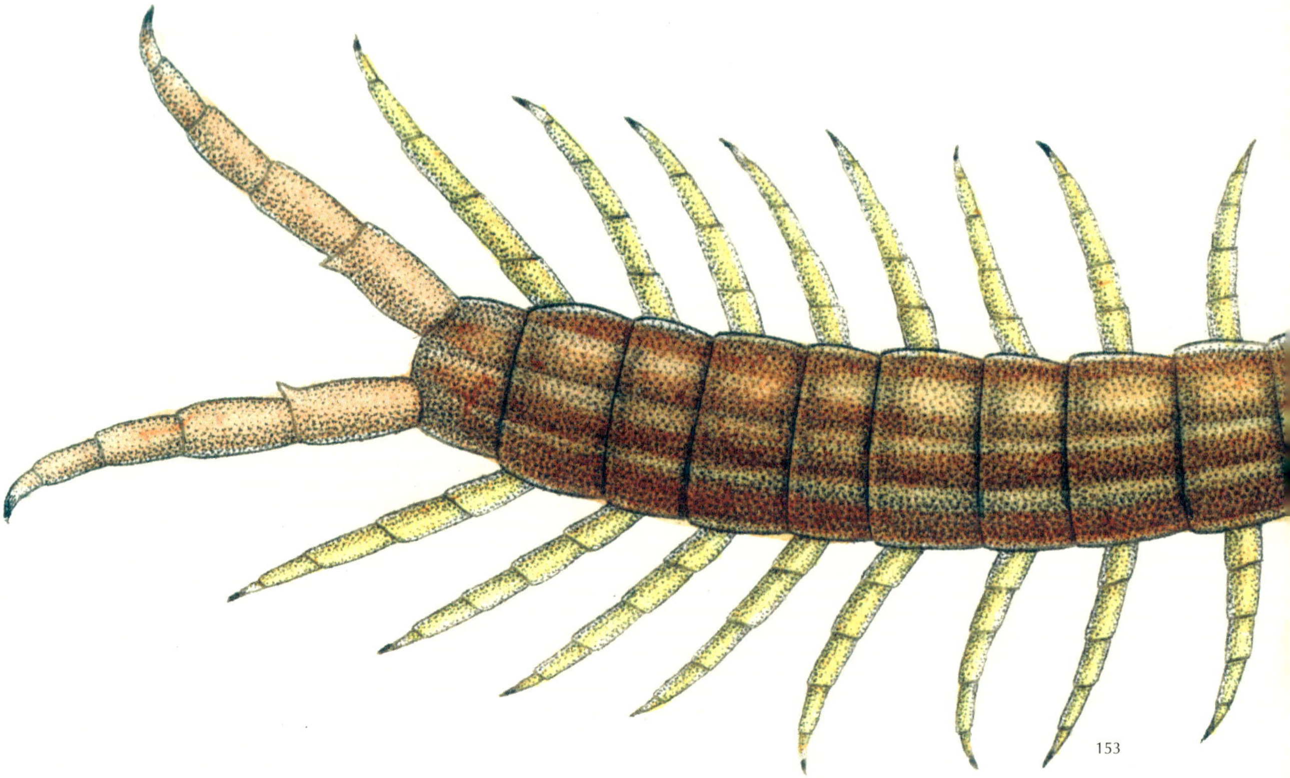

153

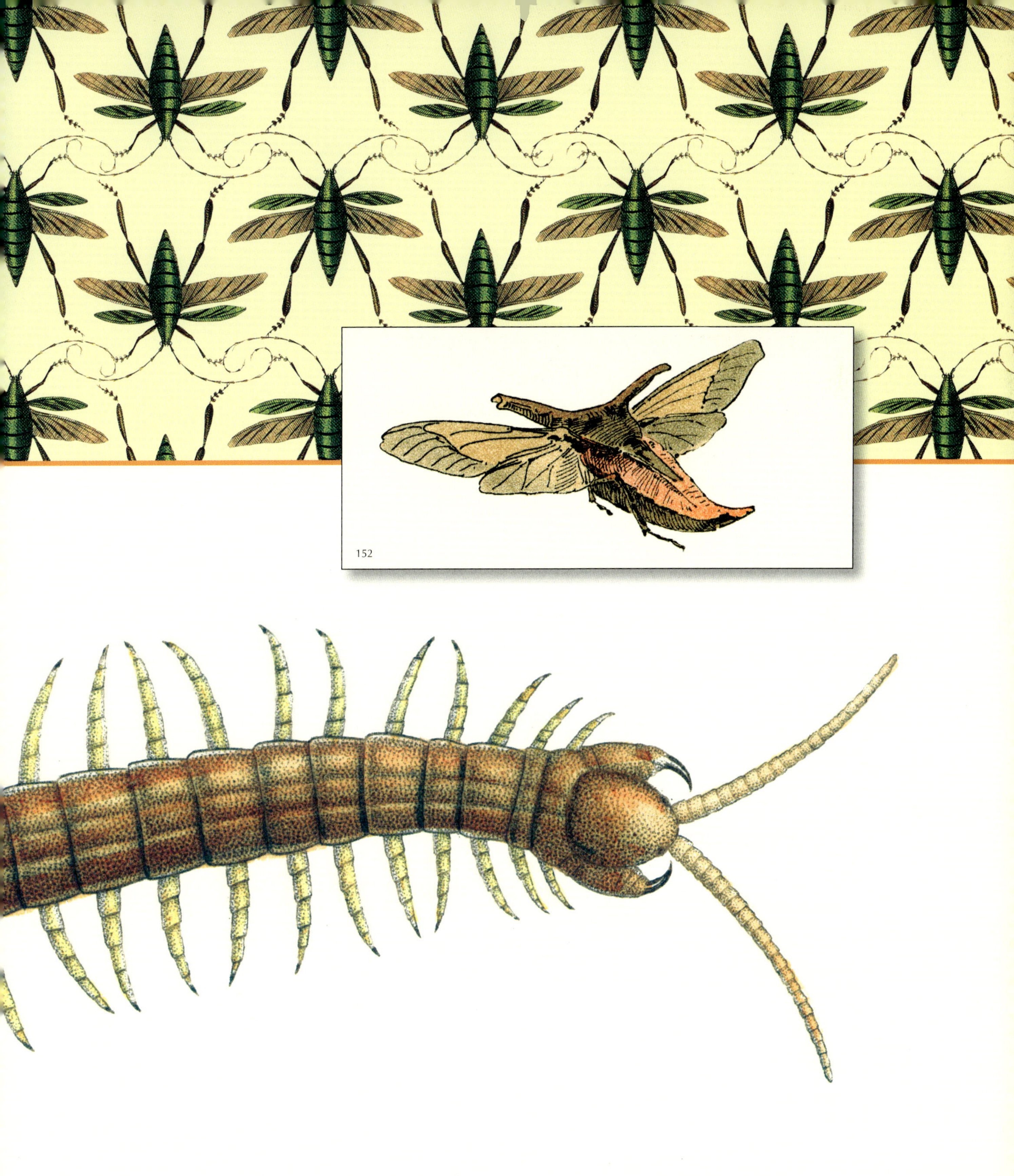
152

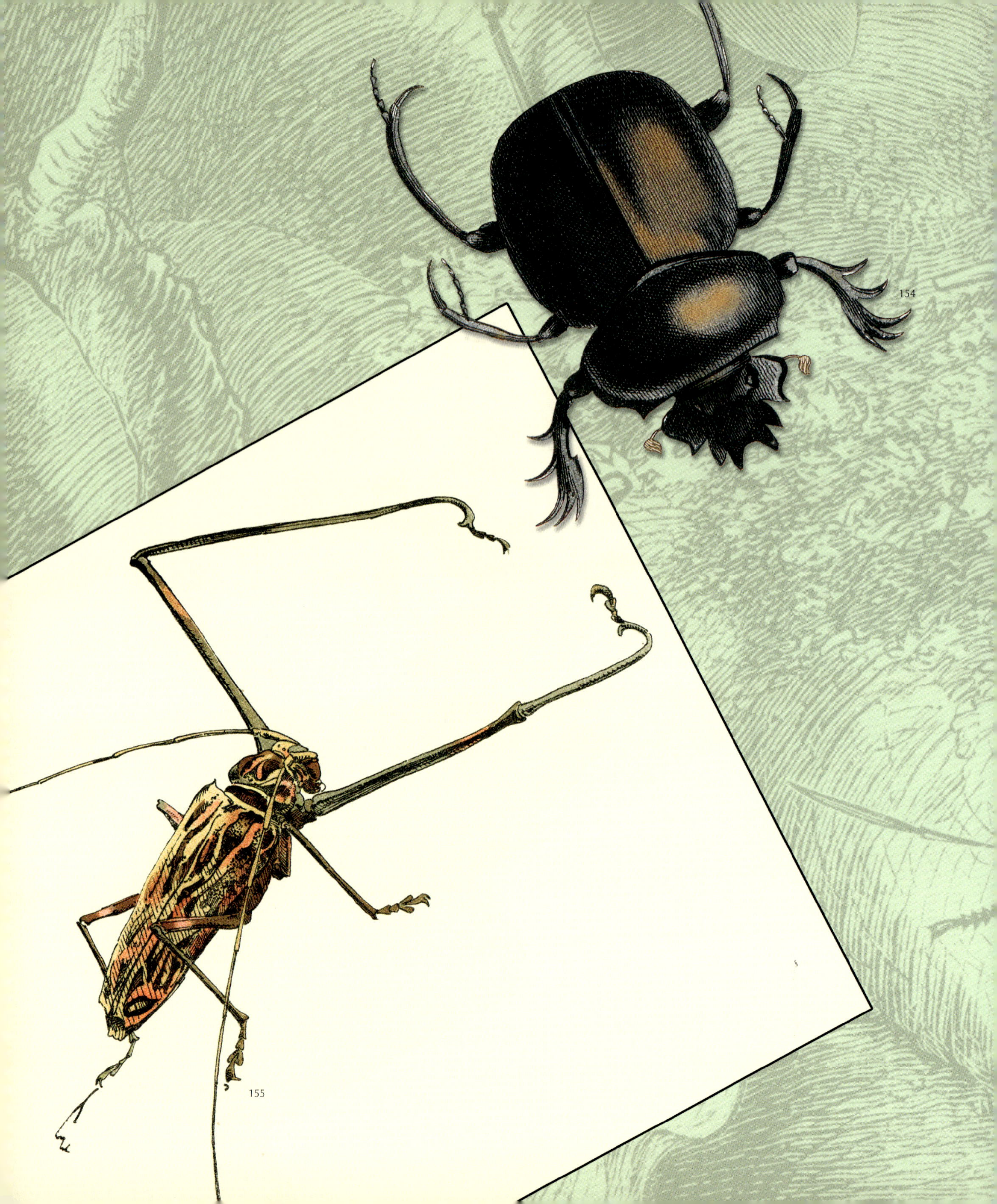
154

155

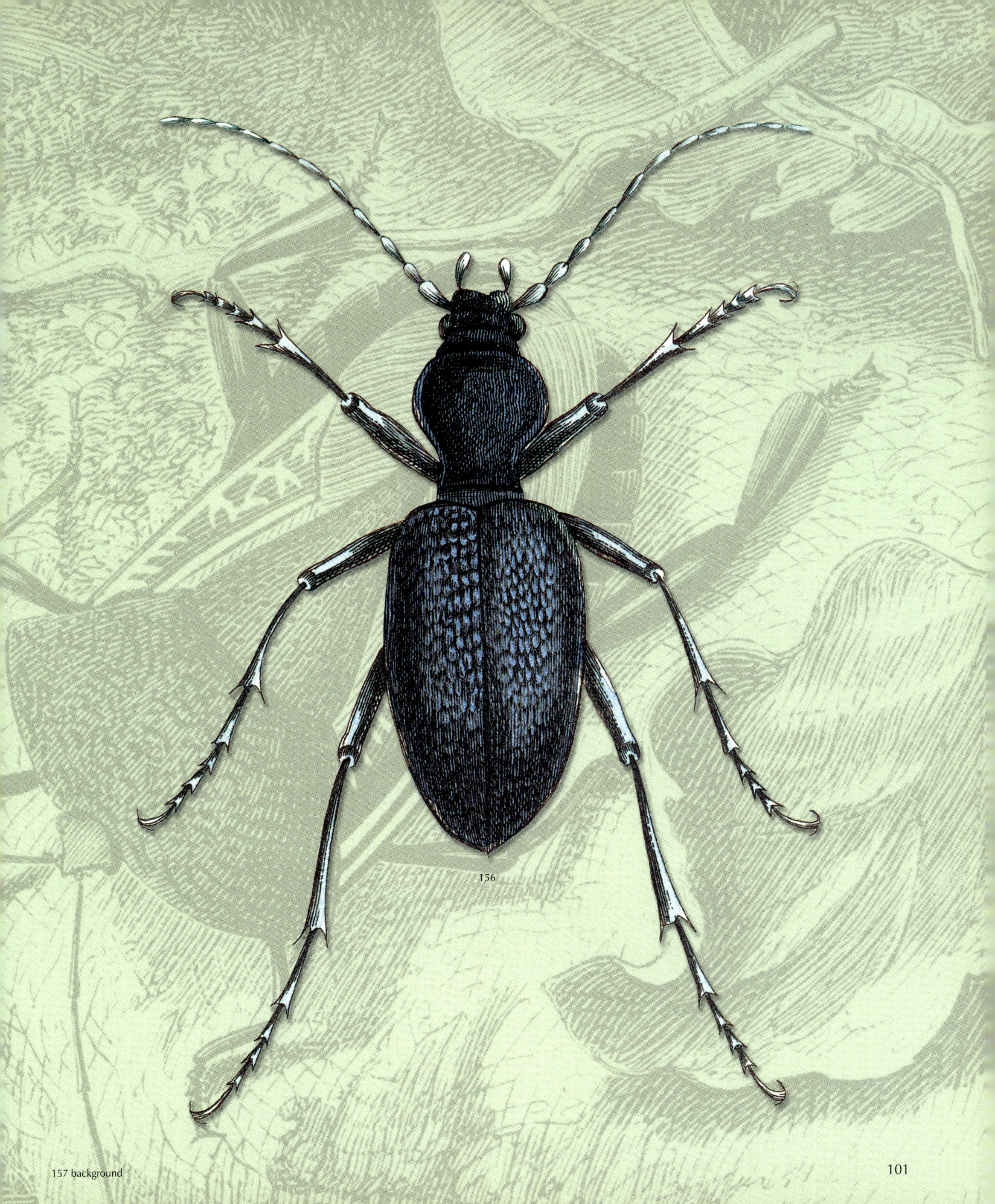

156

157 background

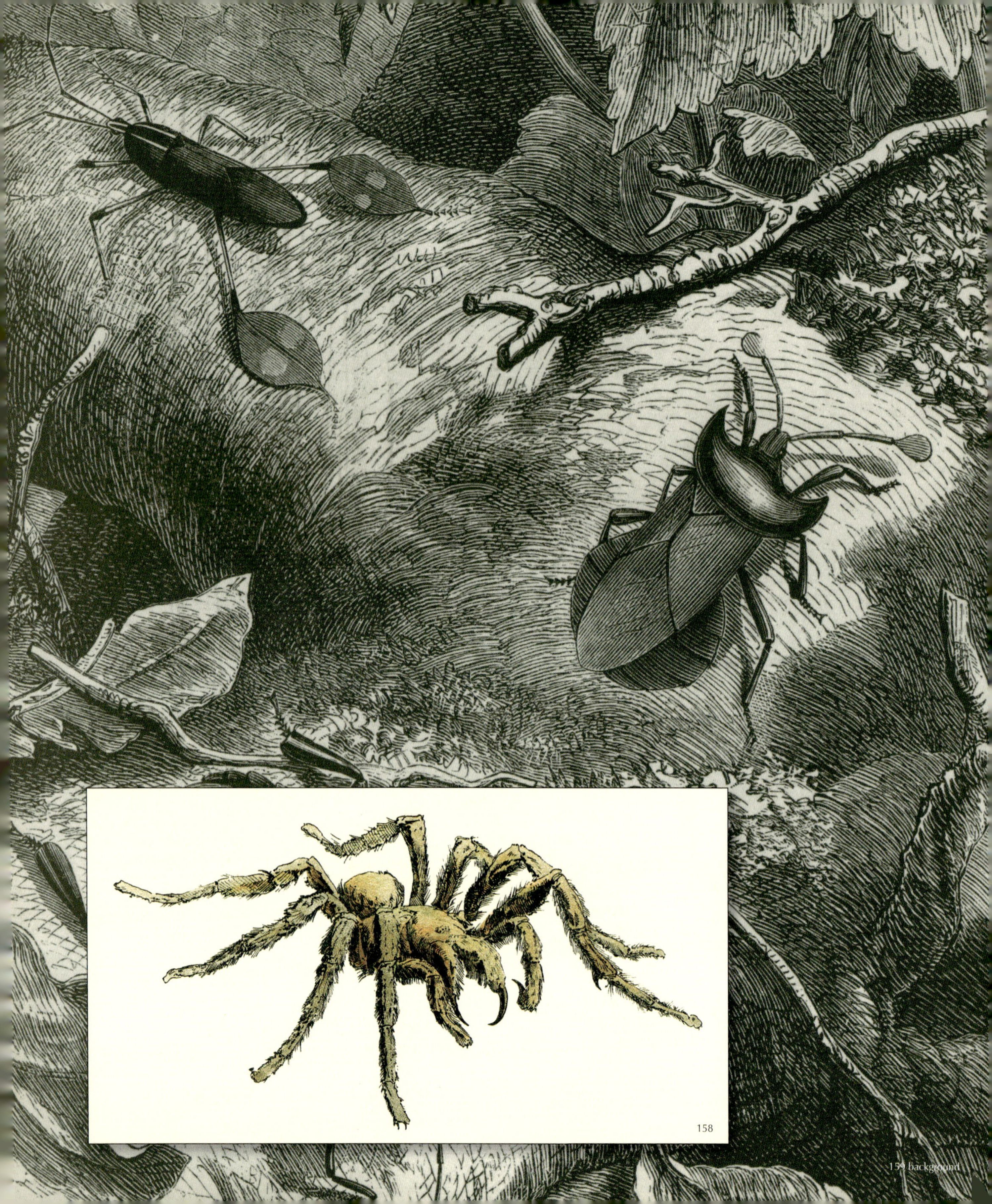

158

159 background

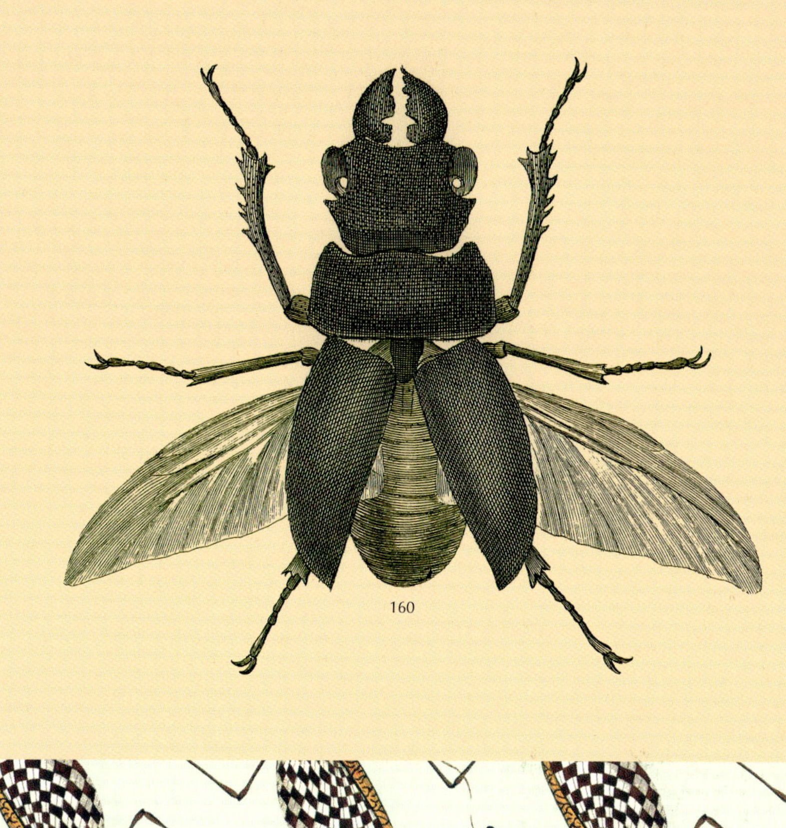

160

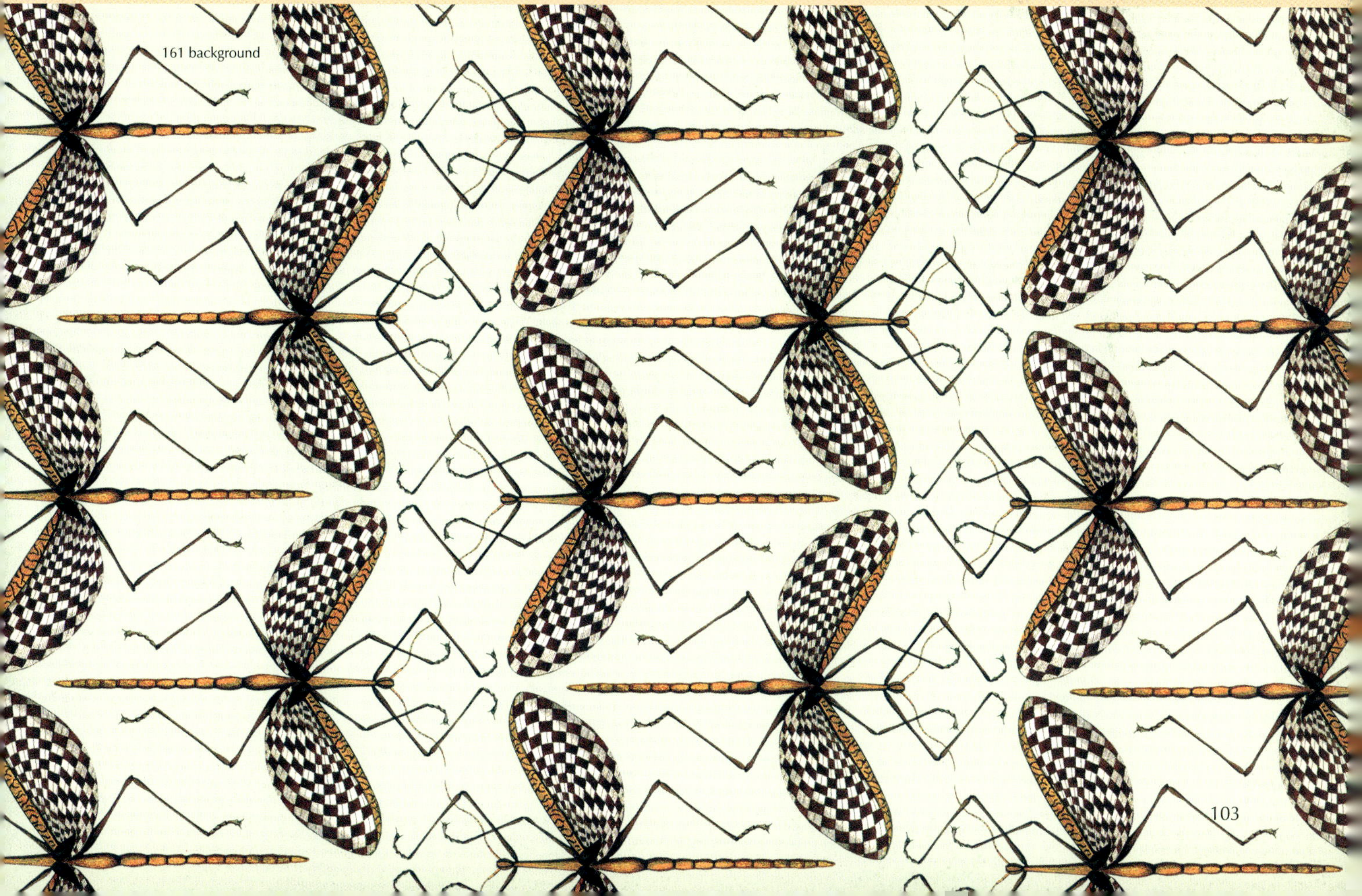

161 background

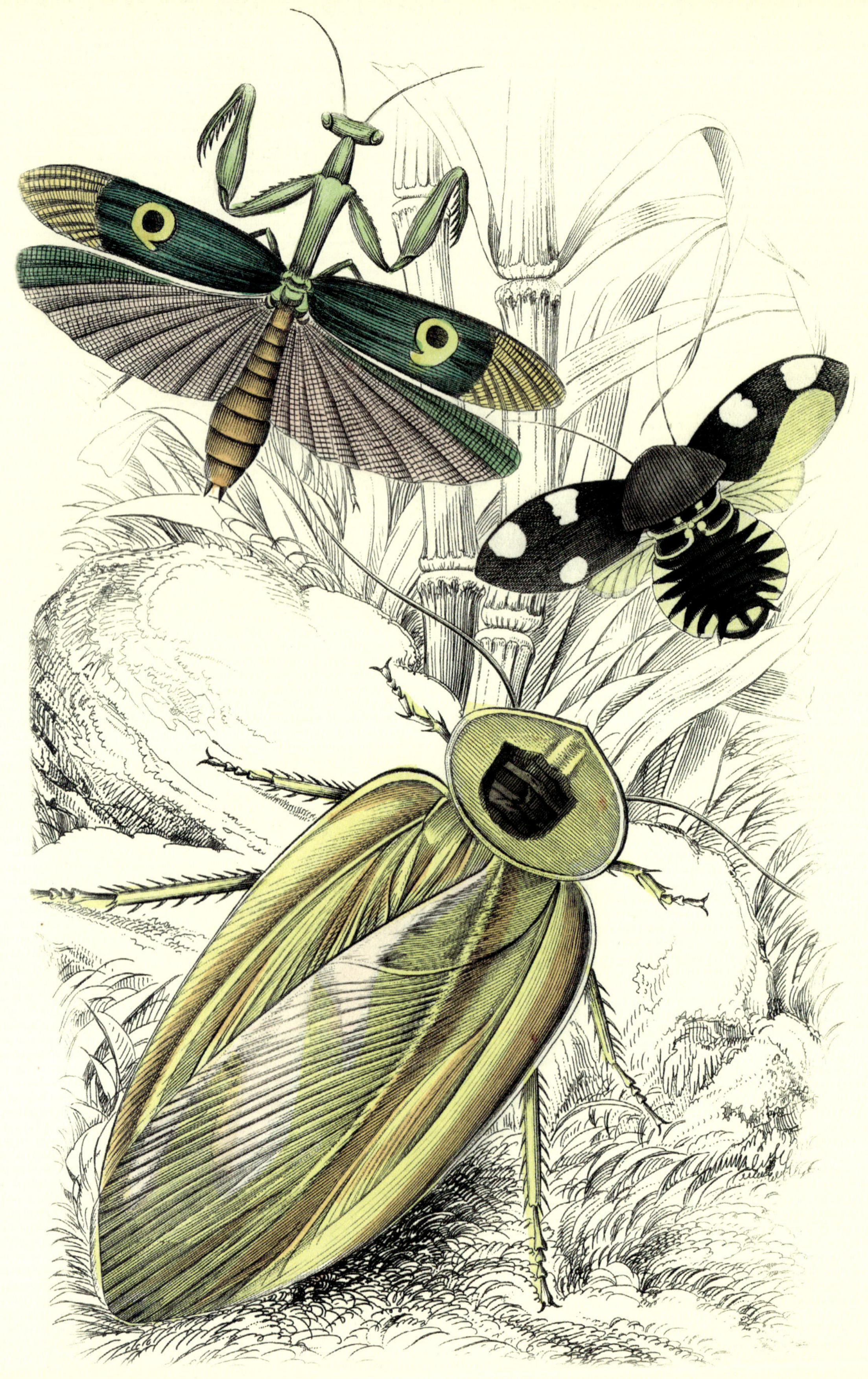

162

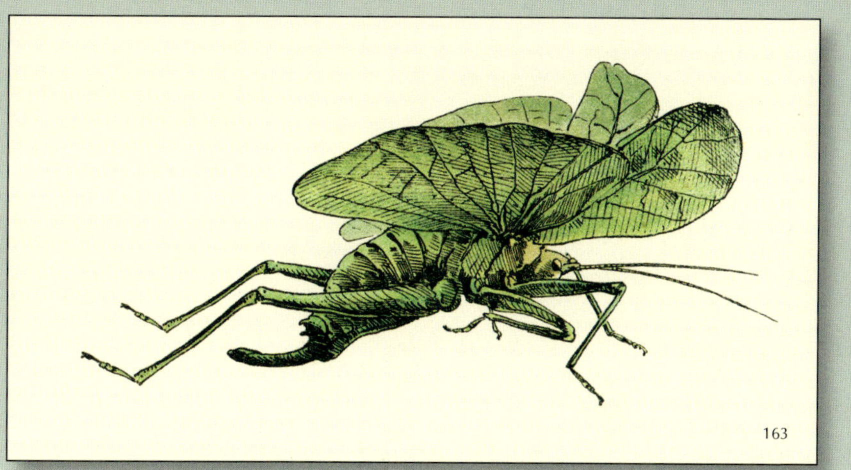

163

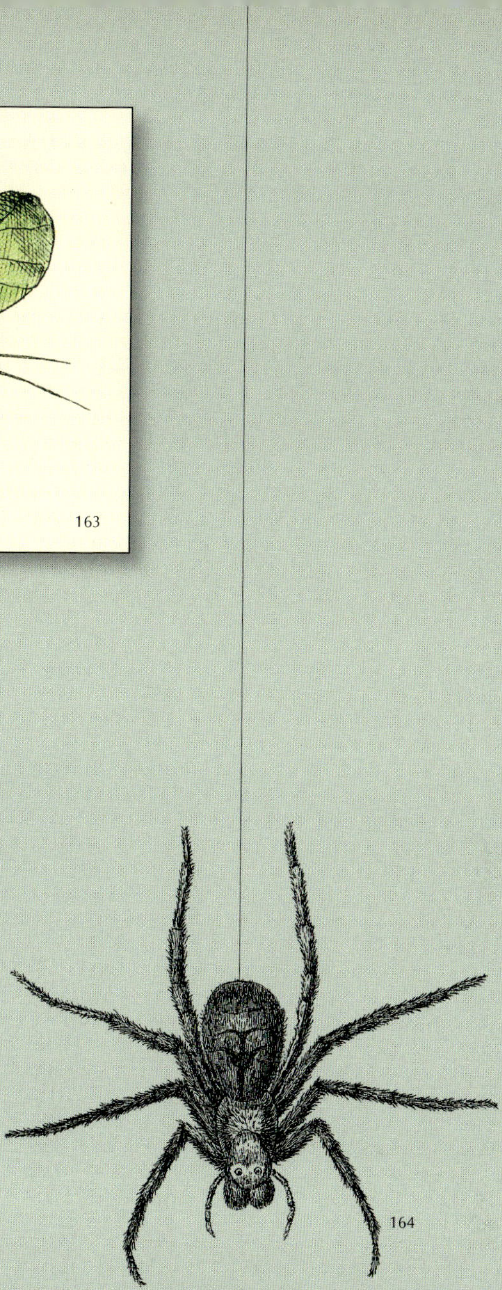

164

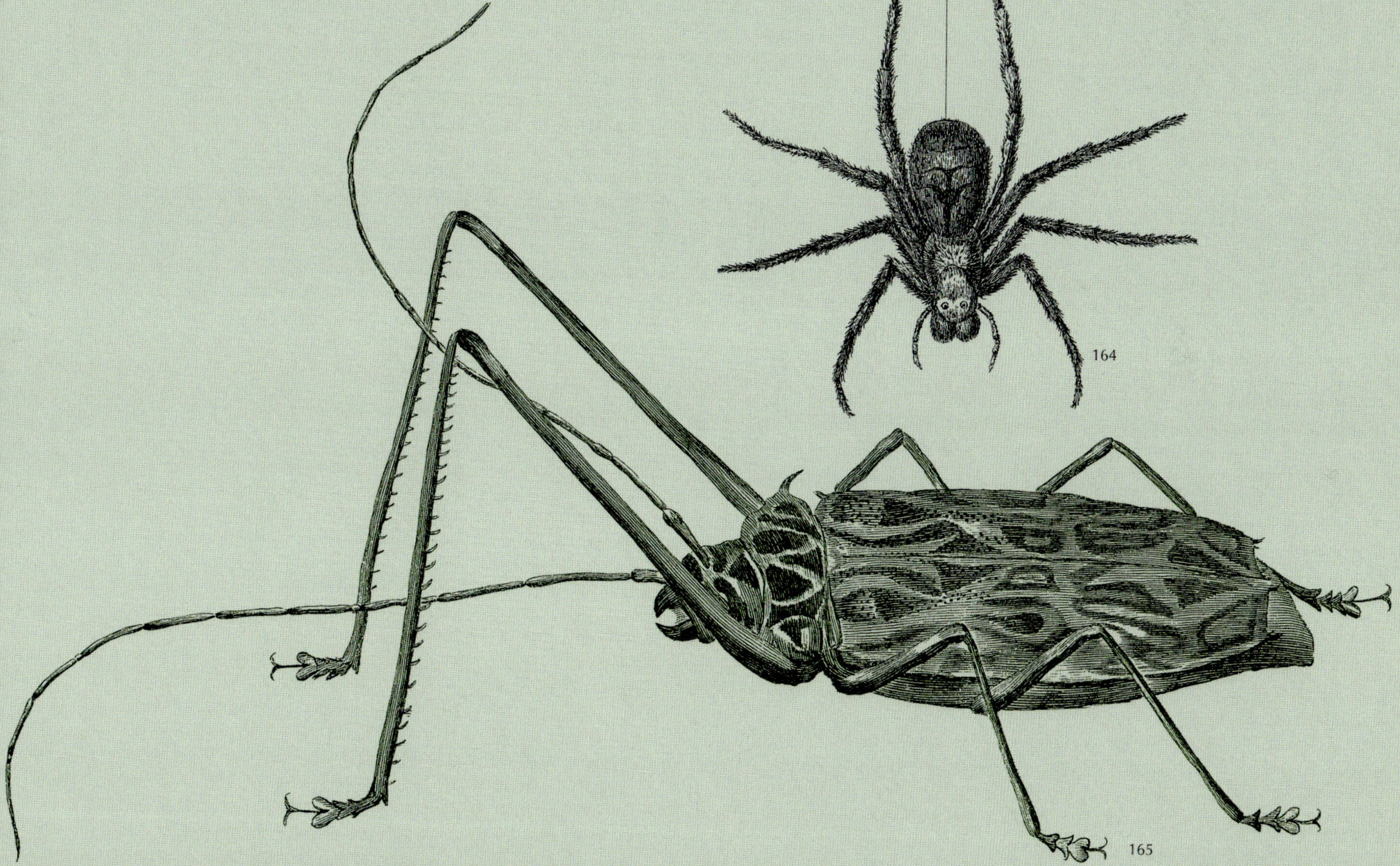

165

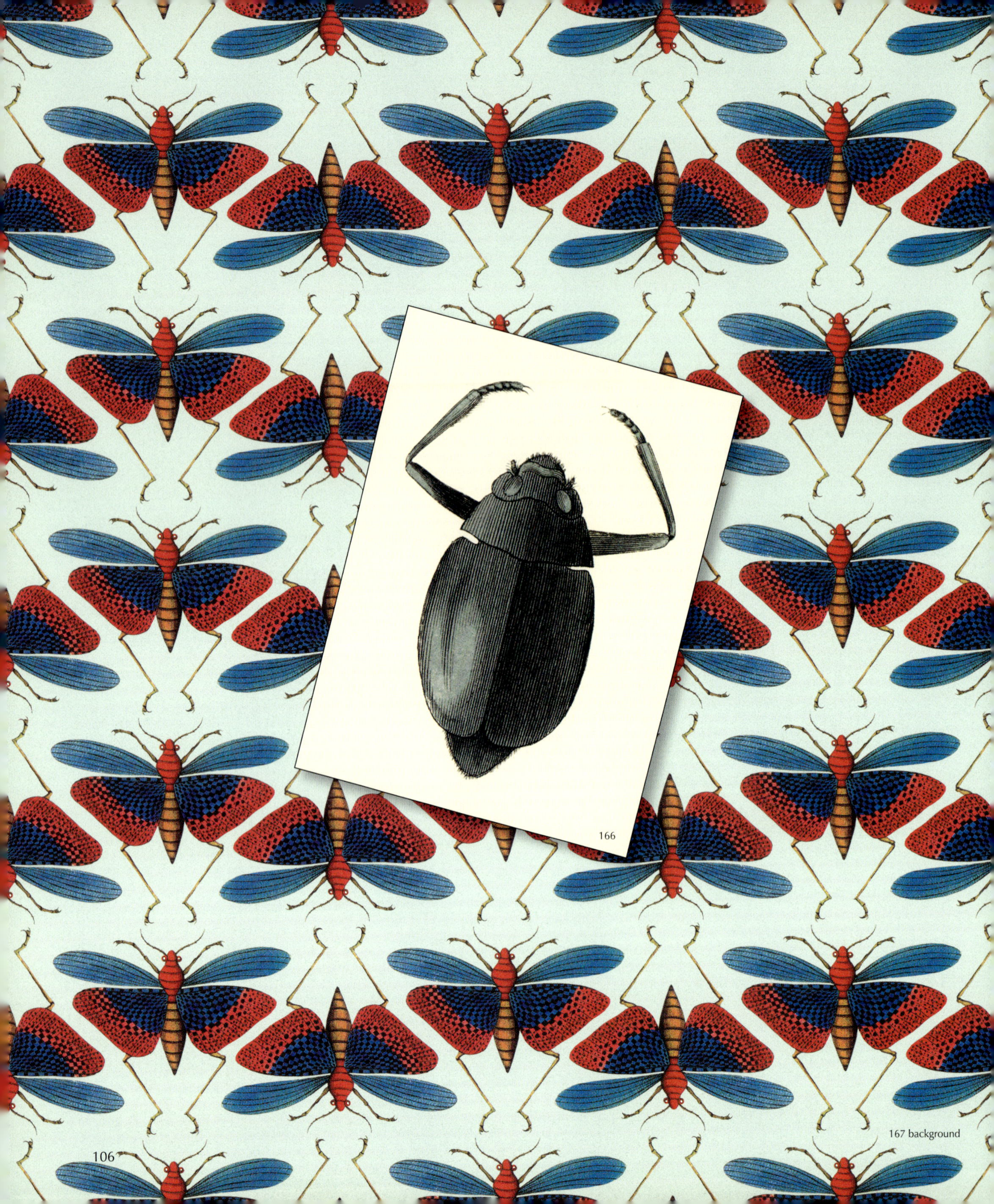

167 background

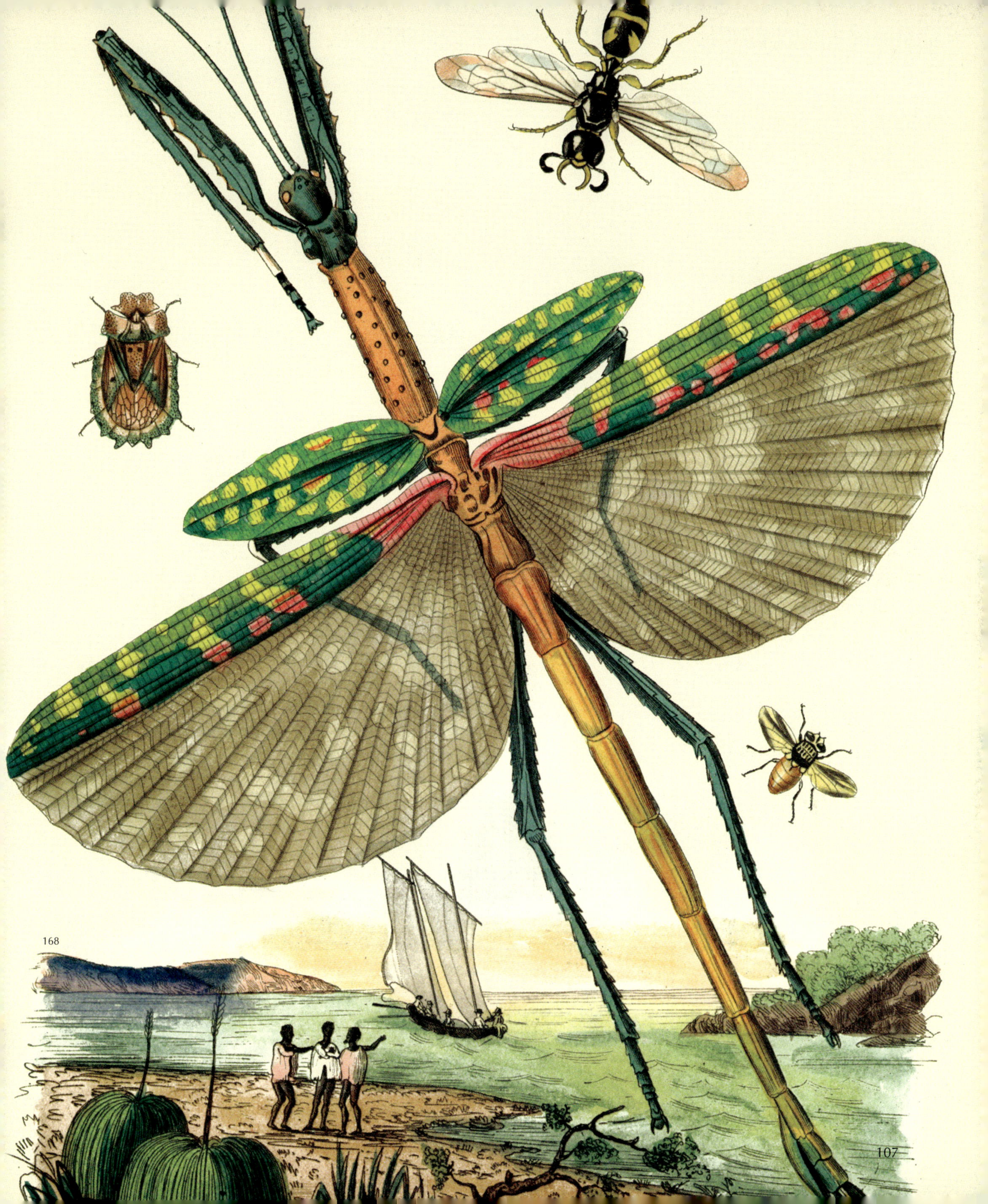

168

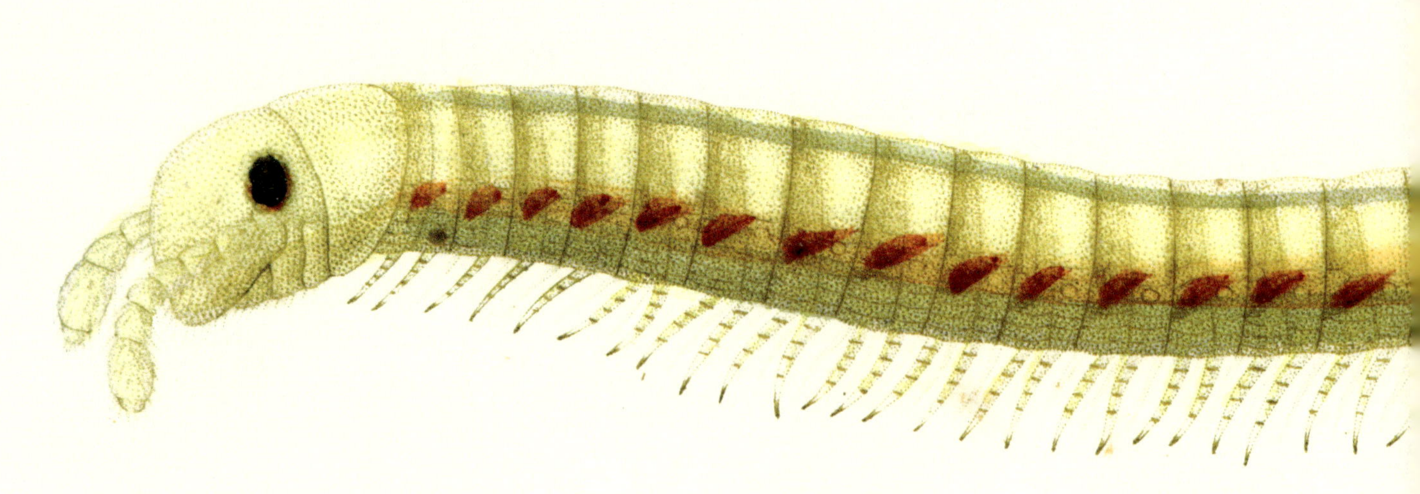

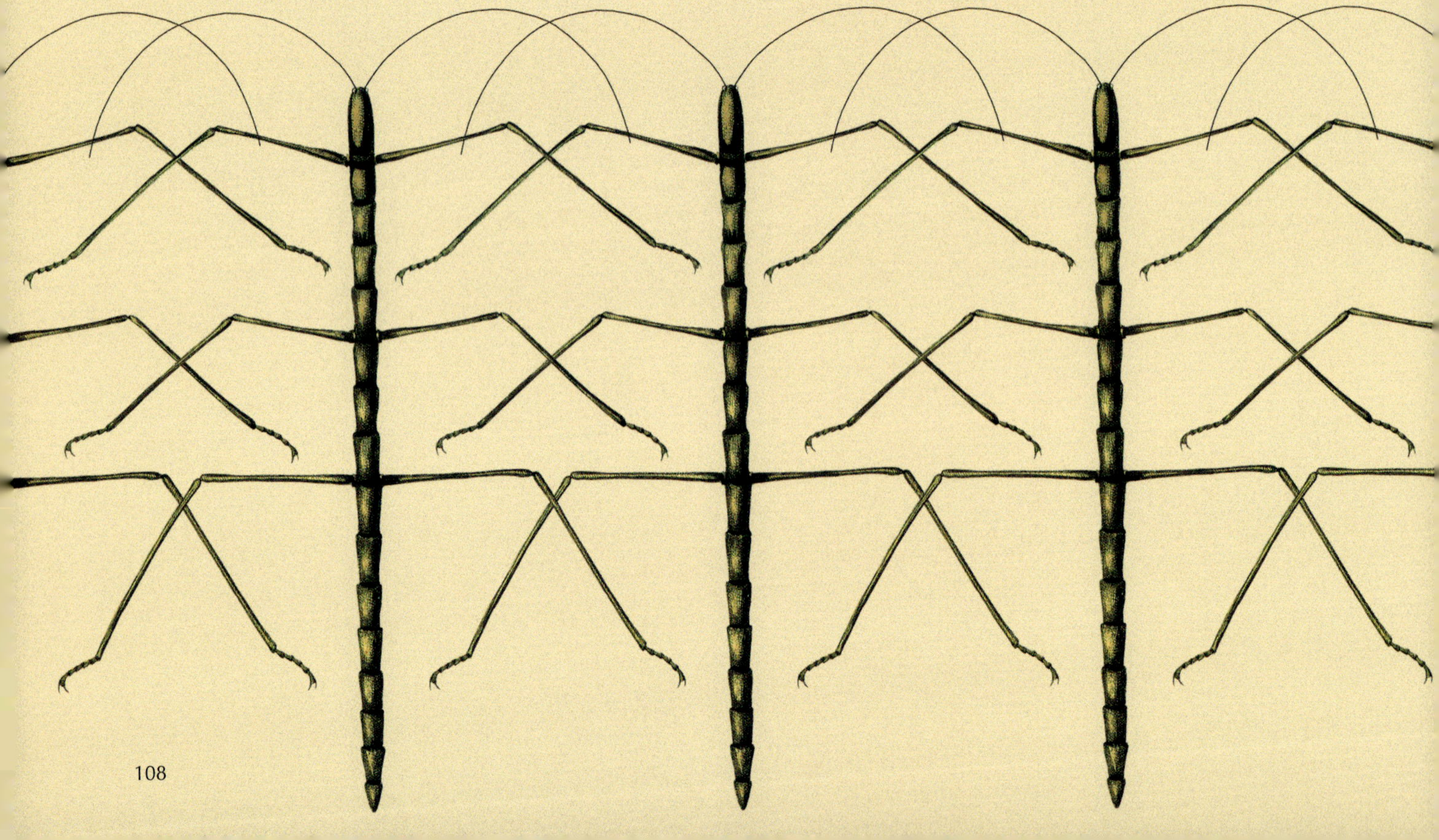

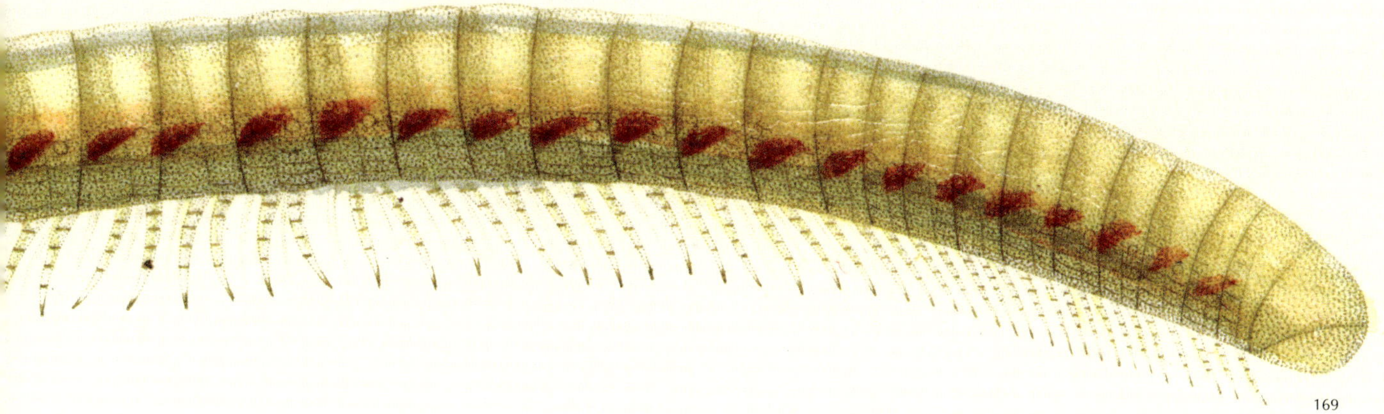

169

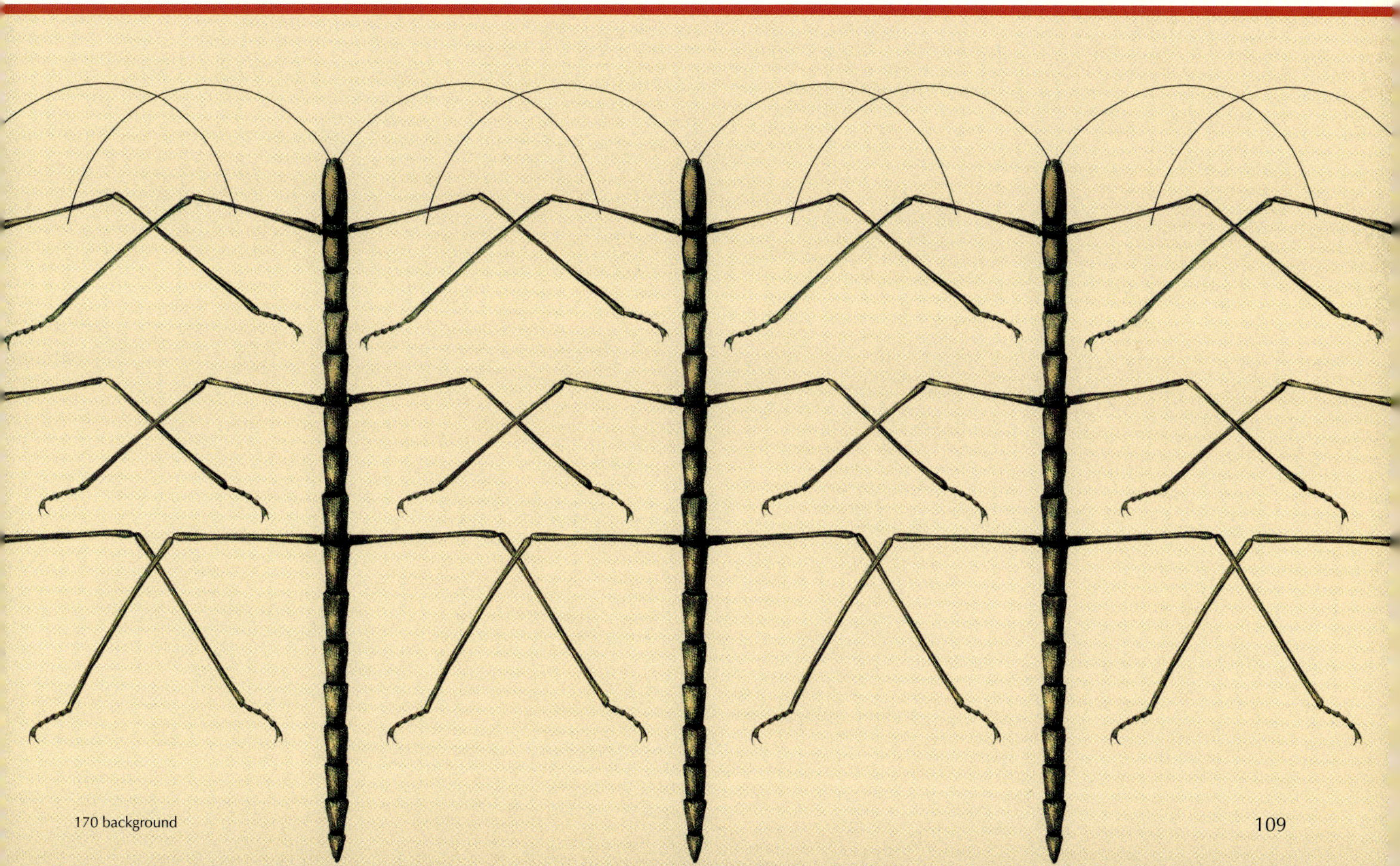

170 background

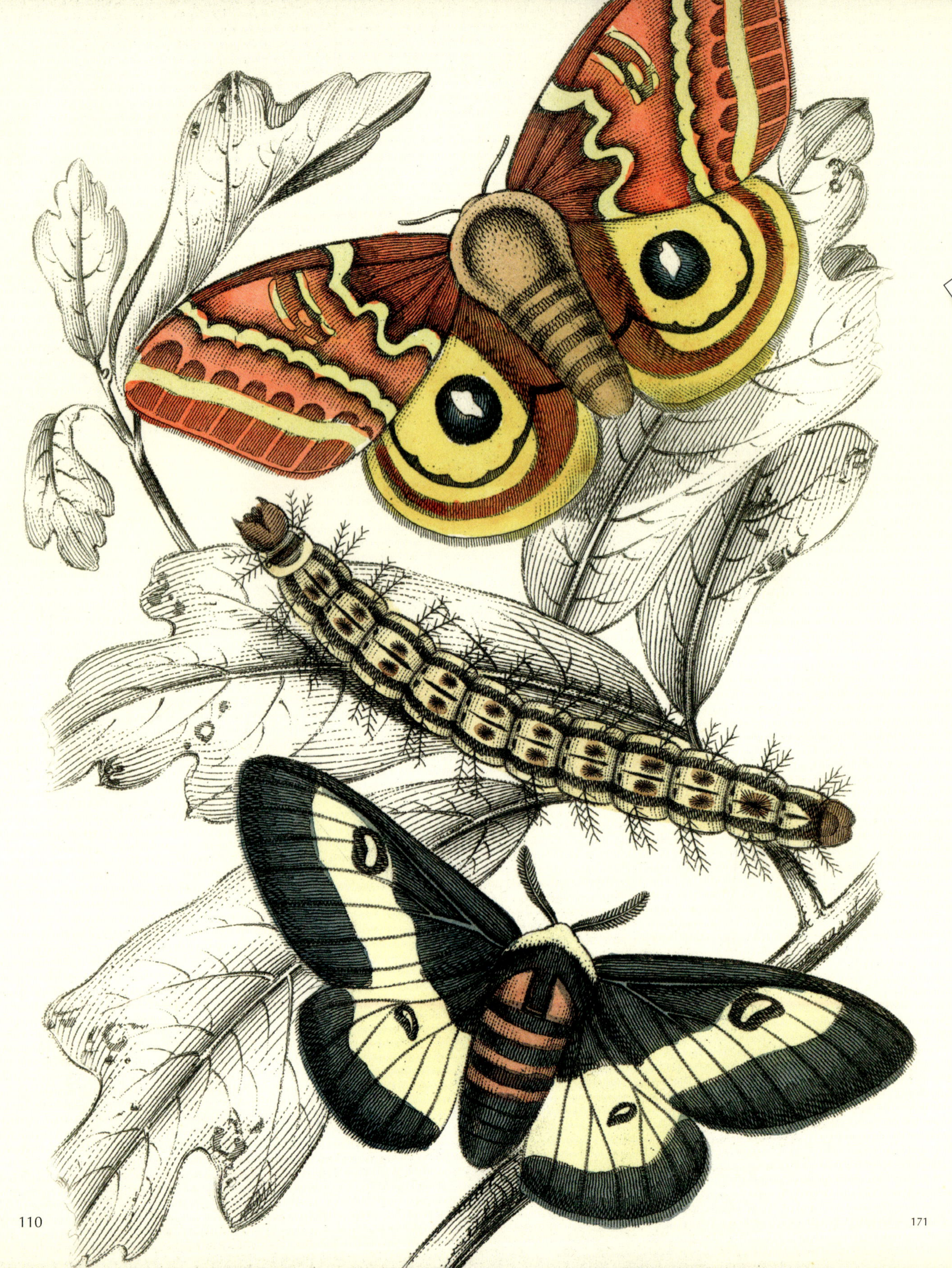

171

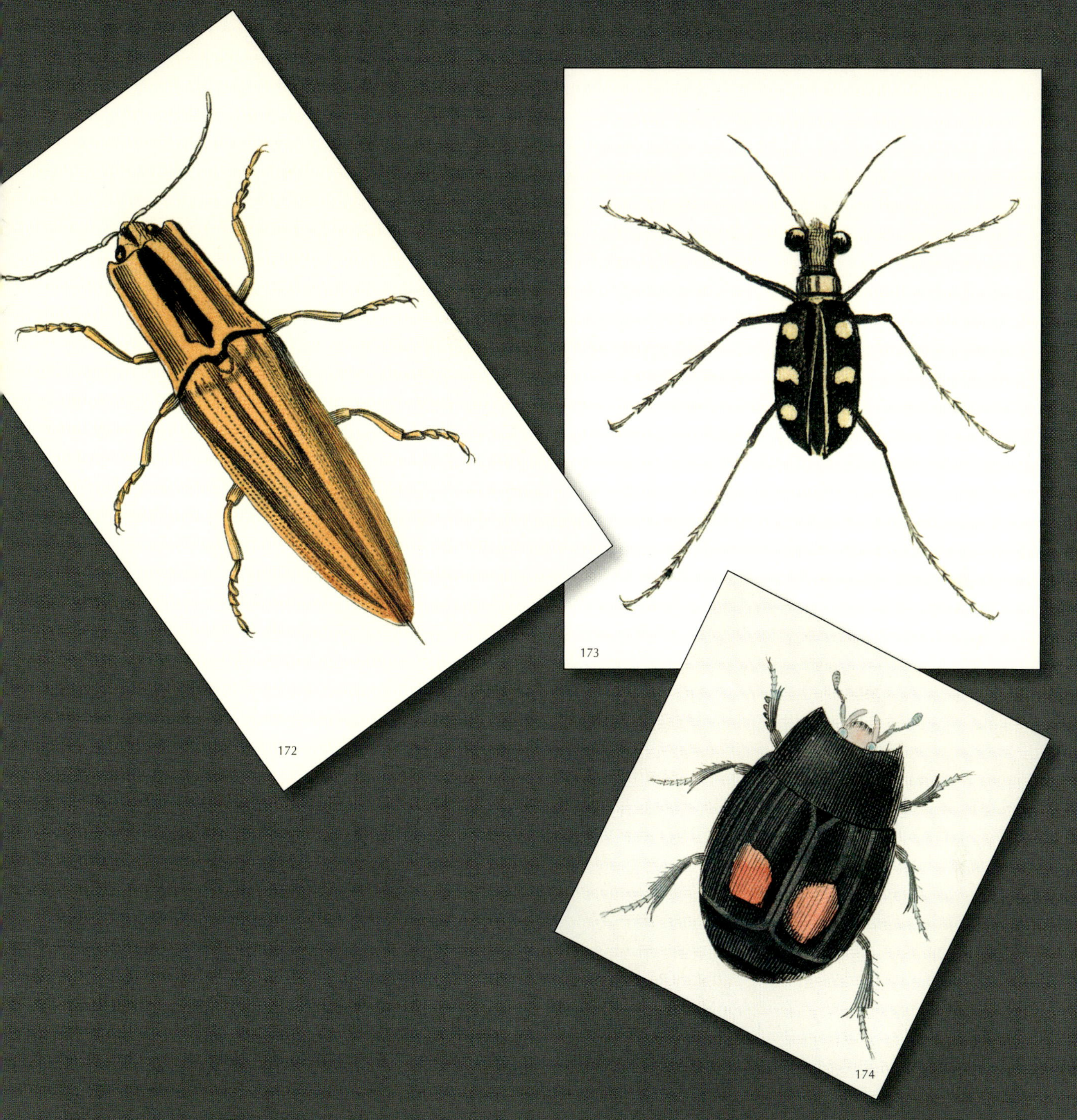
172
173
174

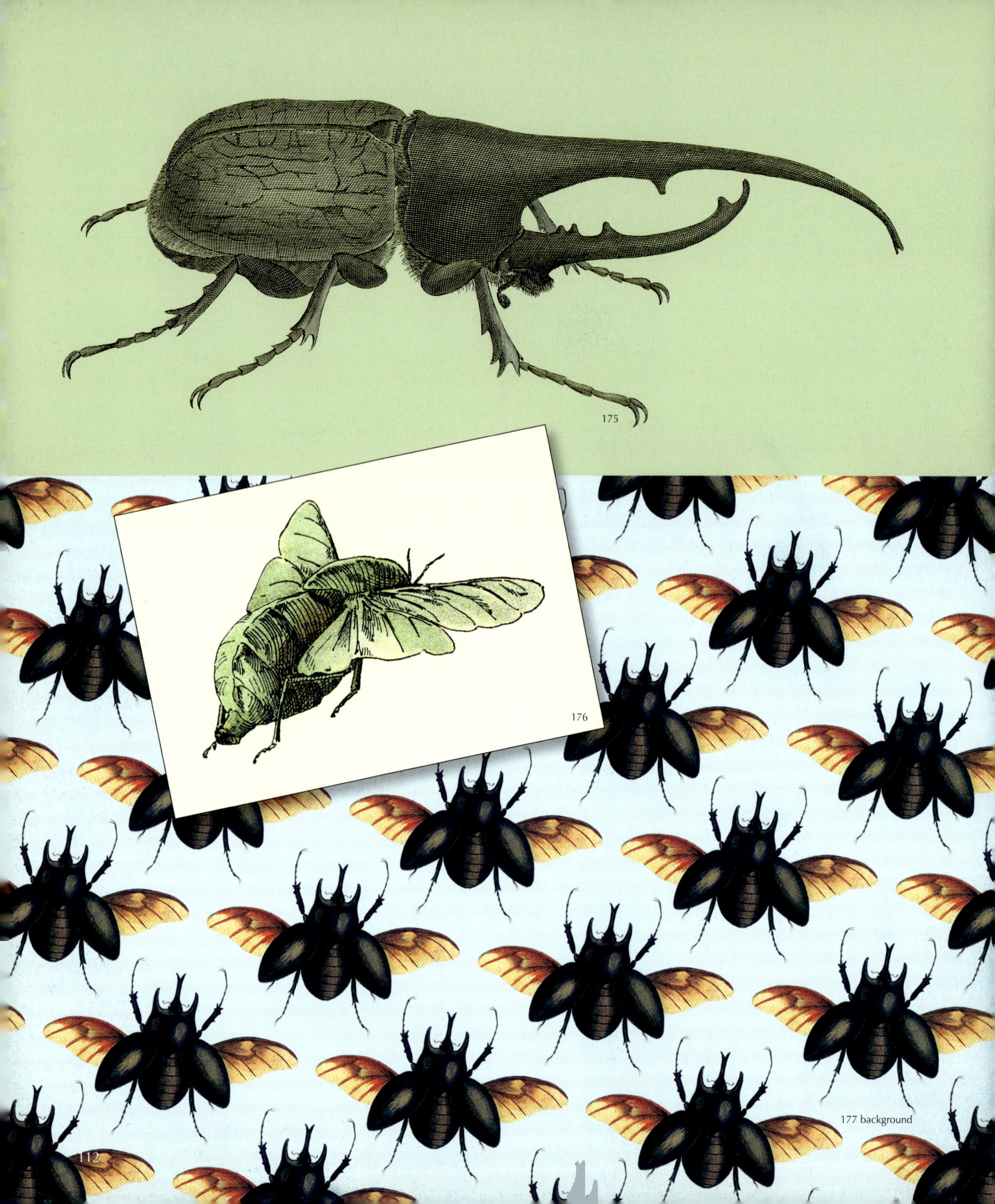
175
176
177 background

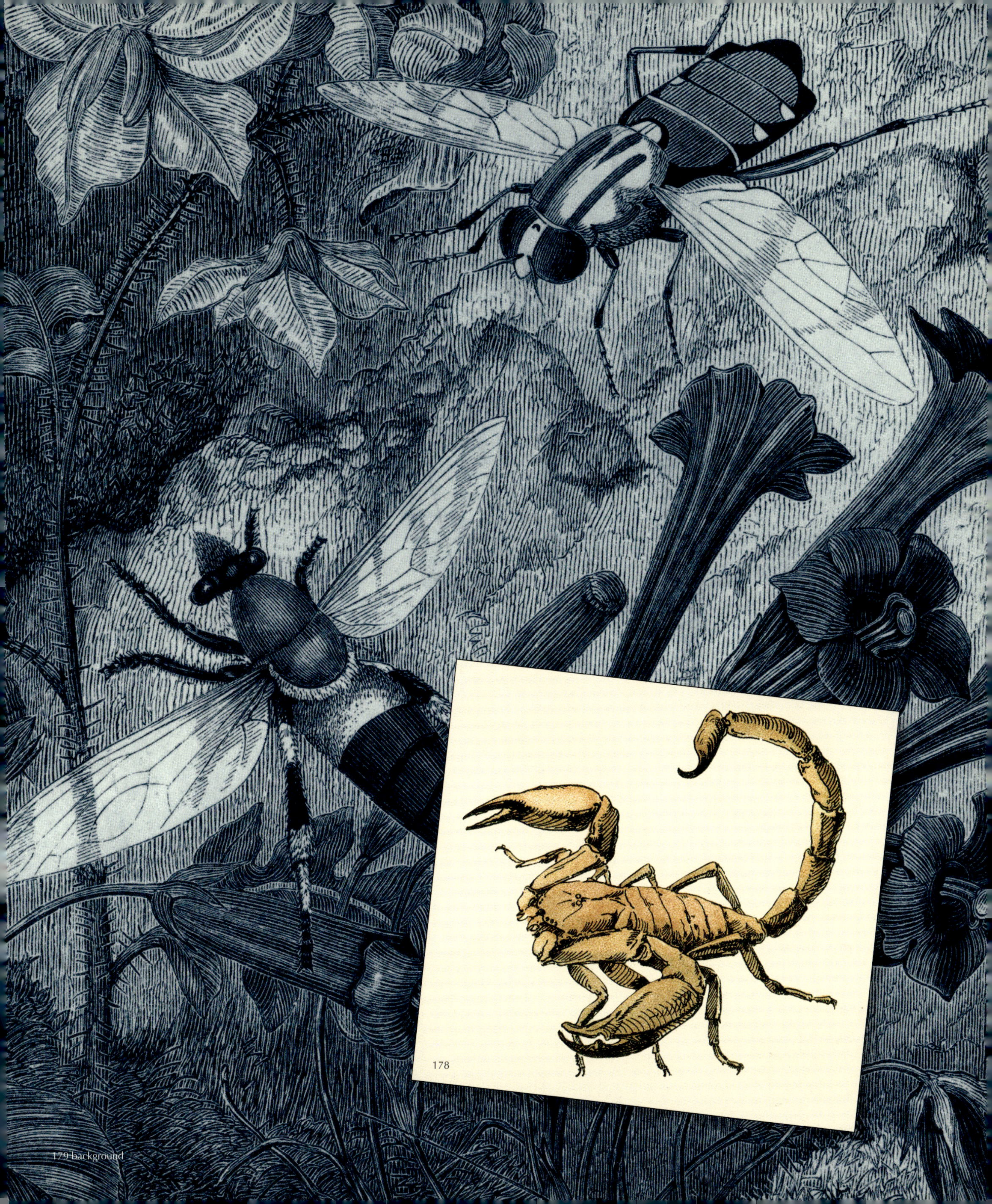

178

179 background

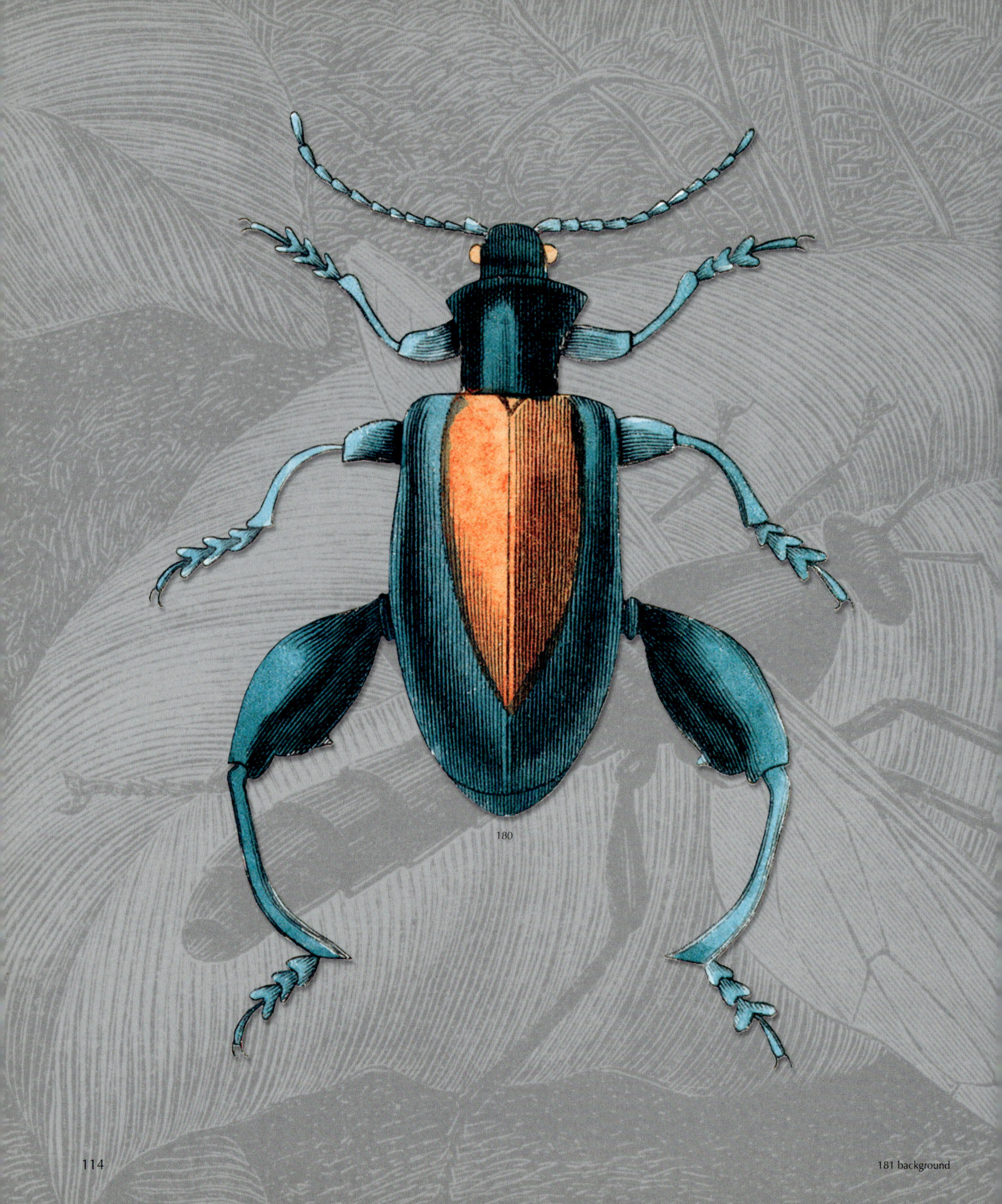

180

181 background

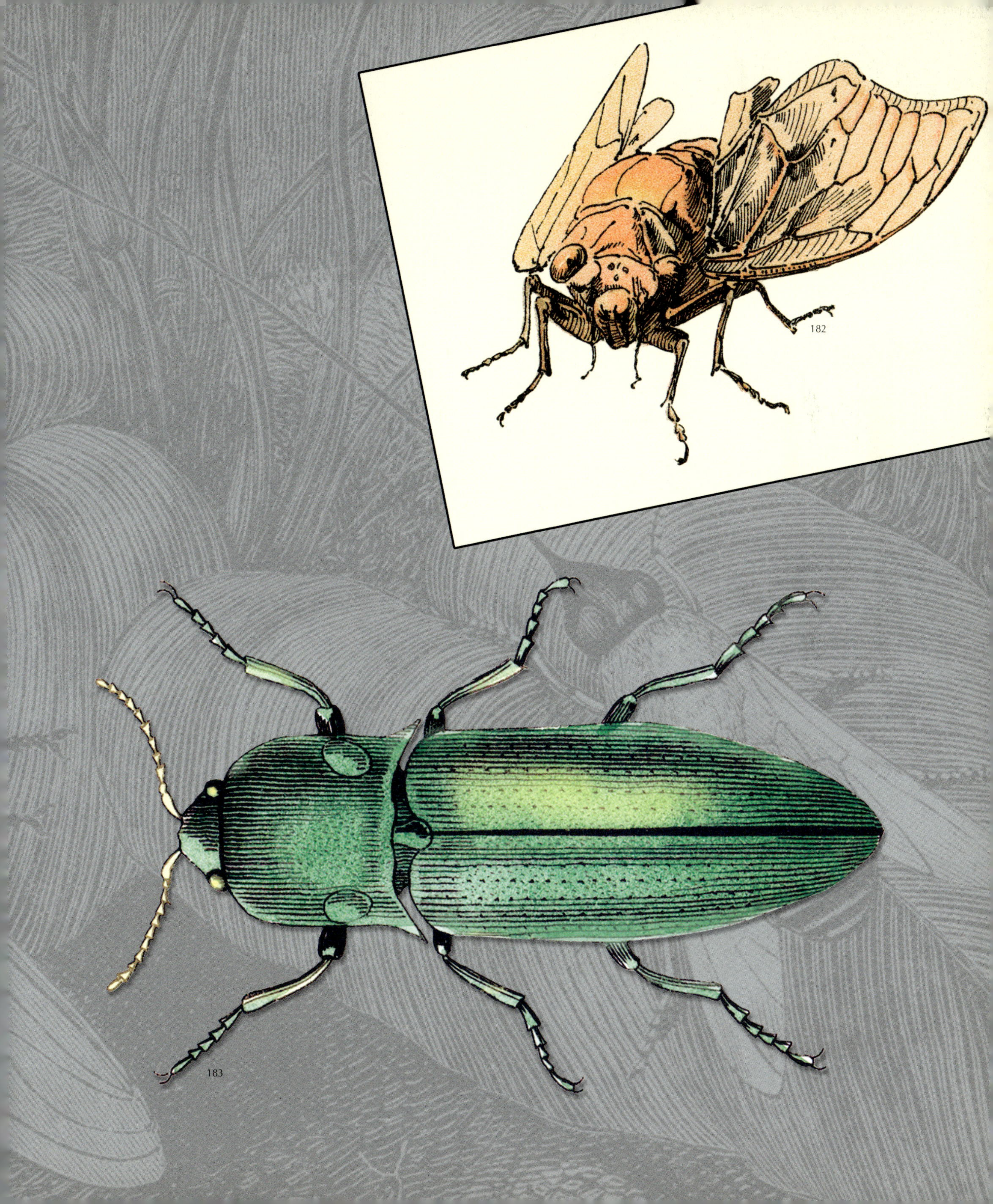

182

183

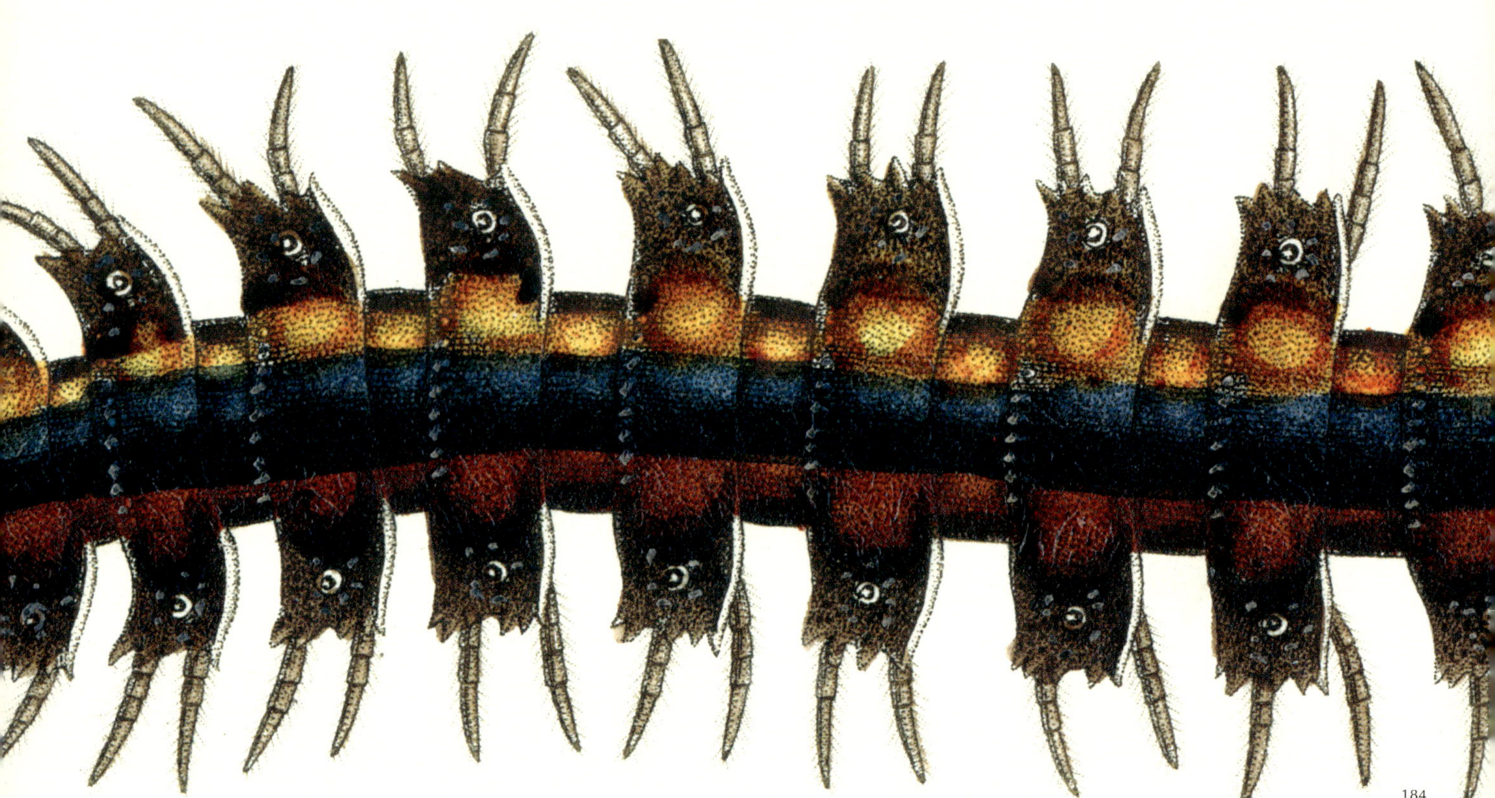

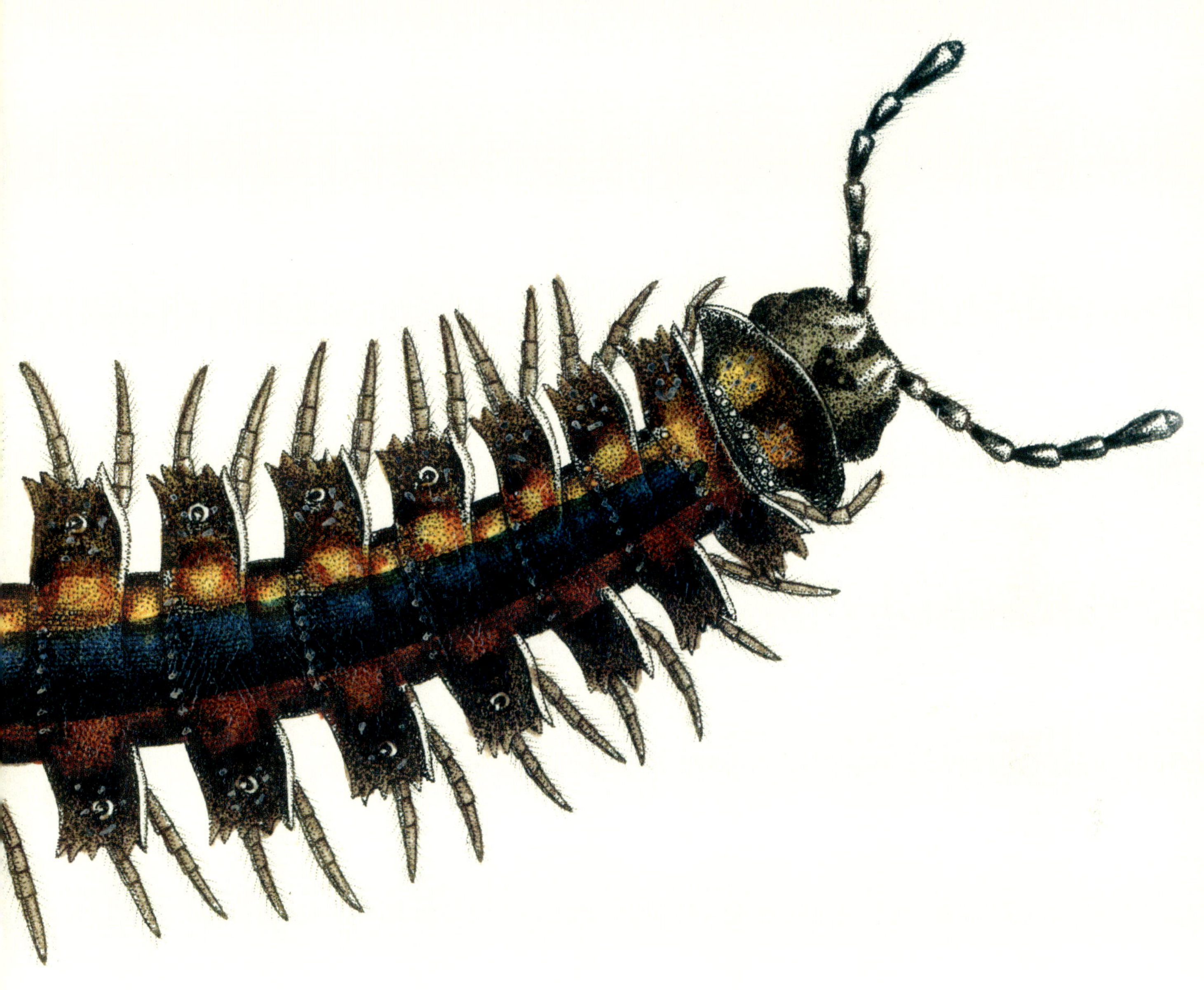

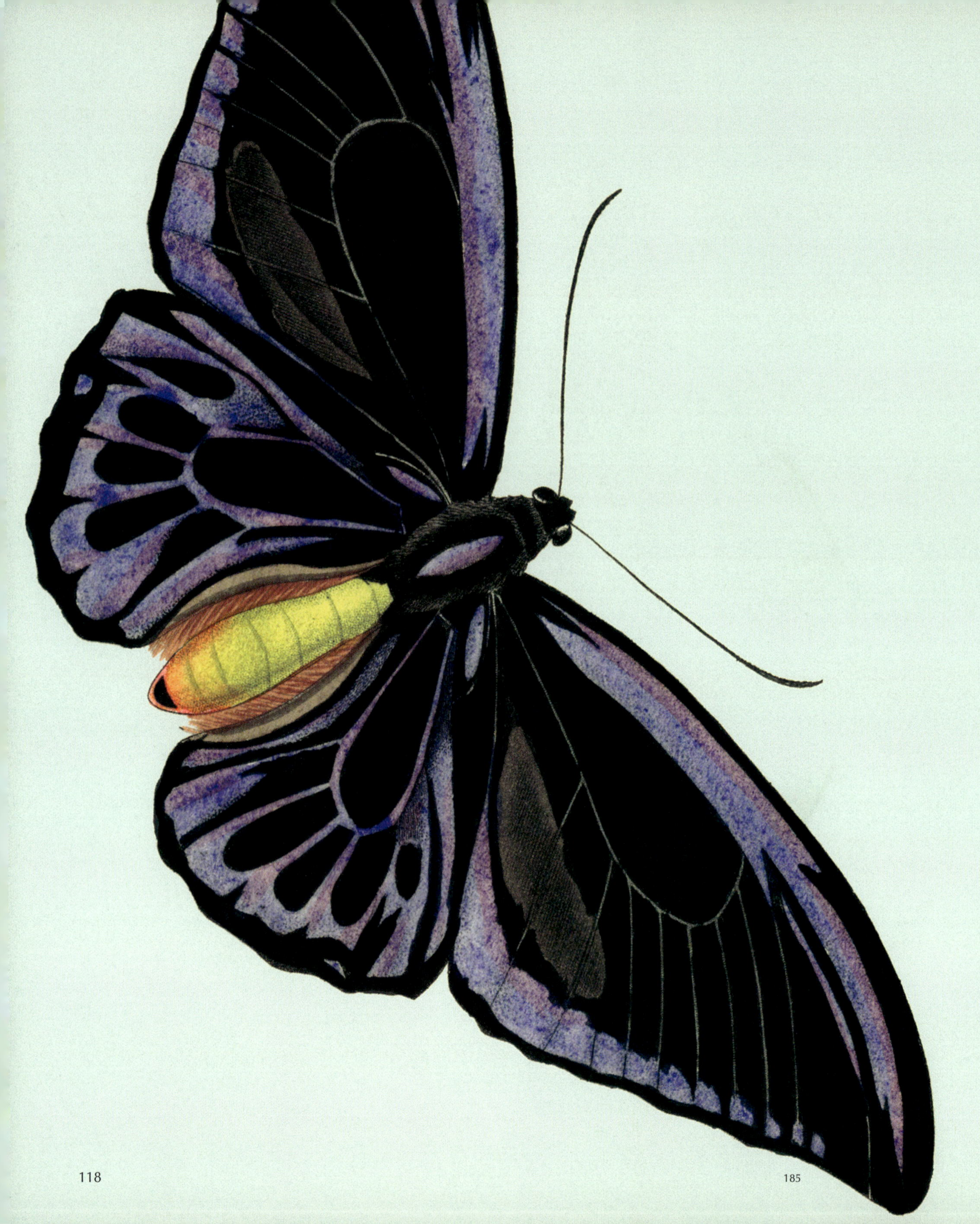

185

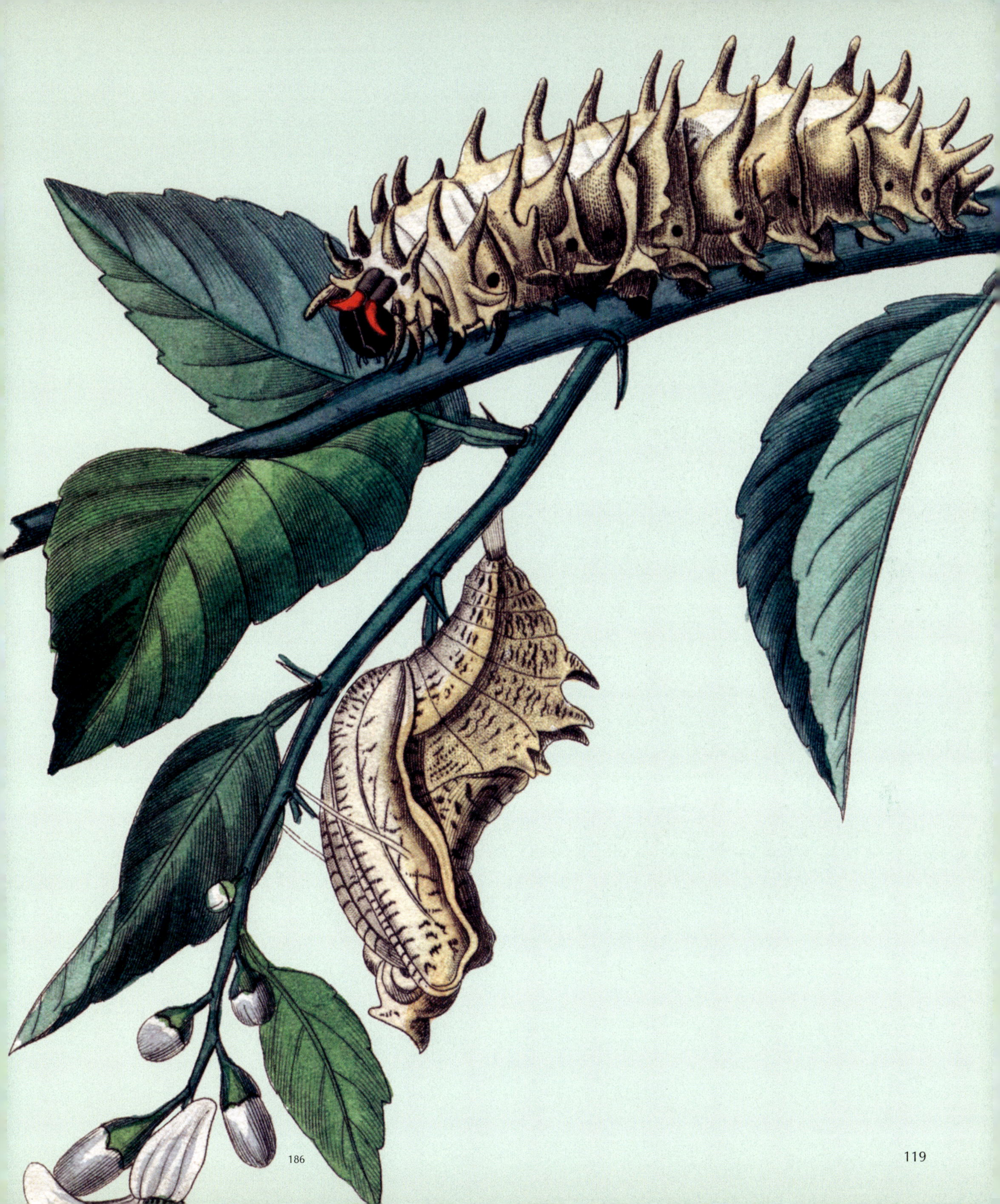
186

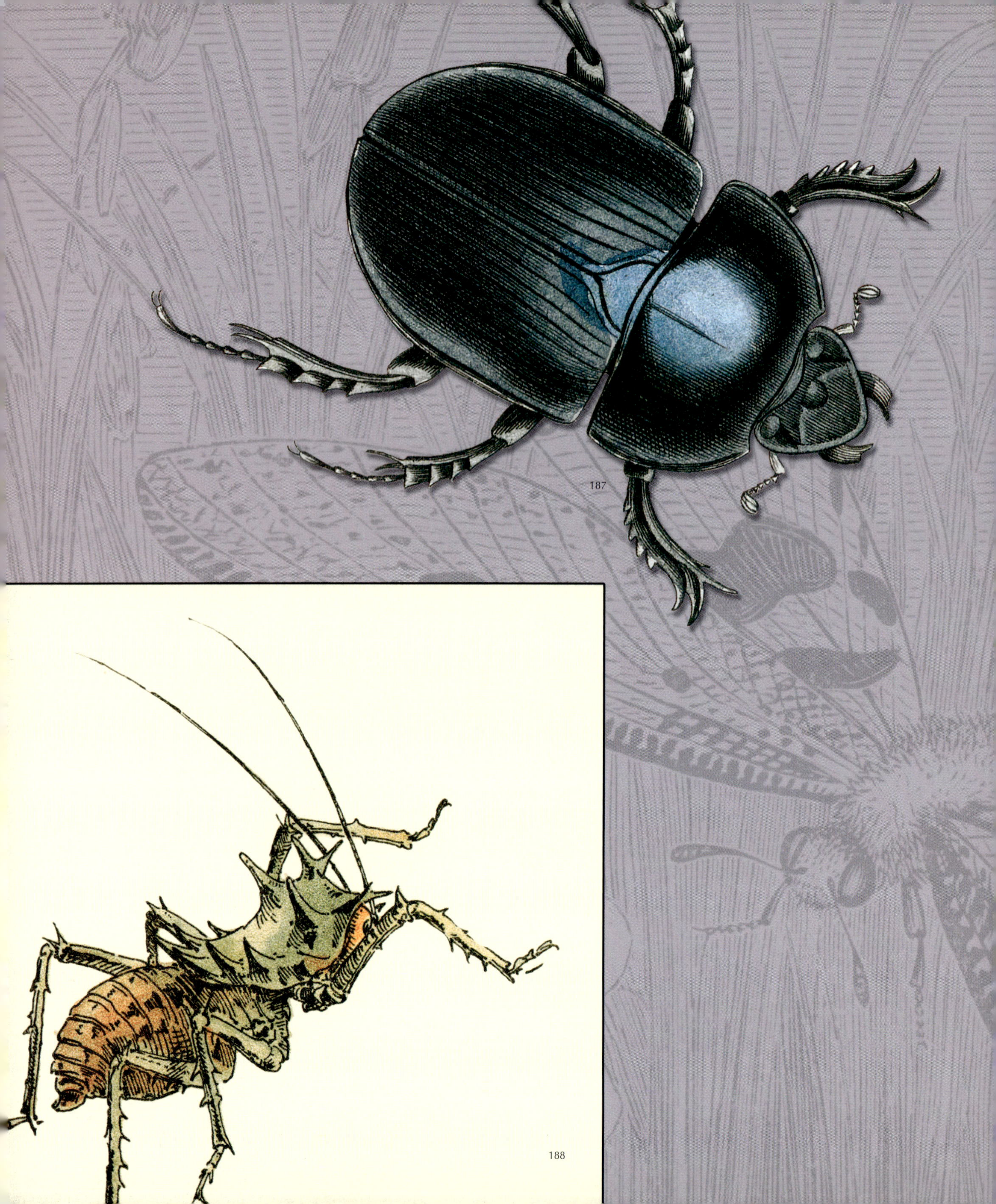
187
188

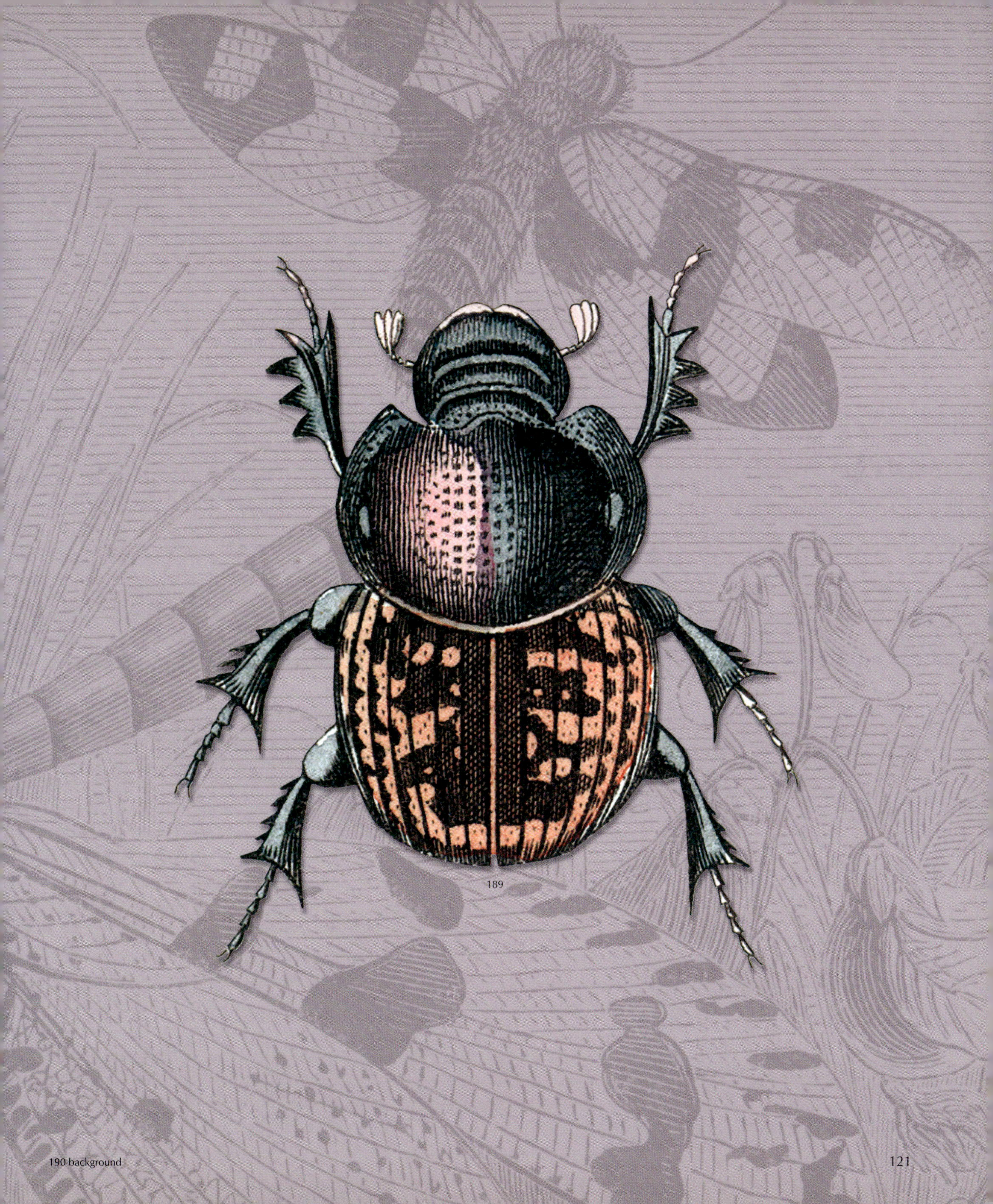
189

190 background

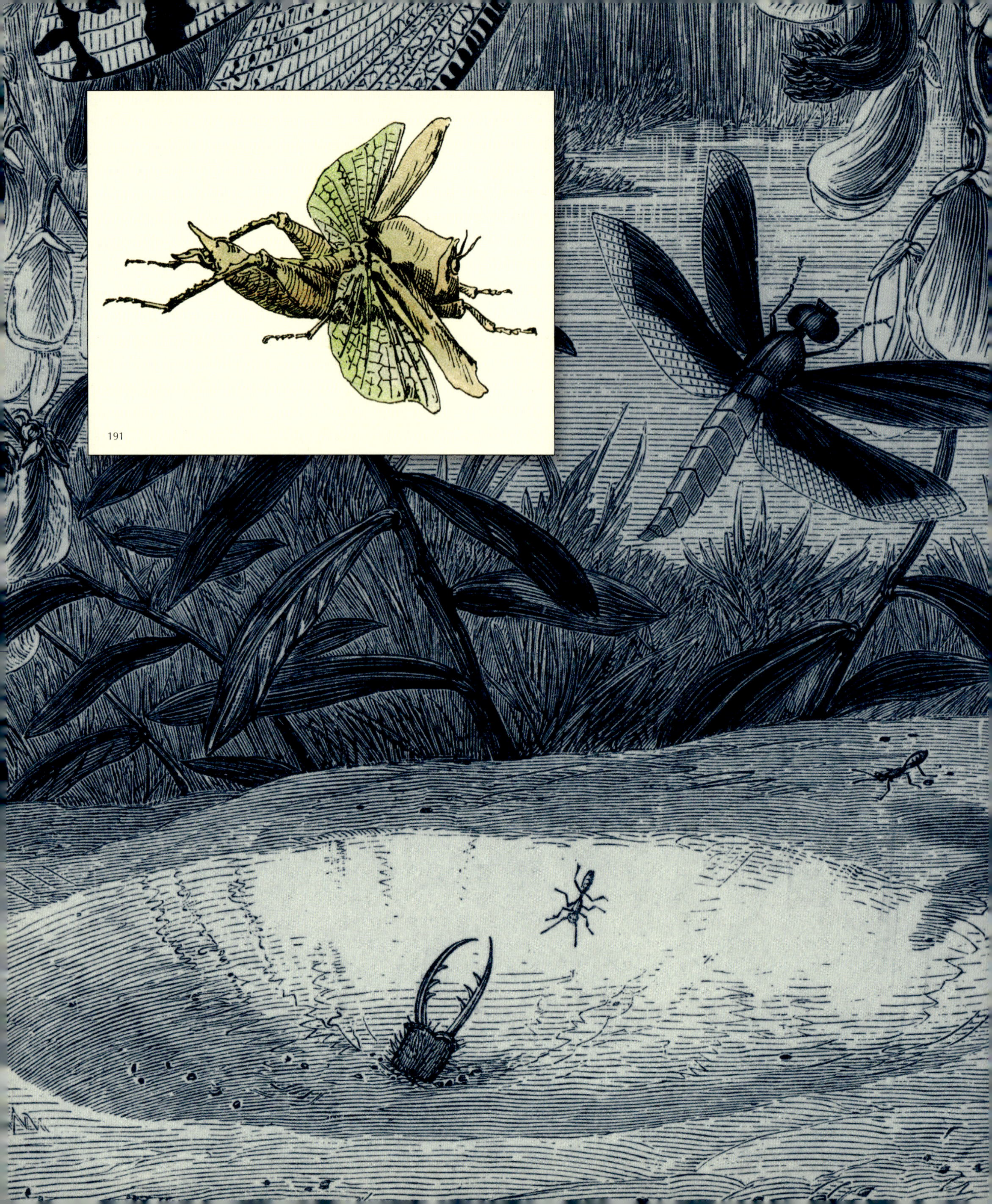
191

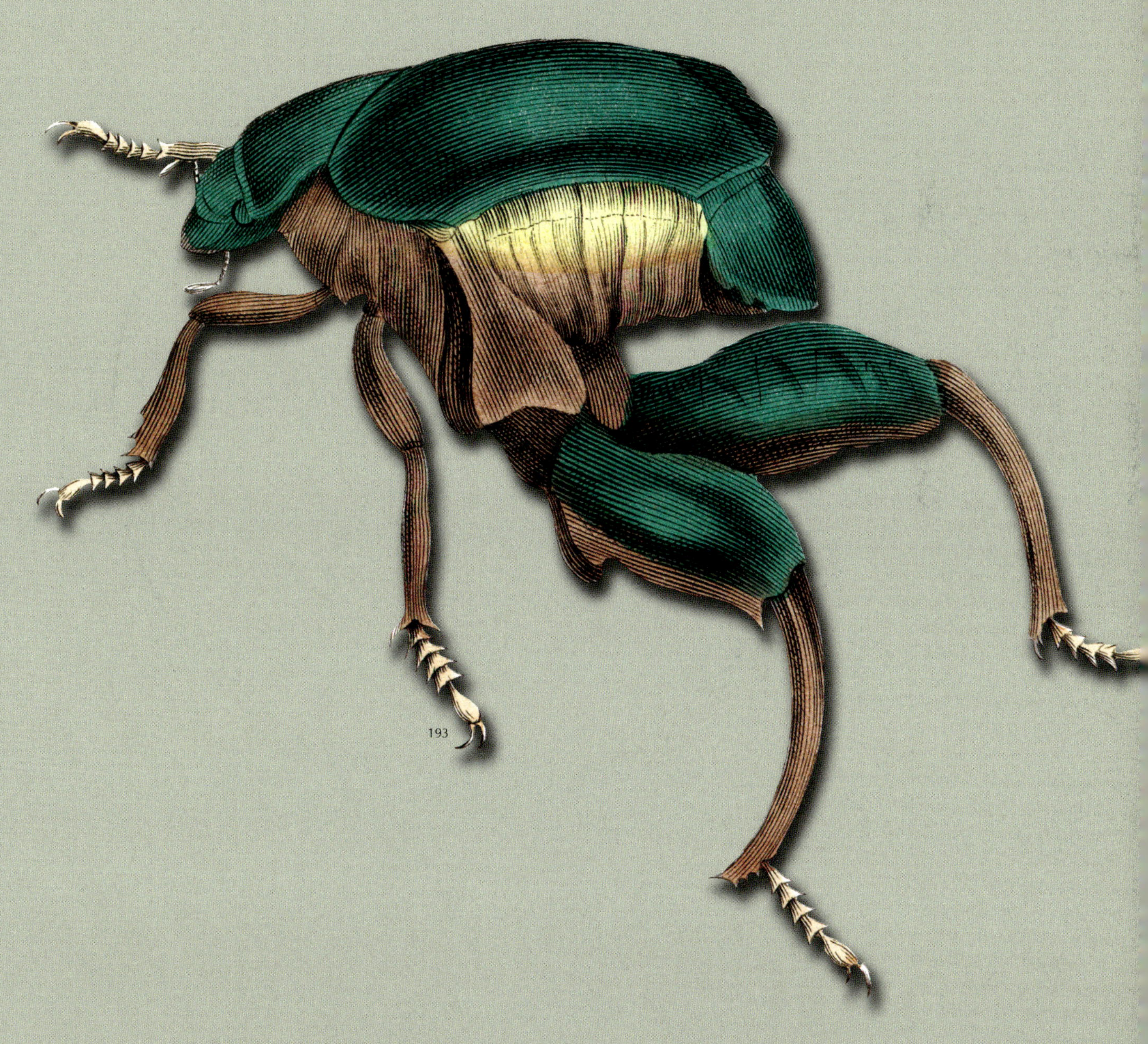

192 background

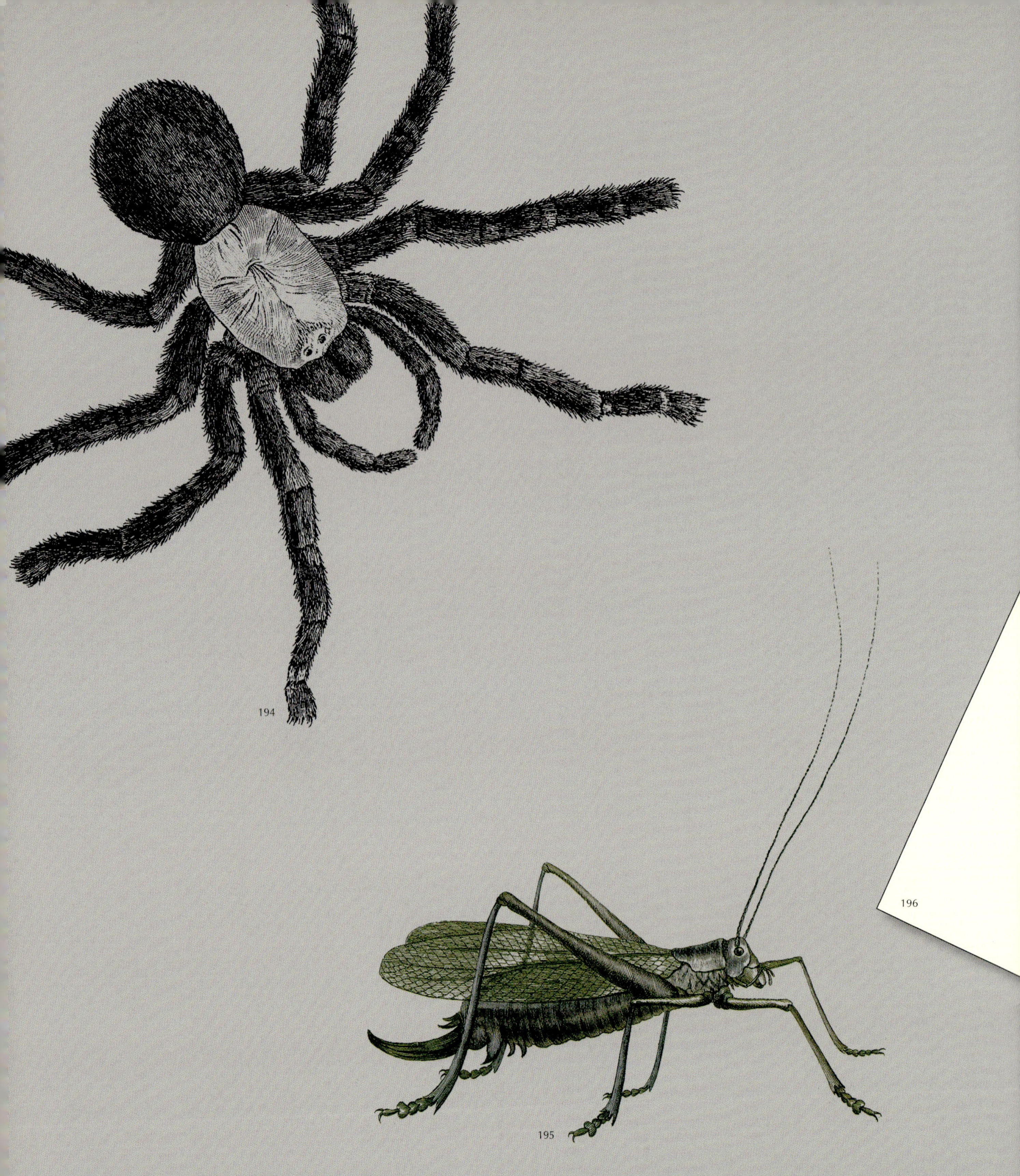
194

195

196

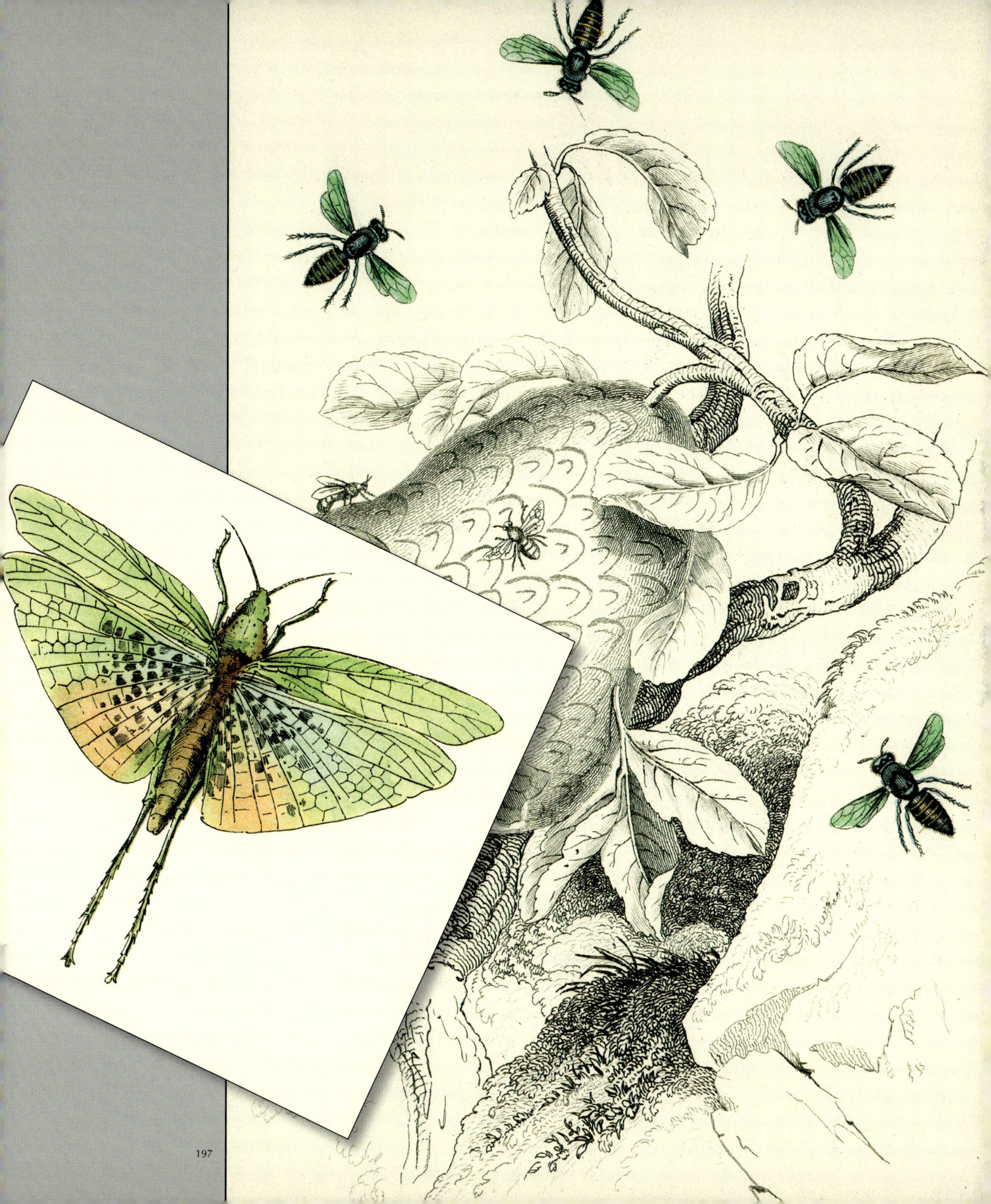

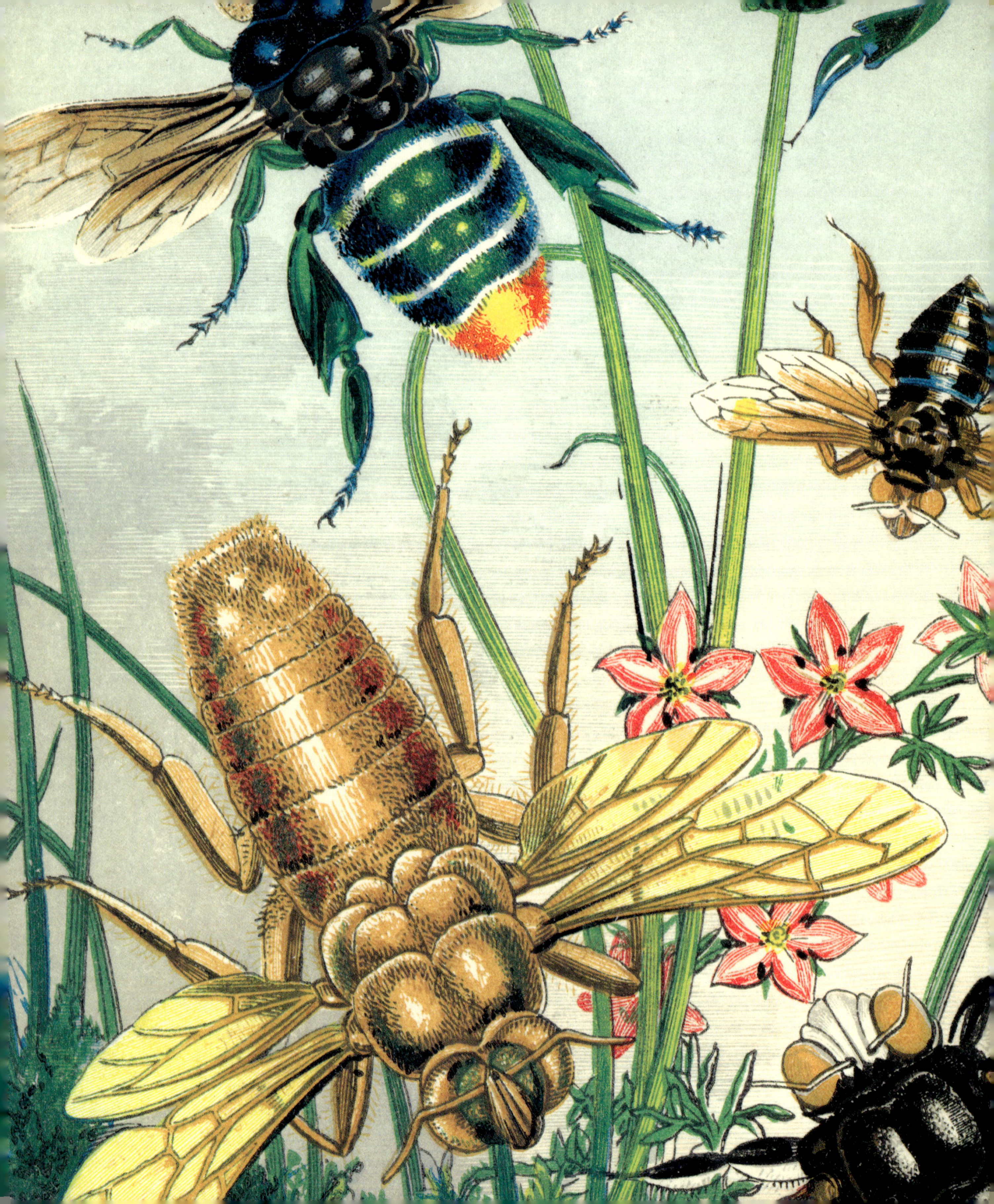

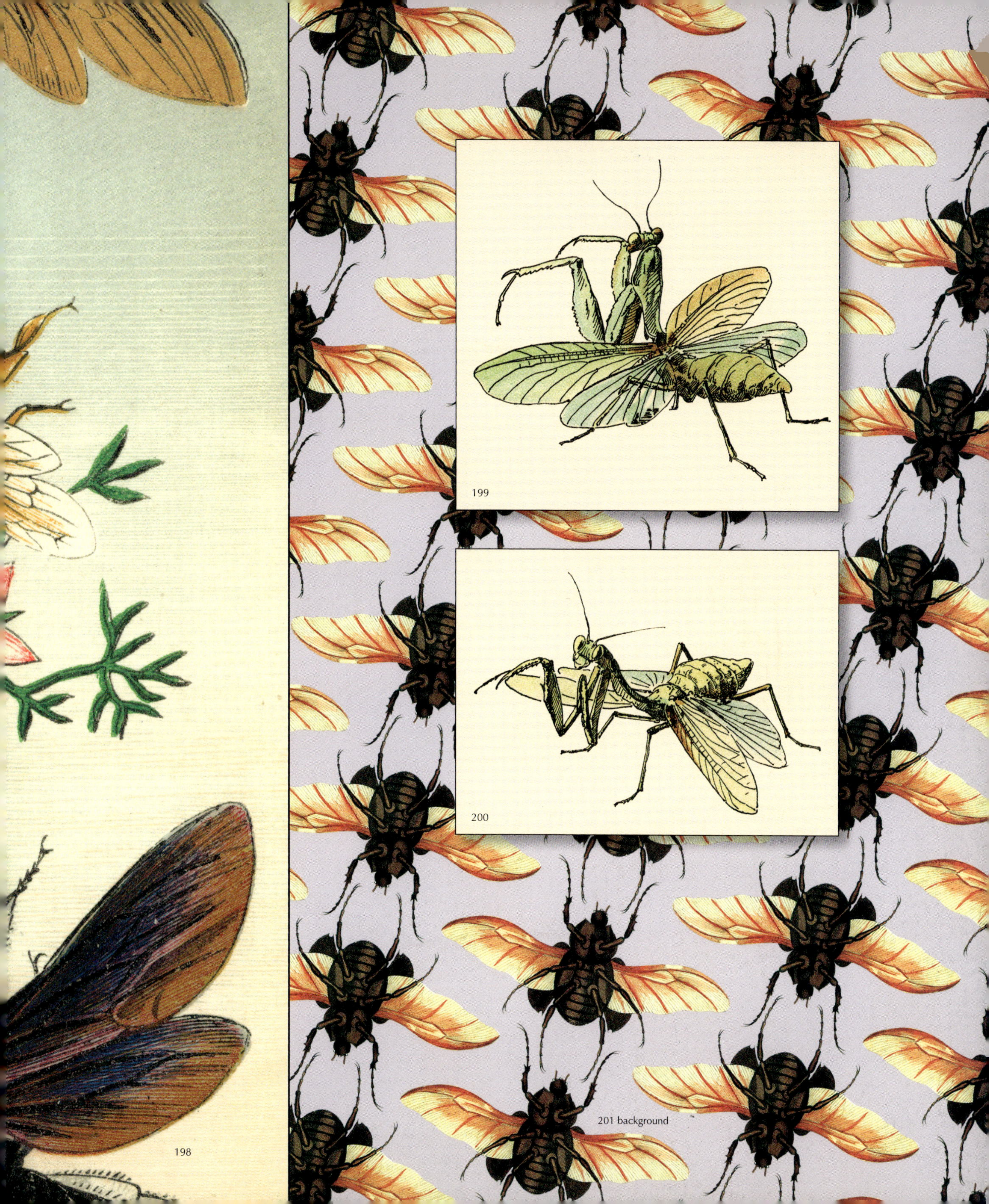

198

199

200

201 background

List of Vector Images

002 040 072 085
019 057 083 122

List of Insects

001 - British beetles
002 - Wasp, *Meteorus hyphantria*
003 - Fly
004 - Beetles
005 - *Coleoptera imperialis*
006 - *Phyllium siccifolia*
007 - Bees
008 - Rhino beetle, *Scarabeus chorinaeus*
009 - Click beetles
010 - Katydid
011 - *Locusta cristata* (lower), *Locusta flava* (upper)
012 - *Aranea avicularia*, Black cuban spider
013 - Click beetle
014 - Harlequin beetles, Beetles
015 - Long-horned beetle, *Prionus cervicornis*
016 - Beetle, *Prionus corticinus*
017 - Harlequin beetle
018 - Hercules beetle
019 - Wasp, *Aphycus annulipes*
020 - Praying mantis, *Mantis religiosa*
021 - *Myrmoteras binghami*
022 - Scarab beetle
023 - Metallic wood-boring beetle
024 - Katydids
025 - Stag beetle
026 - Katydids
027 - Dragonfly
028 - Cricket
029 - Grasshopper
030 - Violin beetle
031 - Praying mantis
032 - Goliath beetle
033 - Dragonfly
034 - Death's head hawk moth
035 - Death's head hawk moth
036 - Death's head hawk moth
037 - Harlequin beetle
038 - Beetle
039 - Violin beetle
040 - Wasp, *Aspidiotiphagus citrinus*
041 - Longhorn beetle
042 - Katydid
043 - Bottom, Cranefly; middle, Fly, *Tabanus tropicus*; top, Guinea fly
044 - Centipede
045 - Spider
046 - Hooded cricket
047 - Longhorn beetle
048 - Stag beetle
049 - Sand wasp
050 - Ground beetle
051 - Ground beetle
052 - Sand wasp
053 - *Dorymyrmex* (*conomyrma*) *exsanguis*, Ant
054 - *Dorymyrmex ensifer*, Ant
055 - Ant
056 - Longhorn beetle
057 - Wasp, *Ablerus clisiocampae*
058 - Ant, *Iridomyrmex detectus*
059 - Ant, *Camponotus myrmosphincta* imitator
060 - *Zirophorus exaratus*
061 - Centipedes
062 - Darwin's beetle
064 - Grasshopper
065 - Tail-less whip scorpion
066 - Scarab beetles
067 - *Curculio sexdecempunctatus*
068 - Wasp and nest
069 - Locusts
070 - Dragonfly
071 - Harlequin beetle
072 - Wasp, *Habrolepis dalmanni*, female
073 - Bottom, Robberfly; Fly, *Acanthomera zimmanis*
074 - Cicada
075 - Wooden hives
076 - Great humble-bee of Valparaiso
077 - Darwin's beetle
078 - Brazilian bees
079 - Elderberry longhorn beetle
080 - Longhorn beetle
081 - Brazilian bees
082 - Scorpion
083 - Honey bee
084 - Bees swarming
085 - Honey bee
086 - Moth caterpillars
087 - Tiger beetle
088 - Walking stick
089 - Beetle, *Heliocopris gigas*
090 - Butterflies
091 - Dragonfly
092 - Tail-less whip scorpion
093 - Giant king cricket
094 - Flea
095 - Tiger beetle
096 - Soldier beetle
097 - Oil beetle
098 - Butterflies
099 - South American bird spider
100 - Rove beetle
101 - Net-winged beetle
102 - Buffalo carpet beetle
103 - Small snail-eating beetle
104 - Hemipterans
105 - Walking stick
106 - Scarab beetle
107 - *Spheniscus erotyloides*
108 - *Horia maculata*
109 - Butterflies
110 - Metallic wood-boring beetle
111 - Violin beetle
112 - Butterflies
113 - Click beetles
114 - *Silpha 4-maculata*
115 - Whirligig beetle
116 - Spitting spider
117 - Beetle, *Heliocopris gigas*
118 - Beetle, *Phanaeus*
119 - Stag beetle larva
120 - Moth, *Philampelus vitis*
121 - Diving beetle
122 - Lunate long sting, *Thalessa lunator*
123 - Beetle, *Phanaeus*
124 - Moths
125 - Dragonfly
126 - Rhinoceros beetle
127 - Scarab beetle
128 - Kangaroo beetle
129 - Moths
130 - Tunnel web spider
131 - Grasshopper
132 - Hercules beetle (male)
133 - Hercules beetle (female)
135 - Great African white ant
138 - Lantern fly
139 - Coleoptera, Ground beetle
140 - Left, Wandering violin mantis, *Empusa gongylodes*; right, *Empusa lobipes*
141 - Beetle, *Batocera*
142 - Moth
144 - *Necrophorus humator*
145 - Diving beetle
146 - Moth
147 - Moth
148 - Grasshopper
149 - Hercules beetle
150 - Hell diver
151 - Longhorn beetle
153 - Millipede
154 - Dung beetle
155 - Harlequin beetle
156 - Ground beetle
158 - South American bird spider
160 - Scarab beetle
161 - Walking stick
162 - Middle, bottom, Cockroaches; top, Mantis, *Harpax ocellaria*
163 - Katydid
165 - Harlequin beetle
166 - *Cyclous vittatus*
167 - Grasshopper
169 - Millipede
170 - Walking stick
171 - Top, Moth, *Aglia io*; bottom, middle, Moth, *Saturnia maia*
172 - Click beetle
173 - Tiger beetle
174 - *Hister reniformis*
175 - Hercules beetle
177 - Atlas beetle
178 - Scorpion
180 - Kangaroo beetle
182 - Cicada
183 - Click beetle
184 - Tanzanian blue ringleg centipede
185 - Butterfly
186 - Butterfly caterpillar and cocoon
187 - Earth-boring dung beetles
188 - Katydid
189 - Scarab beetles
190 - Dragonflies
191 - Grasshopper
192 - Dragonflies
193 - Kangaroo beetle
194 - Tarantula
195 - Grasshopper
196 - Grasshopper
197 - Nest of the Lecheguana
198 - Bees
199 - Praying mantis
200 - Praying mantis
201 - Cockchafer